Saggistica 34

This Hope Sustains the Scholar

THIS HOPE SUSTAINS THE SCHOLAR
Essays in Tribute to the Work of Robert Viscusi

Edited by
Siân Gibby
Joseph Sciorra
Anthony Julian Tamburri

BORDIGHERA PRESS

Library of Congress Control Number: 2020930990

Cover photo courtesy of
ombretta diaferia
abrigliasciolta.it

© 2021 by the Authors

All rights reserved. Parts of this book may be reprinted only by written permission from the authors, and may not be reproduced for publication in book, magazine, or electronic media of any kind, except for purposes of literary reviews.

Printed in the United States.

Published by
BORDIGHERA PRESS
John D. Calandra Italian American Institute
25 West 43rd Street, 17th Floor
New York, NY 10036

SAGGISTICA 34
ISBN 978-1-59954- 167-9

much of the day i think of nothing except the broom and shovel
tall cornices that shade us with deep colors

in my cage without bars i place people by their understandings
which if i do it long enough and quietly enough
teaches me to say things that make sense to them

each book i study requires me to learn another simplicity
so that the more i read the stupider i get
this hope sustains the scholar

Robert Viscusi, *Ellis Island*

Table of Contents

Preface	xi
Introduction: The Scholar with the Red Scarf: Personal Reflections on Robert Viscusi *Anthony Julian Tamburri*	1
Italian American Literary Studies and Robert Viscusi's Buried Treasures *Mary Jo Bona*	9
Existential Universalisms, Epistemological Diversity: A Social Historian Reads Robert Viscusi's *Astoria* *Donna Gabaccia*	27
Robert Viscusi's *Ellis Island* and the Sense of History *Peter Carravetta*	43
Alternative Modernisms: A Contrapuntal Reading of *The Great Gatsby* and *Christ in Concrete* *Donatella Izzo*	61
Augusto Bassetti and the First English Grammar for Italian Speakers Written and Published in the United States (1885) *James J. Periconi*	89
The Life and Poems of Simplicio Righi *Francesco Durante*	115
Living on the Hyphen: Italian Writers in the United States *Paolo Giordano*	161
Dancing with Italians in American Culture *Fred Gardaphé*	181
"He made us all look like gavones": Marking *Cafoneria* and Policing the Boundaries of Propriety, Taste, and Ethnic Identity among Italian Americans *Joseph Sciorra*	193

How Cultural Memory Builds a Narrative Past in Forming
Individual Identity 233
Donna M. Chirico

Italian Diaspora Studies and the University: Professional
Development and Curricular Matters 243
Anthony Julian Tamburri

Contributors 259

Index 265

Preface

Much has happened since this book was first proposed in the fall of 2018. In September of that year, our dear colleague Robert Viscusi—the Broeklundian Professor in the Department of English at Brooklyn College—was feted for his thirty-six years of service as the executive officer of the Ethyle R. Wolfe Institute for the Humanities. The following spring, Bob was named Professor Emeritus upon retiring from the City College of New York. But since 2015 Bob had suffered several transient ischemic attacks that left him with vertigo and other symptoms. This confluence of events and circumstances made it more than appropriate that a review of Bob's scholarship and inspiration written by his peers was in order.

Anthony suggested inviting a small group of scholars who knew Bob well and had worked with him over the years to contribute. Everyone we contacted responded enthusiastically, submitting new and original essays several of which engage directly with Bob's creative and scholarly work.

In the course of the book's production, Francesco Durante, the Italian journalist and literary scholar with whom Bob, Anthony, and James Periconi had collaborated on the translation and publication of *Italoamericana: The Literature of the Great Migration, 1880–1943* (Fordham University Press, 2014), died suddenly on August 3, 2019. We were working with him on his entry to the book when we learned of his untimely passing.

Our hope was to present this published tribute with much fanfare in a public setting and with Bob in the seat of honor, but his health took a turn for the worse when he was diagnosed with pancreatic cancer; he died on January 19, 2020, at age seventy-nine. Before he passed, we were able to show him the book's table of contents and some of the completed articles.

In the spring of 2020, the COVID-19 pandemic swept through New York City and the East Coast, closing the Calandra Institute's office and throwing a momentary hitch into the book's production.

We have finally completed this book two years after it was first discussed, as the second wave of the coronavirus is rising.

Many people have contributed to the publication of this book in one shape or another. We are grateful to all the authors for their brilliance and patience in creating this intellectual tribute. We want to acknowledge Bob's immediate family: his wife Nancy and his children Robert, Jr. and Victoria, especially the latter who helped us locate the photo of Bob that graces the cover. Thanks to ombretta diaferia of abrigliasciolta for this beautiful image of Bob, who kindly allowed us to use her work. Thanks also go to James Periconi who met with Bob in his final days and updated him about the book project. We are also thankful for two coworkers at the Institute: Nicholas Grosso who designed the compelling book cover and Rosangela Briscese who assisted in the compiling and creation of the index.

Bob's legacy for us, for the book's contributors, and for many other colleagues and friends, is a deep and lasting one. His written body of work challenges us to think about the historical and ongoing Italian American creative presence in the United States by engaging with the artists and the myriad characters they have conjured into existence.

For those of us who knew Bob—who studied with him, who collaborated with him, who were encouraged by him—there is also the remembrance of a timeless scholar, whose insightful evocations and often playful turns of phrase have helped us all move beyond the parochial to the universal.

Siân Gibby
Joseph Sciorra
Anthony Julian Tamburri
November 2020

Introduction
The Scholar with the Red Scarf: Personal Reflections on Robert Viscusi

Anthony Julian Tamburri

I first met Robert Viscusi in Chicago in the fall of 1987 at the annual convention of the American Italian Historical Association (AIHA; now Italian American Studies Association). To this day, I recall two thoughts that immediately came to mind on seeing him: (1) "Wow, that's the guy who wrote that great essay on the language of Italian/American[1] literature," and (2) "What's with the red scarf?" Well, I came to realize over the years that the red scarf was a signature of his. I remember it so well because I had one just like it, and after that initial meeting, I laid mine aside for a number of years whenever I was in his company.

The Intellectual

I was supposed to meet Bob Viscusi earlier than I did; we both had been scheduled to deliver papers as part of what was then the "Italian-American Seminar" of the annual convention of the MLA (the Modern Language Association) in Los Angeles in 1981. Unfortunately, he could not be there. However, a friend of his did present his paper.[2] And while my first inclination was to wonder why he did not attend the conference, once his paper was delivered, I was delighted; hearing it, I was witness to an acute reading of Pietro di Donato's *Christ in Concrete* and, further still, I was introduced to what I would discover soon thereafter was one of (if not) the most fundamental critical voices of and on Italian/American literature to date.

I realize that such statements are often considered hyperboles, but in this case—indeed, especially as I work in the same field—I state it as a simple matter of fact. It is true that we owe an invaluable debt to Rose Basile Green for her work on Italian/American literature.[3] Having first published an essay on five stages of Italian/

Anthony Julian Tamburri

American narrative in the proceedings of the second annual conference of the American Italian Historical Association (AIHA 1969), Basile Green was truly the first to offer an in-depth history of Italian/American narrative with her subsequent book (1974).

It was Bob, nonetheless, who first engaged in the theorization of Italian/American literature with his classical and ever important essay "*De Vulgari Eloquentia*: An Approach to the Language of Italian American Fiction" (1981).[4] This was the first comprehensive postulation of a theory of Italian/American literature whose purpose was to uncover the unique power of the "American Italian's Italian American eloquence," as he so poignantly and carefully described it, and with the unique aim "to awaken Italian America to a sense of self" and inevitably to establish a "secure place that no one can confuse with its lost homeland or its fabulous landfall" (305). This is the double-edged sword that challenges Italian Americans from within, something that underscores the predominance of Bob's critical thought. Italian Americans must be able linguistic and hence cultural acrobats, capable of moving between both worlds, inhabiting the one while recalling the other, and vice versa. This is tantamount to a tarantella-type dance on the hyphen, the inhabitance of that interstitial space that Arnold van Gennep aptly described as the "liminal," that "transitional period" (11) of a "passage from ... one social world to another" (10). Here more than a one-way passage we can speak in terms of a to and fro, or, better, the constant state of *in-betweeness* of the metaphorical dance on the hyphen, an image that is dear to Bob's heart; one need only read his thoughts on language in *Christ in Concrete* (1986).

To be sure, this became Bob's *ragion d'essere* as critic: that cultural and literary Italian America acquire this necessary sense of self that eventually transforms its absence within the dominant culture into a presence. Such a requisite manifesto for an intellectual movement is, without doubt, his *Buried Caesars and Other Secrets of Italian American Writing* (2006). It is, I would contend, required reading for anyone, lay or academic, interested in and, more significant, committed to a sort of social activism with regard to Italian America.[5] Indeed, this is a book, in some ways, for the general reader precisely because Bob infuses in his textual analysis historical references and social commentary that, on the one hand, educate and, on the other, lead the reader to consider the critical act in general and its varying potential.

Thus, for those who are interested in the literary act, they have much both to explore and use as a jumping-off point for other readings that may be stimulated by Bob's analyses. Equally so, for those who are interested in any form of activism with regard to Italian Americans today, it is imperative that they have a sound knowledge of Italy's history and how it might relate to today's world of Italian America. It is not enough to know the dates and key-word facts that many individuals and associations—local, regional, and national—have complied from time to time. These are good for the public schools, those tidbits and facts on which children can eventually acquire and construct their preliminary knowledge of Italian Americans. But for the individual who claims to be in the forefront, who declares, if by action only, to be the spokesperson, it is imperative to know all of what Bob supplies to the reader with this book, especially in his preface and introduction. Anything short of a solid knowledge of these data—and how to relate them to other Italian/American phenomena—is grossly insufficient (or clearly inadequate).

What we eventually come to understand from Bob's critical work is that language is both a vehicle for communication as well as a marker for identification, so that Americans of Italian descent came to English "with the mental habit of people who have lived forever in a dialect" (2006, 26). Such being the case, language became the marker of class ("dialectal," Bob underscores, equals *low class* and, consequently, little to no social power), and "dialectic," he ultimately tells us, is, rightfully so, "verbal struggle" (26). Language thus fixes us initially in a social locale (read: class) and then categorizes us, brands us, so to speak, in order to assign us a "set of possibilities and positions in the process of history" (27). Bob goes on to apply this theoretical mind-set to the readings of various literary works that we might readily call classics, unearthing the numerous "buried Caesars," the many facets of Italian nationalist and, as he underscores, imperialist ideology that Italian emigrants exported with them, including those "impossible ideals and exaggerated claims to which Italian Americans still give their devotion" (6). These are indeed the beliefs that have now been "written in new countries and in new languages" (6). But these beliefs, Bob warns at the outset, require a certain capability: "Reading Italian American writing well means understanding its secret themes, where they come from, how they work, and what they accomplish" (6).

In order to know well all of Italian/American culture—both Bob and I have always agreed on this point—requires both a sound knowledge of Italian history and, at the very least, a working knowledge of Italian language. Hence, as the late Felix Stefanile often declared, "there is no ontology without archeology."[6] This lack of the archeological is what we might consider a major flaw in the various discourses that emanate from certain corners of Italian America, where self-proclaimed spokespeople, monolingual and slightly read, elbow their way, so to speak, to the forefront in order to monopolize the podium. This, we must sadly recognize, is our greatest and most grave challenge in Italian America.

THE INDIVIDUAL

After our initial meeting in Chicago, I got to know Bob well and we struck up a friendship that lasted until his death on January 19, 2020. At first it was based on our work. My own professional preparation—an Italianist and not an Americanist—moved me to come to Italian/American studies through the back door of methodology and theory, I like to say. Indeed, Bob's work guided me greatly in these first few years. His ideas and the rhetorical craft through which he articulated them served as a model for me.

Only two years after the Chicago AIHA meeting, Bob participated in our inaugural conference at Purdue University. While the Italian section was indeed that, a gathering of primarily thirty-five or forty professors of Italian, it afforded those of us who were also working in Italian/American studies the opportunity to discuss the field further. At around the same time, Fred Gardaphé, Paolo Giordano, and I submitted the final manuscript for our anthology *From the Margin: Writings in Italian Americana*. We had included some of Bob's poetry, and he also had the lead essay in the book's second section. This was also when Bob and I realized that we had much more in common than we had thought. It was for me the period in which I was working on my notions of hyphenation, and together with my regular interlocutor at the time, Peter Carravetta, Bob's presence rounded out a triad of theoretical and methodological discussions and debates that have continued ever since and through the production of various books we each published over subsequent years.

Additionally, during these years Paolo, Fred, and I founded Bordighera Incorporated, which eventually led to the creation of Bordighera Press. Bob played an integral role from the outset. The inaugural issue of Bordighera's journal, *VIA* (*Voices in Italian Americana*), for instance, opens with yet another fundamental essay by Bob, "Breaking the Silence: Strategic Imperatives for Italian American Culture" (1990). Alongside his "*De Vulgari Eloquentia*," this essay remains foundational to a reconceptualization of Italian America and all that it pertains conceptually, intellectually, and actively.

These two essays remain, in many ways, bookends to an entirely new way of looking at Italian/American culture. They deal with the "hows" as well as the "whys." More significant, they each call for an intellectual and social activism as they accompany each other, a process that is essential to the changing awareness required of all who work within the world of Italian America.

There was a second moment in which Bob played a pivotal role with regard to Bordighera Press. In 1992 he introduced at an AIHA conference his fourteen-page poem titled "An Oration upon the Recent Death of Christopher Columbus," a wonderful satire in verse on the variety of feelings and opinions about the role of Christopher Columbus. The poem was too important to be lost in a journal, so we decided to publish it as a book, and as such it was the first book Boridghera published, the inaugural volume of the series *VIA* Folios, and the reason for which we constituted under the aegis of Bordighera Incorporated the imprint Bordighera Press.

I have often complimented Bob over the years on these and other accomplishments and on how impactful his work has been and continues to be. Always the gracious listener in these moments, he had on occasion been embarrassed by such commentary, believing that he could have developed further certain notions, that his writing, for instance, might have benefitted from yet another revision.

In turn, he was always generous and equally inquisitive about other people's work. I consider my own development, from my essay on the hyphen (1989/1991) to subsequent work on a new taxonomy of the Italian/American writer (1994), as a natural progression. Well, indeed it may have been. Nonetheless, while still in the Midwest, I would make regular trips to the greater New York City metropolitan area, and I would meet up with both Bob and Peter. And we would ponder the state of affairs of Italian America and, in so doing, discuss our own work as well. My essay on the hyphen and other related matter constituted on various occasions the topic(s) of conversation. More than a conversation, it was a discussion if not at times a debate. Often demanding and always respectful, Bob made observations and put forth opinions that were crucial to the progression of my own thought processes during those intertwining three years. When my subsequent essay on the "(re)cognition" of the Italian/American writer finally appeared as the lead essay in a special issue of *Differentia* (1994), the first and most effusive set of compliments came from Bob. He had nothing but positive things to say in outlining how such a set of ideas can be useful for future pondering and writing on the subject matter. His generosity in all of this was second to none.

I hope that the tripartite structure of my essay reminded him of a similar architecture that undergirds his classical essays I have mentioned here above (1981, 1990). He had continued the compliments over the years, something I always appreciated because, after all, if the writer of "*De Vulgari Eloquentia*" thought well of my two essays, I must have been doing something right and of some value. Bob was a friend, and he was also a teacher. That kind of mentorship, regardless of its roots, is invaluable. Bob has offered that same mentorship to others, and those conversant with Bob's work can see the impact. In my own case, at the end of 1994 when I came back to the northeast for my annual visit, I felt a certain comfort in donning once again my red scarf.

NOTES
1. For my use if the slash (/) in place of the hyphen (-) see my essay "To Hyphenate or not to Hyphenate" (1989). There, and in a later version (Tamburri 1991), I spoke to the disjunctive quality of the hyphen (-) being canceled out by the more conjunctive quality of the slash (/).
2. "'The Semiology of Semen': Questioning the Father" was eventually published in 1986.
3. I refer here to both her 1969 essay and eventual book on Italian/American narrative (1974).
4. I am quoting here from the anthologized version (2000).
5. The absolute and unique quality of this book has been underscored by the reviews. See Bona (2006), Kvidera, Plasse, and Jacobson. See also Bona's essay in this volume (2020).
6. Felix articulated this expression in a conversation with a number of us at the Purdue University Conference on Romance Languages, Literatures, and Film, which ran from 1989 to 2000. I remember it vividly because along with Peter Carravetta, Fred Gardaphé, Paolo Giordano, and others, Bob was also present, and at one point both he and Felix engaged in a theoretical dance that was extremely constructive for all.

There was space for Italian/American studies at the Purdue University Conference because my then colleague Ben Lawton and I, co-founders of the event, were also working in the field and decided that we needed to make room for Italian/American studies within the general field of Italian studies. Bob's initial presence was fundamental to this specific gathering.

WORKS CITED

Basile Green, Rose. 1969. "The Italian-American Novel in the Mainstream of American Literature." In *The Italian American Novel. Proceedings of the Second Annual Conference, October 25, 1969*. John M. Cammett, ed., 1-5. Staten Island, NY: American Italian Historical Association.

Basile Green, Rose. 1974. The *Italian-American Novel. An Interaction between Two Cultures*. Madison, NJ: Fairleigh Dickinson University Press.

Bona, Mary Jo. 2006. Review of *Buried Caesars and Other Secrets of Italian American Writing*. Melus 31, no. 2 (Summer): 271-274.

Jacobson, Matthew Frye. 2009. Review of *Buried Caesars and Other Secrets of Italian American Writing*. Italian Americana 27, no. 2: 224-226.

Kvidera, Peter. 2007. Review of *Buried Caesars and Other Secrets of Italian American Writing*. American Literature 79 (September): 620-622.

Plasse, Marie A. 2008. Review of *Buried Caesars and Other Secrets of Italian American Writing*. Italian Culture 26: 194-197.

Tamburri, Anthony Julian. 1989. "To Hyphenate or not to Hyphenate: The Italian/American Writer and *Italianità*." *Italian Journal* (The Italian Academy) 3, no. 5: 37-42.

Tamburri, Anthony Julian. 1991. *To Hyphenate or not to Hyphenate: the Italian/American Writer: Or, An* Other *American?* Montreal: Guernica Editions.

Tamburri, Anthony Julian. 1994. "In (Re)cognition of the Italian/American Writer: Definitions and Categories." *Differentia, review of italian thought* 6/7 (Spring/Autumn): 9-32.

Tamburri, Anthony Julian, Paolo A. Giordano, Fred L. Gardaphé, eds. 1991/2000. *From the Margin: Writings in Italian Americana*. West Lafayette, IN: Purdue University Press.

van Gennep, Arnold. 1960. *The Rites of Passage,* translated by Monika B. Vizedon and Gabrielle L. Caffee, introduction by Solon T. Kimball. Chicago: University of Chicago Press.

Viscusi, Robert. 1986. "'The Semiology of Semen': Questioning the Father." *The Italian Americans Through the Generations.* Proceedings of the 15th Annual Conference of the American Italian Historical Association. Rocco Caporale, ed. 185-95. Staten Island: AIHA.

Viscusi, Robert. 1990. "Breaking the Silence: Strategic Imperatives for Italian American Culture." *Voices in Italian Americana* 1.1: 1-13.

Viscusi, Robert. 2000. "*De Vulgari Eloquentia*: An Approach to the Language of Italian American Fiction." *Yale Italian Poetry* (Winter 1981): 21-38; now in *The Review of the Italian American Studies*. Frank M. Sorrentino and Jerome Krase, eds. 303-322. Lanham, MD: Lexington Books.

Viscusi, Robert. 2006. *Buried Caesars and Other Secrets of Italian American Writing*. Albany, NY: SUNY Press.

Italian American Literary Studies and Robert Viscusi's Buried Treasures

Mary Jo Bona

This essay emerges from a position paper written and published after the 2014 Bellagio Italian American Studies Networking meeting.[1] Focusing on the interdisciplinary nature of our work in Italian American and diaspora studies across a range of fields encompassing the social sciences and the humanities, I chose to write about the challenges literary scholars faced in the academy when claiming the literature of Italian America as worthy of canonization. This struggle has ranged across generations for scholars whose expertise should enable them to shape and disseminate new knowledge. As we know, new knowledge elicits changes in the university curriculum, departmental offerings, and class syllabi. My entry into the field of Italian American literary studies was enabled by those scholars of feminist and ethnic studies who preceded me in the academy and challenged monolithic understandings of literary worth. One of those preeminent scholars whom I met early in my career is Robert Viscusi. His foresight about matters of Italian Americana was both intuitive and insistent: He believed in the importance of developing this field through scholarship, teaching, symposia, conferences, fellowships, and book fairs. I could not have agreed more about this kind of deep and broad focus. However, unlike me, Viscusi was unabashed about examining smash hits (pun intended!) like Mario Puzo's *The Godfather* (1969), examining the complex reasons underlying this novel's popularity and the cottage industry it spawned, and producing sequels and spinoffs for decades thereafter.[2]

Americans have demonstrated that they still know something in the twenty-first century about Puzo and *The Godfather*, though the Francis Ford Coppola trilogy may have eclipsed in scope even the book's huge success.[3] In a 2008 episode of the quiz competition game show *Jeopardy!*, the $800 clue under the category 20th Century Novels featured this declaration: "In 1955 he got an offer he couldn't refuse: the publication of his first novel, *The Dark Arena*" (Puzo 1955). Neither knowledge of the author's oeuvre nor the focus of his postwar novel was needed to answer correctly in the required form of a question: "Who is Mario Puzo?" The most famous—or infamous—idiom in Italian American vernacular goes hands down to Mario Puzo, whose Don Corleone utters this statement, and, like Nora's slamming door in Ibsen's *A Doll's House*, the sound reverberated round the world, especially through its cinematic incarnations in Coppola's film adaptations. To those of us working to develop the field of Italian American studies and in particular its literature, Puzo's *The Godfather* has presented both a challenge and a burden. For Viscusi, however, writing about *The Godfather* seemed like pure joy and a creative challenge. In the discussion below, I should like to engage parts of Viscusi's (2006) important monograph *Buried Caesars and Other Secrets of Italian American Writing* in order to showcase his ability to reveal the skeleton in the closet and teach us all something more about literature and American culture.[4] In addition, I shall consider Viscusi's contributions to literary Italian America as an invitation to explore how I have attempted to make canonical gestures on behalf of this body of literature within academic culture.

In *Buried Caesars*, Viscusi expands on Rose Basile Green's (1974) prescient commentary[5] on Puzo's *The Godfather*: In the United States, one of the most egregious and visibly available examples of grandiosity has been the gangster figure—both real and imagined.[6] Viscusi scrutinizes the history of Italian Americans whose marginalization pre- and postmigration has kept them in a state of suspended colonization, permanently equated with an American ideology that both popularizes and denounces criminality. Viscusi explains that, although second-generation Italian Americans became upwardly mobile, Italian American writers reflect their cultural group's subaltern position to reveal an "ideological double bind that constitutes their condition" (Viscusi 2006, xvii). Viscusi asserts that authors of

Italian America embody both Italian nationalist and imperialist ideologies *and* an American ideology that has class interests "more in common with Italian national culture than with Italian immigrant culture" (Viscusi 2006, xvii). One of the ways Italian American literature finds entrance into an American national discourse is through depictions of multiple forms of violence. Powerful sources in the old world harmed and debased impoverished Italians, who migrated en masse to a new world that inflicted equally violent forms of discrimination against them during the great migration period (approximately 1880–1924). The alignment of Italian ethnicity with criminality during this time was neither surprising nor original, but this association has been as pervasive as it has been durable. Troubling Italian Americans since at least the 1880s, images of violence involving Italian immigrants found their way onto the pages of the *New York Herald*, where Black Handers were featured wielding stilettos.

With the 1969 publication of *The Godfather*, Puzo brilliantly managed to resurrect and romanticize the criminal figure by creating a god in Don Corleone, whose distancing measures (from the sordid world of narcotics, for example) reflect Puzo's "will to canon" with a middle-brow book of popular fiction.[7] This feat poses a challenge for scholars who must approach the novel on several fronts, accepting the fact that "*The Godfather* has done more to create a national consciousness of the Italian American experience than any work of fiction or nonfiction published before or since" (Gardaphé 1996, 89). Puzo's literary forebears Bernadino Ciambelli, Garibaldi Lapolla, Guido D'Agostino, Pietro di Donato, and John Fante (all of whom he read voraciously) prepared him to extend the critique of U.S. capitalism through the filter of Sicilian American family justice, paving the way in the second half of the twentieth century for the creation of Don DeLillo's filmmaker Frank Volterra in *The Names*, whose comment that "Italians have made the family an extremist group" (Viscusi 2006, 202) reverberates around the market industry produced by *The Godfather*. How indebted is Italian American literature to *The Godfather*? Tremendously so. Is this problematic? I think not.

When characterizing the bent of Italian American discourse, Viscusi clarifies one of its founding myths: "this memory of how the rich expelled the poor into the world" (Viscusi 2006, 148). This mythologizing gets encapsulated in Puzo's portrayal of the immigrant who has "'made America' —who has, in effect, paid the price of making real the theoretical continent" (Viscusi 2006, 149).[8] Writing about the Mafia allowed Puzo to address "the problem of Italian subordination in the United States by constructing a version of the world in which Italian Americans are in charge" (Viscusi 2006, 197–198). The "constructing a version of the world in which Italian Americans are in charge" part of Viscusi's statement epitomizes his recognition underlying the psychic toll of extreme forms of marginalization Italians suffered in the homeland and the new world. Undergirding Viscusi's comment is a profundity that seems to have no bottom as represented by authors whose thematic loyalty focuses on criminality. The phrase "I'm in charge" reflects feelings of powerlessness and its puerile response to being put in control of something or someone else, with that control typically coming from a person with more power: a teacher, a parent, a president.[9] The power given is often perceived as illegitimate and its holder pathetic. This idea emerges from a condition of abjection for Italians who migrated because they were mistreated and penniless after the Risorgimento; but it also emerged for those whose colonial condition persisted when they moved from their immigrant parents' Little Italy to the suburbs after World War II. According to Viscusi, the message that immigrant Italians received from the country they left and the one they entered was one and the same: They "cannot achieve cultural equality" (Viscusi 2006, 4).

To combat if not rebut that sense of the abject, writers of Italian America to varying degrees and with arguable success used literary art to disinfect the wound, demonstrating how criminality in effect reified the very systems of order that debased Italian immigrants in the old and new worlds.[10] Viscusi puts it this way: "The Mafia fable dramatizes the truth that Italian Americans secretly belong to the order of prestige established by Roman aristocrats thousands of years ago," whose "Roman Caesars built altars to themselves." Forms of Caesarism in the new world become part of the colonial imagination of Italian immigrants and their progeny and include "impossible ideals and exaggerated claims to which Italian Americans still give their devotion: the notion that Rome was noble; the belief that the Family was sacred; the axiom that Italians discovered America" (Viscusi 2006, 6).

Such impossible ideals and exaggerated claims are on display almost as a form of pageantry in many of the novels, films, and other media Viscusi examines in *Buried Caesars*, from Garibaldi Lapolla's *The Grand Gennaro* to Mario Puzo's *The Godfather*; from *Little Caesar* to *The Sopranos*. This profound conflict in the (Italian American) colonial imagination is partly rooted in masculine culture with young men being socialized into behavior reinforced by a cautionary narrowness in the family home and surrounding neighborhood. Robert Orsi's use of the term *domus* in referring to the community of Italian Harlem of the early twentieth century is instructive here as it underlines the profound importance of the family and household on the larger urban village in which the Italian community's collective faith was performed in the streets through religious procession and *festa*—forms of community pageantry. The term *domus* recalls the houses occupied by the upper classes and some wealthy freedmen during the republican and imperial eras (Orsi 1985). The writers Viscusi examines focus on "the case of the house"—less murder mystery and more passion, but an Italian America in which family and house are interchangeable and a response to abjection (Viscusi 2006, 59). In chapter 3, "Il caso della casa," Viscusi isolates four kinds of houses that exemplify the profound influence of the colonial imagination on Italian Americans that their authors have portrayed. Shrine, villa, palazzo, or embassy, the house remains both sacred and conflicted space for its immigrant inhabitants. Viscusi explains this phenomenon in Kristevian terms:

> *House* must also become *community*. The logic, it may be, is the psychologic of the communion supper: in consuming a corpse,

one must spread the guilt. Instead of consecrating oneself alone to the magic relic of abandoned Italy—the murdered parent—and instead even of merely planting the corpse to grow a new paternal tree, one must call together assemblies of fellow criminals and share the guilty meal. (Viscusi 2006, 64)

Keeping in mind this profound conflict in the colonial imagination, how did its most devoted conjurer, Puzo, benefit from this focus? And, moreover, how to teach this body of Italian American literature in the face of the continued hegemony of Anglophone and Anglo-American writing? Does knowing all this make more tenable the inclusion of Puzo's *The Godfather* in the university classroom? Doubtful, but a monograph like Viscusi's *Buried Caesars* offers professors a theoretical entry into, let us say it, crime fiction. Popular fiction is still disparaged or at least found suspect among U.S. English professors since the professionalization of reading developed as an academic endeavor.[11] It is useful here to take an example from the mid-nineteenth century of Harriet Beecher Stowe's magnificent *Uncle Tom's Cabin*. This best-selling novel was relegated to the historical bins and faulted in the twentieth century for its sentimentalism and racism.[12] Puzo himself denigrated the very genre of popular fiction that gave him his greatest success and fame, admitting that he "wrote below [his] gifts in that novel" (Gussow 1999, 7).

While it is not my purpose to argue for Puzo's canonization within the category of Great Books, *The Godfather* remains an example of a *classic* novel, like Stowe's, in the popular fiction category, and as such the novel "perhaps more than any other kind of literature has always blurred the distinction between popular and high art" (Torgovnick 1994, 114). Blurred distinctions invite reappraisal, especially of disparaged genres such as popular fiction, including sentimental novels, detective fiction, and yes, crime novels. Puzo's *Godfather* blurs distinctions further because it is neither solely a typical crime novel nor a melodrama, but rather a combination of both: a "melodrama of beset manhood," set within a criminal enterprise.[13] For this idea, I am indebted to another superb monograph, solely devoted to the *Godfather* phenomenon: Chris Messenger's (2002) *The Godfather and American Culture: How the Corleones Became "Our Gang."* Published four years before *Buried Caesars*, Messenger clearly influenced Viscusi's appreciation of the allure Puzo's novel held for U.S. readers. As Messenger explains, Puzo uses the genre of sentimental domestic fiction, "putatively the locus of real female authority and multiplicity," and subsumes it through a "male takeover" as a Sicilian peasant boy turned immigrant father goes bad "in search of American power and authority" (Messenger 2002, 175). Assuring visibility within the domus, Don Corleone exhibits a persistence, in the face of outside threats and the brutal realities of drug warfare, that encapsulates the fantasy of "unqualified American security and success: the fantasy of a self-reliant, upward mobility within a total identity in family" (Messenger 2002, 174). Because it functions as popular fiction, *The Godfather*, Messenger explains, "licenses a terrific mobility and freedom," allowing readers vicarious pleasure in believing for a while that Don Corleone, the "avenging peasant" (41), was as morally scrupulous as his avenging celestial counterpart, St. Michael, victorious over the horrors of hell. For better or worse, Puzo placed Italian Americans on the literary map more visibly than any other writer before or since.

The erasure of literary Italian America, whether popular or elite, was neither entirely systemic nor systematic but occurred in the 1930s along with the elimination of black, white female, and all working-class writers from the American literary canon. As Paul Lauter outlined, "the professionalization of the teaching of literature, the development of an aesthetic theory that privileged certain texts, and the historiographic organization of the body of literature into conventional 'periods' and 'themes'" (Lauter 1991, 27) together create intrinsic barriers to teaching lesser-known writers. The hegemonic force of U.S. literary anthologies, which decreased focus on a variety of writers in favor of promoting "major writers," all but guaranteed the exclusion from syllabi of ethnically identified writers. Along with primarily Anglo-Saxon male professors, who influenced the teaching of literature and reading choices, were editors themselves who, in their untested acceptance of the inherent value of certain literary works, neglected or refused to recognize "their own role in determining which are the truly great works" (Tompkins 1985, 188).

Despite the publishing achievements of early writers of Italian America such as John Fante, Pietro di Donato, and Jerre Mangione, they did not reap the benefits of sustained secondary criticism or anthology inclusion (within the academy) until the latter half of the twentieth century. Their narratives and those of many others unflinchingly portray the experience of being colonized by both a homeland that starved them and a new world that exploited them. In several chapters of *Buried Caesars,* Viscusi creatively discusses the dialectical impact of Italian immigrant languages on the development of an Italian national identity in the United States and as a rhetorical device in writing that offers both continuity with the homeland and a way to negotiate with the new world. Those of us devoted to the ongoing recovery work of Italian American writers recognize that we are thoroughly involved in determining how this literature will be valued and interpreted in the future. As a result, we must make a deliberate mental shift away from the limiting confines of traditional departments in order to introduce underrepresented texts, aware of the intersection between redefined modes of scholarship and pedagogy. The academic shifts in the 1970s and 1980s that brought conversations—often contentious ones—about canon reformation to the forefront and in the 1990s brought the "culture wars" to a fever pitch, required us to work fast and proficiently to develop the late-arriving field of Italian American studies.[14] Aware that academic canons exert hegemonic force in traditional departments, I continue to align my classes with general education requirements for idealistic and pragmatic purposes: to expose a larger swath of the Stony Brook University student population to the field of Italian American studies and to assure that our courses would garner the numbers to keep them running. Donning several hats beyond what counts in academia as worthy of promotion, those of us who have built programs recognize the necessity of touting the discipline in various venues, enriching the field of Italian American studies through new historicist and feminist approaches that address social and political contexts within literary analysis. As Jane Tompkins (1985) said, "*[L]iterary* judgments of value do not depend on literary considerations alone, since the notion of what is literary is defined by and nested within changing historical conditions" (195; italics added).

Comparative approaches, for example, move us away from a consensus-oriented syllabus in which textual themes are shared across a culture and toward a perspective that has potential to offer counter-readings, which are fundamentally interventionist in purpose. Ethnic literatures in the United States, Italian American literature included, often articulate counterhegemonic textual practices, mapping out, as David Palumbo-Liu (1995) explains, possible "spaces of resistance" (2). Even within the same cultural group, comparative perspectives illuminate conflicting sides of a debate close to the hearts of its readers: Nathaniel Hawthorne's *The Scarlet Letter* reads differently when read alongside Harriet Beecher Stowe's *Uncle Tom's Cabin*, compelling us to redefine motherhood through institutions of religion and slavery and illuminating societal evils from different eras as combatted by the moral righteousness of mothers.

No less fruitful would it be to place two generically different works by the same author side by side, thereby inflecting the experience of reading them together. Puzo's second novel, *The Fortunate Pilgrim* (1965), allows readers to deconstruct the romance of the third, provoking a rereading of *The Godfather* that *resists* the tendency to be seduced by the *comparatico* (godparent) world represented by the insularity of Sicilian Americans. Add to this example of provincialism a feminist reading and a woman might ask the same question that Judith Fetterley suggests be asked about that earlier misogynistic tale of America "Rip Van Winkle": What is a woman to do? Like Irving's seductively amiable tale, Puzo's novel invites the female reader to be "co-opted into participation in an experience from which she is explicitly excluded; she is asked to identify with a selfhood that defines itself in opposition to her; she is required to identify against herself" (Fetterley 1978, 9, xii). For in *The Godfather*, there is only one person with whom to identify—Don Corleone—and the identification is illusory and impossible for any reader, resisting or not. When juxtaposed with *The Fortunate Pilgrim*, however, *The Godfather* can be deconstructed and the very mythology of Sicilian justice critiqued by the earlier novel's central character, Lucia Santa, whose resiliency and strength emerge from an impregnable understanding of honor and loyalty disconnected from masculine notions of power.

That said, I remain vigilant with regard to how I go about teaching and developing a canon of Italian American letters, keeping in mind Toni Morrison's admonition that "there must be a way to enhance canon readings without enshrining them" (Morrison 1990, 205). The analysis of Italian American texts (including visual media) faces a similar challenge of being subsumed under the rubric of "homogenized difference," to quote David Palumbo-Liu (1995), and these works can be managed in such a way as to erase or at least neutralize conflict (5). In his reflection on the discourses of transnationalism and African American studies, for example, Mark Sanders examines the ways ethnic disciplines in U.S. universities are limited by academic institutionalization. Largely U.S.-focused, such disciplines produce scholars who are trained in "longer-standing disciplines and thus often specialize in fields that are nation-specific, that do not need to be comparative, and that most frequently require the use of only one language, usually English" (Sanders 2007, 813). In order to achieve cultural equality, Viscusi believes that a historically nuanced understanding of the Mafia as a myth of the Italian American colonial condition must be examined alongside the preeminent marker of their historical social subordination, which is language itself.

Viscusi hails as Dantean the decision to write in the vernacular by Italian American writers whose linguistic daring makes it possible to celebrate the power of a mythical Italy and to mediate between two languages. Citing Pietro di Donato's (1939) *Christ in Concrete* as a novel that speaks in tongues—liturgical, patriarchal, heroic, and diplomatic—Viscusi recapitulates this linguistic masterpiece throughout *Buried Caesars*, examining the interrupted history of Italian American writing and di Donato's early national fame. In "The Semiology of Semen: Questioning the Father" (chapter 6), Viscusi explores the truncated literary career of di Donato, attributing the suspension of the development of Italian American letters to World War II when Italy became an enemy nation and a generation of Italian Americans were under suspicion, interned in camps, and forbidden to speak their native tongues (2006). As Viscusi eloquently shows, *Christ in Concrete* is all about recovering the language and subsequently recovering *italianità* (Italianness) after its disparagement by Benito Mussolini's Fascism and the American wartime antipathy toward Italian Americans.

Throughout *Buried Caesars*, Viscusi reveals the aftershocks of post-Risorgimento Italy for those Italians who migrated and those Americans whose perception of Italy before the mass migration were indubitably altered after decades of poor Italian immigrants coming to seek work. However, what occurred in the aftermath of those years of Italian migration might seem counterintuitive, but in fact it makes perfect sense in light of the centuries-long love affair Anglo-Americans had for Italy. In a terrific analysis of the effects of the great wave of migration, Viscusi argues that Italian immigrants indeed assimilated into the U.S. economy partly because of the longtime investment Americans already had made in the aesthetic wonders of Italy:

> [T]he Italian Sign in the United States had very little trouble assimilating the Italian immigrants to its economy. The American Renaissance had what appears in retrospect a fated meeting with the Great Migration ... [which was] not accompanied by a withdrawal from things Italian in Anglo-America. Indeed, the opposite occurred. The late nineteenth century was a time of unparalleled Italianate splendor in the U.S. cities. (Viscusi 2006, 165)

Once immigrants discovered they were Italian (after migration to the United States), they entered the English language "bearing the Italian sign on their backs" (Viscusi 2006, 169). Viscusi cites the revolutionary poet Arturo Giovannitti, who understood that the English language and "the oppressive system that the immigrants need to negotiate become the same thing" (170). Viscusi explains that in Giovannitti's poem "To the English language" the poet "transfers his enormous resentment of the immigrant condition onto the language that has institutionalized that condition." In the parodic poem, Giovannitti writes: "To the English language . . . / I have put in my hands your hands to grapple with you, / . . . You the deed that has become the word" (Viscusi 2006, 169).

Grappling with English in the United States, Italians became both European and Italian American on new-world shores. Those who became writers empathized deeply with the stories they heard from parents, extended families, and kinship communities, incorporating voices of folk wisdom and American lingo to produce a multivocality unique to Italian American writing. Viscusi gives the lie to the assumption that immigrant Italians were *all* "inarticulate and uneducated undesirables" (174), and he has spent a lifetime proving doubters wrong. If the field of literary Italian American studies falls through the cracks in academia, then it is up to us to get on our knees and start digging.

Robert Viscusi has been one of those intrepid excavators who has always appreciated the inseparable nexus of personal advocacy, word-of-mouth sponsorship, supportive publishers, scholarly critiques, conference panels, books, exhibits, and — not least — syllabi inclusion. He has uncovered buried treasures of literary Italian America through a theoretical lens that compels us to recognize the colonial condition within the tradition and reflect further on the aftershocks of the migratory experience. This is a story worth investing more time in unearthing. Viscusi's *Buried Caesars* offers us a way into that space without getting trapped inside narrow confines. His work helps expand the literary territory of Italian America. Lest we despair, let us remember that during the terrible Depression of the 1930s, the literary landscape shifted, illuminating the works of immigrant and minority writers, including Italian Americans. Consider the careers of John Fante, Pietro di Donato, Jerre Mangione, Mari Tomasi, Marion Benasutti, and certainly Frances Winwar, who is in need of recuperation. Should other fortuitous events embrace us, I imagine here a future episode of *Jeopardy!*, in which, under the category of 20th Century Novels, the $2,000 clue reads as follows: "In her only published novel of Italian American Chicago, this author wrote the line, 'When you fight to come home, you beautiful.'"[15] Of course, Robert Viscusi knows the answer, given in the form of a question he has relentlessly pursued throughout the course of his storied career.

NOTES

[1] For more essays on the topic of Italian American studies and diaspora-related curricula, please see the resulting publication, *Transcending Borders, Bridging Gaps: Italian Americana, Diasporic Studies, and the University Curriculum*, edited by Tamburri and Gardaphé (2015).

[2] See also the 2008 special issue *Reconsidering Mario Puzo*, guest edited by Chris Messenger, Michele Fazio, and JoAnne Ruvoli. My essay, "Puzo and the Power of Fictional Mythography," was my first entry into a critical analysis on the literary criminal enterprise of Mario Puzo. Writing this essay helped me to understand my father better.

[3] Puzo won acceptance for his first two books with the publication of *The Godfather*. A "genuinely mythic" work of fiction, as Puzo wrote in *The Godfather Papers* (Puzo 1972, 33), this best-selling novel catapulted its author into the national limelight, exceeding in critical praise all works of Italian American fiction prior to it, including Pietro di Donato's popular *Christ in Concrete*. One of the most widely read novels of the twentieth century, *The Godfather* spent sixty-seven weeks on the *New York Times* best-seller list. *The Godfather* continues to be the best-known book by an Italian American writer.

[4] I reviewed *Buried Caesars and Other Secrets of Italian American Writing* for the journal *MELUS*, the primary organ for the dissemination of multiethnic literature of the United States. A continuous and primary goal for literary Italian American studies must be sustained inclusion in peer-reviewed journals devoted to *all* American literatures, especially for works that are less known than but equally commendable as their more famous peers.

[5] One of the earliest and most astute critics of *The Godfather*, Rose Basile Green believed that the Italian American novel came of age with the publication of Puzo's third novel (*The Godfather*, 1969). Green declared that Puzo's "art [was] evaluated on equal terms with other writers" (Green 1974, 368). Aware of America's "psychic obsessions" with violence and criminality, Green noted the benefit Puzo's novel gained from such obsessions, "since he deals aggressively with areas of Italian American experience to which the mass media have given national notoriety" (336).

[6] Mario Puzo's best seller has inspired a plethora of evocative interpretations, including the aforementioned Rose Green's assessment (Green 1974) of *The God-

father as a quintessential American story. For Fred Gardaphé (1996), *The Godfather* functions strategically as a tale of reverse assimilation, teaching American readers how to assimilate to Sicilian ways. Thomas Ferraro extends such an analysis by focusing on Puzo's novel as a story of the fusion of kinship (Italian) with capitalism (American) (Ferraro 1993). Interpreted as a tale of seduction, Pellegrino D'Acierno (1999) argues that *The Godfather* makes an offer to the reader he can't refuse. Chris Messenger (2002) argues that *The Godfather* was at the same time Mario Puzo's gesture of "going bad," responding to the betrayal he felt for the lack of popular success of *The Fortunate Pilgrim* (1965): "*The Godfather* counters all the authorities that function like the invisible government of literary culture to keep Puzo from validating his 'belief in art' as a talisman to ward off any lifeworld interference. … The Corleone historical situation is such that the 'Family' replaces 'Art' as the first principle, even as *The Godfather* replaces Puzo's earlier fiction. Puzo believes in Don Corleone as he had in art; he finds in *him* the protection that he 'could find in no other place'" (Messenger 2002, 33).

[7] I borrow the phrase "will to canon" from Wenying Xu (2006), who analyzes the poetry of Li-Young Lee and his disavowals of ethnic identification as a deliberate "*will to canon* that is tied to the dominant sociocultural practice of exclusion in the name of universalism and aesthetics" (145). See also Chris Messenger (2002) for a comprehensive analysis of Puzo's best seller in the context of popular versus elite fiction.

[8] Viscusi's (2006) comment here echoes William Boelhower's (1987) theoretical cartography in *Through a Glass Darkly*. Of Hector St. John de Crèvecoeur and his 1782 *Letters from an American Farmer*, Boelhower writes, "By making America, Americans could make themselves" (42) — explanatory language Viscusi uses to examine the Italian migration story a century later. Of Boelhower, Viscusi (2006) writes: "Boelhower occupies so richly elaborated an intellectual space [and is] the literary geographer … an originator of very considerable poetic power" (235).

[9] A memorable example occurred in 1981 after an assassination attempt on President Ronald Reagan when then Secretary of State Alexander Haig famously declared on television that "I'm in charge here and not to worry."

[10] I am taking my cue from Julia Kristeva's (1982) formulation of the abject in *Powers of Horror*. Kristeva associates literary art with the sublime and the abject, explaining that "literature is probably a version of the apocalypse that seems to me rooted … on the fragile border … where identities … do not exist or only barely so — double, fuzzy, heterogeneous, animal, metamorphosed, altered, abject" (207).

[11] In the past twenty years, the proliferation of memoirs and graphic narratives (to name just two genres) has re-shifted the literary landscape in many U.S. academic departments, including my own: Women's, Gender & Sexuality Studies and English. Reading "popular fiction" continues to be treated with skepticism in canonical departments like English but syllabus reading choices are increasingly tempered by trends in popular culture, which, candidly, do not feature crime novels from the Italian American oeuvre.

[12] The first book edition of Stowe's *Uncle Tom's Cabin* appeared in 1852 "and sold more than 300,000 copies in the first year. This bestselling novel of the nineteenth century was extremely influential in fueling antislavery sentiment during the

decade preceding the Civil War" (Books That Shaped America, n.d.). In her copy of the novel, Susan B. Anthony acknowledged in 1903 that "blacks are still not fairly treated" (Books That Shaped America, n.d.). James Baldwin (1949) excoriated Stowe's novel for its dishonesty and sentimentality.

13 I am referring to Nina Baym's 1982 groundbreaking essay in which the author argues convincingly how literary theories throughout most of the twentieth century excluded women from the canon.

14 The genealogical provenance of the culture wars emerges from the *Kulturkampf* (literally, culture struggle) of the 1870s German Reich. For historical context and background to the culture wars in America, see Chapman's (2015) three-volume reference work, *Culture Wars in America*, and, in particular, his introduction to the first edition. See also James Davison Hunter's (1991) *Culture Wars*, especially chapter 3, "The Historical Roots of the Culture War," and Todd Gitlin's (1995) *The Twilight of Common Dreams*. For an overview of the intersection between the culture wars and the canon debate in 1980s America, see "The Culture Wars and the Canon Debate" (Bona 2017).

15 The answer is Tina De Rosa (1980, 1996).

WORKS CITED

Baldwin, James. 1949. "Everybody's Protest Novel." *The Partisan Review*; reprinted in *Notes of a Native Son*. https://.loc.gov/exhibits/books-that-shaped-america/1850-to-1920.html (accessed July 11, 2019).

Baym, Nina. 1982. "Melodramas of Beset Manhood: How Theories of American Fiction Exclude Women Authors." *American Quarterly* vol. 33, no. 2 (Summer, 1981): 123–139.

Boelhower, William. 1987. *Through a Glass Darkly: Ethnic Semiosis in American Literature*. Oxford: Oxford University Press.

Bona, Mary Jo. 2008. "Puzo and the Power of Fictional Mythography." *Voices in Italian Americana* 19.2 (Fall): 28–42.

Bona, Mary Jo. 2017. "The Culture Wars and the Canon Debate." In *American Literature in Transition: 1980–1990*, edited by D. Miller, 225–238. Cambridge: Cambridge University Press.

Books That Shaped America. n.d. "1850–1900." Library of Congress. https://www.loc.gov/exhibits/books-that-shaped-America/1850-to-1900.html (accessed July 10, 2019).

Chapman, Roger. 2015. "Introduction to the First Edition: Culture Wars in America—Rhetoric and Reality." In *Culture Wars in America: An Encyclopedia of Issues, Viewpoints, and Voices*, edited by Roger Chapman and James Ciment. xxvii–xxxii. Armonk, NY: M.E. Sharpe.

D'Acierno, Pellegrino. 1999. "Cinema Paradiso: The Italian American Presence in American Cinema." In *The Italian American Heritage: A Companion to Literature and Arts*, edited by Pellegrino D'Acierno, 563–690. New York: Garland Publishing.

De Rosa, Tina. 1996 [1980]. *Paper Fish.* New York: Feminist Press.

Di Donato, Pietro. 1993 [1939]. *Christ in Concrete.* 1939. New York: Signet.

Ferraro, Thomas. 1993. *Ethnic Passages: Literary Immigrants in Twentieth-Century America.* Chicago: University of Chicago Press.

Fetterley, Judith. 1978. *The Resisting Reader: A Feminist Approach to American Fiction.* Bloomington: Indiana University Press.

Gardaphé, Fred L. 1996. *Italian Signs, American Streets: The Evolution of Italian American Narrative.* Durham: Duke University Press.

Gitlin, Todd. 1995. *The Twilight of Common Dreams: Why America Is Wracked by Culture Wars.* Henry Holt: Metropolitan Books.

Green, Rose Basile. 1974. *The Italian American Novel: A Document of the Interaction of Two Cultures.* Rutherford, NJ: Fairleigh Dickinson University Press.

Gussow, Mel. 1999. "Mario Puzo, Author Who Made 'The Godfather' a World Addiction, Is Dead at 78," the *New York Times*, July 3, 7.

Haig, Alexander. 2014. "Moments in U.S. Diplomatic History"; https://adst.org/2014/03/al-haig-and-the-reagan-assassination-attempt-im-in-charge-here/ (accessed July 10, 2019).

Hunter, James Davison. 1991. *Culture Wars: The Struggle to Define America.* New York: Basic Books.

Kristeva, Julia. 1982. *Powers of Horror: An Essay on Abjection.* New York: Columbia University Press.

La Polla, Garibaldi. 2009. *The Grand Gennaro,* rev. ed. New Brunswick, NJ: Rutgers University Press.

Lauter, Paul. 1991. *Canons and Contexts.* New York: Oxford University Press.

Messenger, Chris. 2002. *The Godfather and American Culture: How the Corleones Became "Our Gang."* Albany: State University of New York Press.

Morrison, Toni. 1990. "Unspeakable Things Unspoken: The Afro-American Presence in American Literature." In *Modern Critical Views: Toni Morrison*, edited by Harold Bloom, 201–230. New York: Chelsea.

Orsi, Robert. 1985. *The Madonna of 115th Street: Faith and Community in Italian Harlem, 1880–1950.* New Haven, CT: Yale University Press.

Palumbo-Liu, David, ed. 1995. *The Ethnic Canon: Histories, Institutions and Interventions.* Minneapolis: University of Minnesota Press.

Puzo, Mario. 1955. *The Dark Arena.* New York: Ballantine Books.

Puzo, Mario. 1997 [1965]. *The Fortunate Pilgrim.* New York: Ballantine.

Puzo, Mario. 1969. *The Godfather.* New York: New American Library.

Puzo, Mario. 1972. *The Godfather Papers and Other Confessions.* New York: G. P. Putnam.

Sanders, Mark A. 2007. "Brief Reflections on the Discourse of Transnationalism and African American Studies." Ethnic Studies in the Age of Transnationalism. *PMLA* 122.3 (May): 812–814.

Tamburri, Anthony, and Fred Gardaphé, eds. 2015. *Transcending Borders, Bridging Gaps: Italian Americana, Diasporic Studies, and the University Curriculum.* New York: John D. Calandra Italian American Institute.

Tompkins, Jane. 1985. *Sensational Designs: The Cultural Work of American Fiction, 1790–1860.* New York: Oxford University Press.

Torgovnick, Marianna De Marco. 1994. *Crossing Ocean Parkway.* Chicago: University of Chicago Press.

Viscusi, Robert. 2006. *Buried Caesars and Other Secrets of Italian American Writing.* Albany: State University of New York Press.

Xu, Wenying. 2006. "An Exile's Will to Canon and Its Tension with Ethnicity." In *Multiethnic Literature and Canon Debates*, edited by Mary Jo Bona and Irma Maini, 145–164. Albany: State University of New York Press.

Existential Universalisms, Epistemological Diversity: A Social Historian Reads Robert Viscusi's *Astoria*

Donna Gabaccia

It begins with memory. Sooner or later—whether at age twenty or at age fifty—the experience of growing older causes you to review remembered wisps of your childhood, perhaps with the futile hope that your elders and your memories of them will not disappear as they age and die, as you age and die. The first moment of confronting your own mortality is the start of an existential crisis that accelerates with the mourning of each subsequent death. Yet the universality of that crisis, shared by all humans, provides scant comfort. You want to take action, you have unanswered questions. There is so much you do not know. Descendants of immigrants often begin at this moment to grasp the vastness of the movements that deposited them in their current locations and to be aware of the enormity of transformations, still ongoing, that preceded them. And there are little mysteries too, family mysteries. Your ignorance of them exacerbates your malaise. You want keys to unlock closed doors. Do you ask questions? Do elders refuse to answer? Do they offer confused responses? Perhaps they will share secrets only if you promise to carry the proffered clues to your own grave.

Each person on earth faces the existential crisis differently. Robert Viscusi's acceptance of a mother's request for secrecy powerfully shaped the writing of his astonishing 1995 book *Astoria*. For me, a social historian, reading *Astoria* has been a way to get to know better a scholar whom I have met only very casually at occasional scholarly meetings. Our professional distance is itself an indicator of how significantly epistemology divides scholars, even in the relatively small field of Italian American studies.

Astoria is a book written by a man struggling to know the full significance of the recent death of his immigrant mother. In it, he approaches his mother through memory, allegory, and landscape, often reflecting on the unlikely figure of Napoleon Bonaparte as another "Italian immigrant, short, quick, determined, who made good" (Viscusi 1995, 59). Struggling to uncover new knowledge about a powerful, haunting mother, he tromps boldly through literature, history, philosophy, and semiology. Searching for a path forward, he criss-crosses familiar landscapes around New York City and its suburbs and outer-borough neighborhoods—notably Astoria and Sunnyside—and beyond to Paris and Rome, where he suffers and describes the agony of writing. Once writing, he names some family names and shares some family memories while also leaving much hidden or obscure. *Astoria* offers a vivid account of mourning a parent who remains elusive to the end, in part because she wanted that. It reveals mourning to be the obsessive, vertiginous, and terrifying process that I, too, know it to be.[1] For 276 pages, Viscusi does battle—sometimes tenderly, sometimes brutally—with his mother, his memories of her, and his knowledge of Napoleon. At the book's center is the moment when his mother will not or cannot validate his horrific memory of her threatening him, "If I thought you were going to grow up like him [his father], I would strangle you right now" (168). The author experienced her as angry and powerful enough to do it; he also recounts a terrifying family scene of his mother's father chasing her around the block with a straight razor after cutting himself while shaving. Violence and silence haunt *Astoria*. And they continue across generations.

When it was published in 1995, *Astoria* marked a shift in the epistemological center of migration studies, away from the positivist assumptions of the social sciences and history. Personally and professionally—which is to say, as a writer—Viscusi began with different assumptions and other talents. Recounting his sojourn in Rome, he confesses his unhappiness with the "new faraway cousins with their incredibly precise collections of names and dates and faces, their avid comparative sociology" (247). And he is not afraid to show readers that his own preferences for metaphor and allegory did not satisfy his kin. When Viscusi describes his Sunnyside grandmother working in a basement wearing a factory smock as resembling "the Queen of England in a cage at the zoo" (248), his name-compiling Italian cousin bridles. In the same conversation, Viscusi vigorously declares his impatience with those who write "of migrations like swarming termites" (248). And it is not just faraway cousins that discomfit him, for he has heard with dismay reports of Astoria "*paisani* forming folkdance societies to preserve the dialect and the music" (218). Historians and folklorists, be forewarned!

In its June 15, 1995, evaluation, *Kirkus Reviews* praised *Astoria*'s rich evocations of remembered people and places. But like the author's Italian cousin, it also raised objections to the book's central allegory and to its recurring experiments with authorial positionality. Viewed retrospectively it is obvious how *Astoria* mirrored 1990s academic battles among structuralists, positivists, post-structuralists, and deconstructionists. But reading it twenty-five years later, I felt impatience with both the author (sorry, but I too am no fan of *Astoria*'s playful positionality) and the book's reviewers. To reviewers, I wanted to conjure my own dead father's voice and tell them simply to "let the man mourn, for chrissakes. It's his mother and it's his mourning." The existential challenges of death and desire for transcendence and meaningful existence across time and space may be universals, but each person's response and mourning reveal the considerable depth of humans' epistemological diversity. And that is a good thing—a good thing for all, I assert.

Reading *Astoria* in 2019, I especially appreciated the gauntlet the book throws down before the epistemological assumptions of people much like me—sociologists, family historians, and genealogists. In 2019 more than in 1995 I can assert that Italian American studies has room for queenly metaphors, dancing *paisani*, allegories of Napoleon, swarming termites, and genealogically inclined relatives. So strongly do I feel about such epistemological diversity that I offer here as homage to Viscusi[2] a modest reflection on how I, in addition to all other humans, struggle with the universal existential challenge.

Our responses typically begin with compilations of memory fragments. Beyond memory, we look for other shards, which can be cobbled together in complex fashion and in many different forms. Some compilers ease the existential malaise by reading and writing poetry. Some revisit and reflect on landscapes remembered, preserved, foreign, transformed. Some grasp for the stars and for grandeur, drawing on intensive years of their own unique educations to produce allegory, statistical summations, works of art. Some compile family archives, transforming taped or typed voices and photographs into preserved artifacts. Many—very many, I have learned—search for scraps of paper (now increasingly glowing on computer screens everywhere) and become genealogists, creating family trees heavy with names and dates. While all these activities can offer routes to identity, transcendence, and existential peace, none is universally appreciated. For this homage, I use the naming of names as an articulation of fundamental epistemological difference while also identifying the unifying importance of memory in confrontations with family secrets—whether among the allegorically or the genealogically inclined.

Perhaps because I am a social historian who has used genealogical methods to explore emigration from Sambuca di Sicilia and who has written recently about Italian American genealogists with Sambuca origins as researchers and knowledge-producers, *Astoria* powerfully alerted me to the naming of names as a marker of an epistemological chasm that yawns open at the moment of existential crisis. Producing an emotionally satisfying form of knowledge for some, personal and family names elicit boredom from others. Naming names (or refusing to name names, a central expectation of *omertà*) is always an issue for Italian Americans and thus for Italian American studies. Whether or not to name names was undoubtedly a complex issue for *Astoria*'s author, for it was among his two groups of kin in Astoria and Sunnyside that he, in mourning, sought his path forward.

As a reader of *Astoria*, I quickly recognized how the book's frequent invocations of Napoleon contributed to its allegorical and poetic strengths. Discussion of Napoleon transformed one man's mother into a more powerful and universal figure with well-known qualities—notably great power and political tactical skills—that then adhered, however problematically, to the mother. Napoleon's name linked the small localisms of one mother's life to the vast transformative global historical cataclysms of revolution, nation-building, and exile and to the grand architecture and cities of Europe. These cataclysms defined the experience of mourning the mother's death.

Somewhat similarly, although on a far smaller scale, Viscusi's introduction of the names of Robert Browning and Beato Roberto (the patron saint of Salle [Pescara province], Abruzzo, hometown of his mother's father) layered meaning and significance onto each of the briefly mentioned individual Roberts of his mother's family. These include Viscusi's mother's paternal Uncle Roberto DiRocco, her father's younger and more successful brother, the author himself (fully named only on the title page), and the author's son Robert Viscusi, Jr. (to whom, along with his daughter Victoria, he dedicated *Astoria*). *Astoria* offers readers a maternal lineage of Roberts. The allegories of Robert Browning and Beato Roberto relocate an individual mother and several individual Roberts, repositioning them on a grander social, cultural, and historical scale of importance while leaving the author (and sometimes also the reader) overwhelmed and confused. The grand scale sucks the reader into the large and swirling maelstrom of the mourning the author experienced, allowing them to appreciate and share it.

But whereas Napoleon and Robert Browning are oft named, only a few of Viscusi's kin carry their own given or family names in *Astoria*. Most named are his mother's relatives, a choice that deepens the book's differentiation between the warm but violent emotionalism and *italianità* (Italianness) of maternal Astoria (the DiRoccos and their affines) and the workaday, more American, upwardly mobile and analytical world of Sunnyside where the author lived among his mechanically inclined and entrepreneurial paternal kin, the Viscusis. His maternal "Uncle Mike" (his godfather and the husband of his mother's sister, who was also his godmother) is named several times as an important presence at several key moments of Viscusi's life. Even more important is his mother's "Cousin Bill" who is not only named more often than any other relative, but whose relationship to the author's mother reveals her as both a woman in possession of positive and loving emotions (apparently missing from her fraught marriage) and limited by conventional gendered expectations. She greatly admired her slightly younger, reckless Cousin Bill, son of her father's sister, who swam New York City's treacherous Hell Gate at age thirteen, "not long before he went to jail" (Viscusi 1995, 34). Viscusi later makes Bill's bravura Hell Gate swim and his mother's pleasure in watching it the central scene of the allegorical immigrant Disneyland he creates on the final pages of *Astoria*. Despite his incarceration, Cousin Bill obviously remained the apple of Viscusi's mother's affectionate eye. She enjoyed his reminiscences of adventures in the wartime South Pacific. In late life when the physically powerful Bill needed an influx of cash, she purchased from him (and subsequently benefited enormously from the sale of) a plot of land both of them believed initially to be worthless. In short, although Viscusi's mother may have sworn him to silence on other matters, it is her kin—or at least a few of them—who carry personal names in *Astoria*.

Not so the Viscusis of Sunnyside. There, only his cousin Judy is named more than once—as the keeper of several important memories. Viscusi's Aunt Margaret Giardinelli Viscusi also bears a name but she was simultaneously paternal kin (the wife of the author's father's brother) and maternal kin (the child of his mother's mother's sister). The imbalance in naming maternal and paternal kin persists even among the book's minor figures. While a boarder with the DiRocco family and the DiRoccos' prosperous landlords have names (Tomas the Communist in the first case and the Fanaras, including their skilled cousin Angelina, in the second), the Viscusis' boarder remains a closely described and influential person identified only as an anonymous "Connecticut" or "Yankee tinker." Readers learn the names of the Italian villages of origin of the DiRoccos (Salle and Tivoli, near Rome) and not those of the paternal kin. By rooting the mother's kin in Italy, with its peasant customs and dialects, the book makes the American commitments to success among the DiRoccos appear more obvious through contrast.

A Social Historian Reads Robert Viscusi's *Astoria*

Astoria forced me as a reader to recognize how badly I wanted to attach names to all the people appearing in Viscusi's shared shards of memory. That desire in turn revealed my own epistemological assumptions: Names created necessary knowledge for me. At first I found myself scribbling marginal notes like some social anthropologist with a field journal. Any reference to a "cousin" challenged me to assert, marginally at least, "this is Viscusi's mother's sister's daughter" or "his mother's mother's sister's son." Such marginally identified kinship relations began to interconnect as I read, forming separate webs of connections among maternal and paternal relatives. Each forming web effectively removed "a cousin" from his or her exclusive relationship to the author or to his mother and gave each of them dozens of relationships to one another. Even while trying my hardest to understand existential crisis and mourning as Viscusi lived it, I found I did not want to feel so alone in sharing his experience of mourning: Those webs made social beings of him, his mother, and all his kin, creating a relationship to me as the reader, the creator of the webs.

But I also wanted more. I wanted to know their personal names. In a second round of note-taking, I turned to the shards of written names and dates preserved in the digital collections of ancestry.com: birth and marriage records, census listings, ship manifests of arrival and departure, naturalization papers, city directories, and military registrations. I did not need to become a thorough-going genealogist of the Viscusis and DiRoccos for I found on ancestry.com a small but highly capable group of genealogical researchers who were Viscusi's kin (mainly cousins of varying degrees). These people had clearly devoted many hours to genealogical research, and most chose to share the results of their research with other ancestry.com subscribers. These genealogist cousins had produced family trees chock full of the Viscusi and DiRocco (and many other affinal) names, producing trees naming hundreds of individual persons, along with key life dates and place names. Apparently, I was not alone in creating the kind of knowledge I sought as existential comfort. Still, it remained an unsolved mystery that while genealogists (and I) desired to name names and create webs of relationships, Viscusi often rejected such knowledge. Apparently, one can identify an epistemological chasm without predicting how people will sort themselves out around it.

The epistemological sorting itself fascinated me. One form of knowledge that genealogists and many family and immigration historians create is the short biography; often enough it resembles Viscusi's online professional bio—names, dates, changes of address, honorifics. Obituaries too are like short who's who entries but with kin relationships centrally featured. These forms of knowledge share a purpose. They announce or publish an individual's significance to a group of readers larger than that of immediate relations who presumably already possess that knowledge. Short biographies in any of these forms assume that strangers will want the knowledge they create. By making the individual into a public figure whose basic life details are accessible to a larger group of readers, the genealogists on ancestry.com may well hope to give their family greater significance and to earn for them recognition (among an invisible and much larger society of interested readers) as a kind of honorific.

As a type of knowledge, short bios are more specific and detailed than the family trees that typically ignore such characteristics as occupation while generating long quasi-biblical lists of begettings that reach backward in time, usually to some founding man and his wife. Trees and biblical begetting lists may not be satisfying forms of knowledge for all, but they do position individuals across time and space, creating both a visual representation of transcendence and a location for each related individual, at least for readers with the appropriate epistemological predilections. Even *Astoria*, with its preference for allegory and metaphor, includes acknowledgments of the power of individuals strung sequentially across time as they are on every begetting list or family tree. Describing one long dream sequence (135), Viscusi sees and describes a row of 100 tiny clay shelves that begins with a married clay couple (presumably Rodolfo and Annunziata, 138) on the first shelf. On another shelf they appear to be sailing to America. On another shelf they die—in 1941 and 1942. Assessing the dream, the author connects past and present in ways any genealogist would find familiar:

A Social Historian Reads Robert Viscusi's *Astoria*

> I was born in 1941, my wife in 1942, and I took this dream as a gloss on what you have been reading here, as a clear way of thinking what is born with us when we are born, which is to say the memories of our parents' grandparents, whom we never see, even if they happen to be alive ... like Grandma Marguerite, my cousin Marjorie's great-grandmother and her namesake, who slept in the hall bedroom and moved so quietly through her business that you hardly knew she was there till she broke her hip and died, ninety six years old, while her daughter ruled the whole clan with a quick mind and a settled Sicilian sense of order that showed nowhere in her perfect English. (135)

As this beautifully evoked dream suggests, the combination of memory, webs of kinship, and the naming of names can transform an apparently tedious string of begats (or for that matter portraits of swarming statistical migrant termites or family trees) into existentially significant knowledge for their creators. All three are visualizations of an individual's transcendence, placing him along a family's long temporal arc, which is surely what the writing of *Astoria* was also meant to accomplish for its mourning author.

The power of names can, for some, I believe, equal the power of allegory and metaphor. For thirty-five years, for example, I have carried with me on my many moves 3,500 five-by-seven-inch index cards listing the names, birth, marriage, and death dates, occupations, kinship relations, and addresses in Italy and the United States for the individual migrants of one town in Sicily. These cards acquired meaning and significance for me (whose family origins did not, I want to emphasize, reach back to that town) as I produced them during my dissertation research. With the help of all their "incredibly precise collections of names and dates and faces, their avid comparative sociology" (247), I believed I was creating a kind of documentary of individual dignity—a dignity that is rarely afforded illiterate and poor people who leave behind no personal scraps of paper and who may now be totally forgotten by their American descendants. These index cards are scarcely the equivalent of full-length biographies, but they speak nevertheless of the value of recording the biographies of individual lives and declaring them worthy of remembrance. In short, the naming and compiling of dozens or even hundreds of names function as the equivalents for social historians and genealogists of the allegorical use of Napoleon's or Beato Roberto's names in *Astoria*. As visualizations of kinship relationships, distances traveled, and names repeatedly named, extensive family trees too can achieve such magnitude and complexity that they easily evoke for their creators the kind of vertiginous emotions that defined the author's mourning in *Astoria*. With allegory, Viscusi too asserted the significance and importance of humble people and places, honoring in a different way the modest, illiterate, and often poorly educated migrants of his family and their children. It is impossible, and probably also wrong-headed, to try to assess differential rates of success—whatever that might mean for the existentially challenged individuals—of such epistemological difference.

Attention to kinship networks delivers another possible insight into the epistemological chasm, this one about silence and family secrets. With one exception, it appears that the ancestry.com genealogists researching various corners of Viscusi's family tree are all descendants of the Astoria DiRoccos, and especially of the author's mother's father's prosperous brother Robert, described in *Astoria* as a "ward boss" (35). By contrast, the Sunnyside Viscusis have produced few genealogists. Here is one more confirmation of the sharp difference Viscusi perceived between maternal Astoria and paternal Sunnyside. The differences of the two families and the two Queens neighborhoods are absolutely central to *Astoria*. In *Astoria* the mother's power emerged from her son's adoption of her imagination, he reports, and that imagination included disdain for Sunnyside, his father, and possibly other Viscusi relatives for their practical, workaday, worldly successes and brilliance. The mother's imagination made Astoria (and her kinfolk living there) into a fascinating if puzzling and ultimately inaccessible haven for the child Robert. It produced a son unable to embrace fully either mother's or father's world or to integrate either parent seamlessly within himself, an issue openly discussed in *Astoria*. But ultimately it was the power of the mother and the mother's world, and not that of the father, that drove him to write *Astoria*. At the very least it seems plausible that the power of the DiRoccos persisted for him because of the family's penchant for secrecy and silence. That same penchant may have pushed some of their descendants into genealogy and into ancestry.com's nominal and digital shards.

Genealogists sometimes confess they were initially motivated by secrets adhering to their childhood memories. Children of immigrants may especially sense the presence of mystery if they do not understand the language or dialect spoken by their elders—a possibility raised explicitly in *Astoria* (37, 38). The author recalls a childhood of trying to understand "every possible meaning in every raised bushy grey eyebrow" (153). While genealogists influenced by American popular culture sometimes imagine their families' silences and secrets as originating in criminality, *Astoria* demonstrates the far more important long-term consequences of managing family scandals related to the small irregularities of humans unwilling to respect social or religious rules governing reproduction, marriage, or familial solidarities. Both *Astoria* and the genealogists' family trees suggest that the choice to tell and share small scandal stories or, alternatively, to treat them as secrets in closed boxes locked by silence, can resonate across generations.

For example, in Sunnyside, a foundational family scandal was repeated often, although, according to Viscusi, "I never heard the whole story the same way twice" (147). *Astoria* tells one version of the story. Viscusi's paternal grandmother (the same woman he compared to the Queen of England) married a man who "worked six days a week twelve hours a day in the G.E. factory in Schenectady. The seventh day he played cards and got drunk" (122). After giving him four sons, his wife escaped with the family's boarder; and that somewhat older man—not Viscusi's father's biological sire—became the Sunnyside father of the "four sturdy, brilliant impossible sons" who loved and admired their new father for his boldness and his settled opinions (and perhaps also his lack of diplomacy). No silence surrounded the original status of this grandfather as the boarder who "had made love to the wife" (148). Neither *Astoria* nor any ancestry.com family trees record any evidence that Viscusi descendants still wonder about the subsequent life of the abandoned first husband once he had found another wife with four daughters (146–147) and ceased trying to find and punish the absconded wife and her boarder lover. In Astoria, too, Cousin Bill's incarceration seems to have mattered little to anyone and certainly not to Viscusi's mother. It may even have burnished her appreciation of his bad-boy bravura. The record of Bill's imprisonment is there on full public view as part of at least one of the family trees' collections of documents, thanks to ancestry.com.

Since readers of *Astoria* know that Viscusi promised his mother to protect family secrets, they can be sure that the petty criminality of Cousin Bill is not the secret being protected. There are other breadcrumbs that point the way toward other small secrets, for example, Viscusi's childhood confusion about memories of "babies born in butcher shops" (256) or of his mother's dislike of her middle initial "M" (204). (He explores the meaning of that middle initial rather extensively.) As a reader I concluded, rightly or wrongly, that it was Viscusi's references to mysterious births and the possible exchange of babies that constituted the family secrets that still demanded him to maintain a kind of silence, rather than to recount the family story of an amorous boarder, daring grandmother, or rascal cousin. Struggling to write while in Paris, Viscusi suddenly inserts and recounts a curious memory of going with his aging grandmother to the hospital to visit two of his mother's cousins after giving birth. There he describes finding a tray of loaves of bread at the feet of their adjoining beds. When he asks about the bread, the cousins tell him, "These are our babies. That happens. Sometimes a loaf of bread is born." But surely, the author asks, "You must tell it before it grows up who its real parents are." After purchasing bread himself, he returns to this memory and finishes it inconclusively. As he helped his grandmother to don her coat, he remembers, she had chided him, "You must not let those women take you in like that." Viscusi, along with the reader, is left to wonder "is she angry because I have referred to the family secret or is she telling me something else?" (43). One assumes the family's genealogists also continue to ponder this mystery. But it is not at all clear they find answers or break their family's expectations of silence about its own mysteries.

While searching for clues to family secrets, genealogical researchers can uncover discrepancies in existing family stories and memories. The digital shards from ancestry.com can add nuance and richness for those mourners or seekers who need that kind of knowledge. A naturalization record for Viscusi's Sunnyside grandfather reveals the existence of a wife still living in an Avellino village in 1927, at least a decade after his escape with his landlord's wife. (Presumably it was the death of the wife in Italy that freed the boarder grandfather to marry the grandmother in 1931; their marriage record does little to clarify whether or not the remarrying grandmother, or her abandoned husband, who also remarried, had divorced or had simply married a second time, ignoring laws against bigamy. In either case the Viscusi family seemed uninterested in the details.) Similarly, an avid genealogist can quickly establish that the unnamed Connecticut tinker and boarder in Viscusi's Astoria family story had been born abroad and was thus an immigrant from Austrian Bohemia and not a native Yankee. One can also enrich the story of Cousin Bill with an account of his father's death and his mother's remarriage, events that may have precipitated his confinement in a juvenile home on Randall's Island (overlooking the Hell Gate), where he lived in 1930 before the petty theft that sent him in 1933 to Sing Sing for a few years. In all these cases, however, both families have been telling, re-telling, and even—in *Astoria*—publishing the stories. None of ancestry.com's digital shards seem likely to either alter the existing narrative or point toward silences or secrets within it. At most, the marital irregularities of the Astoria grandmother and grandfather may explain something about the anti-clericalism of the family ("I mean, my father felt it. My grandfathers never went to church. No one went, but they sent us. ... I felt it; I bristled at everything. But I went." 208–209).

It is not the stories already told and retold that motivate family genealogists as they confront their existential challenges: It is the family secrets. Perusal of the family trees created by Viscusi's family genealogists suggests further that any secrets unlocked by research do not release the researchers from a family legacy of protective silence or *omertà*. The raging Astoria grandfather? One census record does show him living in Astoria with his wife and daughter, soon after his arrival, while using a given and family name from his wife's family rather than his own. But there is no evidence of any murder in the family trees, just the story of him chasing his daughter around the block with a razor. At the same time, the family trees point quite clearly toward several possible cases of cousins' children born close together in the 1920s and the 1940s, a not uncommon phenomenon in large families. The trees also identify at least one birth to a particularly young mother and father. Tellingly, their full names are not included in all the appropriate trees. One tree does suggest a hastily arranged marriage with an Italian cousin sent by a father before his own return to Italy; one young child born to this cousin may also have been given as a daughter to older, maternal relatives, with whom the young couple lived temporarily. But in this case, too, that child has disappeared from the public record created by the family genealogists, perhaps because of subsequent name changes, perhaps because of family splits, perhaps because of family commitments to silence.

Minor family scandals like these can be and in many families are easily forgotten; they certainly can lose their power to shock family descendants as time passes and as the rules governing appropriate marriage and birth conventions also change. What is striking about the ancestry.com genealogies created by the descendants in Astoria is that such small scandals have remained alive enough to omit or render them invisible (or "private" in ancestry.com terminology). It is possible the genealogists have solved to their own satisfaction mysteries that Viscusi promised his mother not to unravel or reveal. But if, indeed, that were the case, they continue to hold the secrets close and refuse to reveal them on their otherwise public trees. Ancestry.com routinely marks as private only the biographies of living persons. But in all the cases identified above as possibly linked to the allegory of loaves of bread and exchanged babies, the persons involved are all long dead. It seems, then, that genealogists still do not want others from outside the family to know what they may know or suspect. Their inclination is still to hide scandal behind silence.

That is their good right. But it is also evidence that family habits of silence and secrecy can persist across generations. They can influence genealogists as much as poets who search for answers in very different ways but who both seek to ease their existential malaise by defining their own identities in relationship to past and future.

In this short reflection, I have juxtaposed two epistemologies that can divide individuals who are facing the universal crisis of human existence, the crisis of death and loss. While the epistemological chasm separating the poets and allegorists from the genealogist namers and compilers of names is large, neither apparently produces satisfying knowledge in the absence of shared memories. There is no one predictable or even predictably successful path toward existential peace or toward the satisfying sense of having transcended the brutal facts of death and loss. In *Buried Caesars and Other Secrets of Italian American Writing*, Viscusi (2006) perhaps signals his own progress down the path when he acknowledges by name those who have joined him in the collective memory work that facilitated the writing of the later book — his children, his wife, his sisters, and five cousins of varying degrees of separation and representing both his Sunnyside Viscusi and Astoria DiRocco kin networks.

I did not write this essay with any intent to alter readers' epistemological preferences; I knew I, as author, was much too old for that transformation. At most, I hope my homage to Viscusi serves as a plea for tolerance and appreciation across a chasm that can divide families as well as scholarly fields. Surely, too, Viscusi knew the family genealogists busily engaged in creating his own family's trees on ancestry.com. Their existential crises will never produce a book like *Astoria*, just as he was unlikely to begin researching and producing new knowledge in the form of a family tree that might give life, dignity, and meaning to the biological grandfather, the abandoned man, along with his new wife and her daughters. Still, I saw in *Astoria* the glimmer of appreciation for the names-naming and dates-compiling faraway cousins from Italy who helped him to grasp the ways migration had damaged and transformed people at both ends of the migrants' trajectories (247–250). That enhanced appreciation for names-naming flowered, I believe, in *Buried Caesars*.

Finally, as I read *Astoria* and wrote these paragraphs, I found myself inexplicably drawn into the protective silences preferred by the Astoria DiRoccos. I too faced writerly choices—would I prepare a small biography of the mother? Would I name the names of people and places delivered to me by the family genealogists but missing completely from *Astoria*? At the moment of choice I too experienced, however indirectly, the power of Viscusi's Napoleon, his mother. Vera wanted privacy, she preferred secrecy; her son respected her wishes. And so have I. He names her name only twice in *Astoria*. I have been even more cautious. I have not named any names not named in *Astoria* and have not displayed for readers the full genealogical evidence that might affix names and dates to minor family scandals of Astoria and Sunnyside. I am quite sure a marvelous book could be written about them. But if ever I tackle scandals—whether as a person, an historian, or a writer—I will focus on the secrets of my own family. There are enough of them.

NOTES

[1] My father died in 1997, making me the mourning daughter of a man who had lived as a child in Astoria and Sunnyside and who also, like Viscusi's parents, fled to Florida around 1970.

[2] I struggled over the best way to refer to the author in this piece, since it is as "Bob" that I knew him. It is not a close personal relationship, but the rudimentary explorations into his genealogy that I undertook as I prepared to write this essay about his famously intimate book created a sense of intimacy. The editors preferred to standardize references to the author as *Viscusi*.

WORKS CITED

Viscusi, Robert. 1995. *Astoria*. Toronto: Guernica.
Viscusi, Robert. 2006. *Buried Caesars and Other Secrets of Italian American Writing*. Albany: SUNY Press.

Robert Viscusi's *Ellis Island* and the Sense of History

Peter Carravetta

> everyone you look at has a plan an opinion and a time to leave
> nothing lasts very long in anything like the same condition
> most change comes in subtle increments till one day you need a new battery
> Robert Viscusi, *Ellis Island*

> Those whose reasoning went to the root of things
> Perceived this innate freedom; as a result,
> They left the gift of ethics to the world.
> Dante, *Purgatorio*

EARLY ATTEMPTS AT REWRITING HISTORY

The work of Robert Viscusi has been engaged with the question of cultural identity and historical memory since the early 1980s. Each of his works marks a turning point in our understanding of what it means to be Italian American sandwiched between the greater entities that are Italy and the United States, the latter understood in its allegorical incarnation as *America*. I argue that with *Ellis Island* (Viscusi 2013), undoubtedly his masterpiece, Viscusi shows how the question of cultural identity and its representation in historical narrative has reached its dissolution, in a sense prompting a reflection on the passing of an age. This is of paramount importance to students of the various schools of cultural studies, postcolonial studies, ethnic studies, and theories of history. *Ellis Island* demands that we go beyond the cultural politics of the last half century and turn to more fundamental issues such as migration, biopower, multiplicity, the prospect of existence as a mere cipher, and the arrival of the posthistoric world.

In an earlier article (1994) on Viscusi's *An Oration upon the Most Recent Death of Christopher Columbus* (hereafter referred to as *Oration*), I analyzed how that poem retraces through the historical-mythical figure of Columbus both the social history of Italian America *and* the ideological self-construction of the United States by throwing light upon one another, given that these two entities originate in the same historical continuum (Carravetta 2017, 195–220). In the context of the year it came out, 1993, it soon became clear, while reading it and watching the author performing it at various public venues, that Viscusi was looking at his immediate society while at the same time interrogating the United States' overall sense of itself, with its bragging claims and noisy silences, its litigiousness and continuous rewriting of the National Allegory, even though there were many newer meta-narratives available. But Viscusi has been working on the idea of history since the beginning of his career, starting with a study of the appropriation and relaunching of the work/iconicity of Dante Alighieri in the second half of the nineteenth century titled *Max Beerbohm, or The Dandy Dante* (Viscusi 1986). It deals with Max Beerbohm (1872–1956), the brilliant humorist and parodist of the Oscar Wilde circle, of the Rossettis, and beyond. While analyzing how Dante played such a huge role in nineteenth-century British high culture, Viscusi dwelt on the seductive power of the mask, the paradoxes of reflection (the subtitle of the book was *Re-Reading with Mirrors*), and the techniques of sublimation and re-semantization by a restless, complex, heterodox author who preferred to live as an expatriate in Italy and who, like the Brownings a generation earlier, after decades had mastered only what we can call tourist Italian. Understanding how Dante was "used" within a different culture was instructive in analyzing later how other historical figures-turned-mythological figures and identitarian icons came about, often to say the opposite of what an earlier generation had thought.

This condition of living and writing across a diachronic language/territory divide will return in Viscusi's subsequent critical production, when in the early 1980s he turned to Italian American writing. I note his innovative article *"De Vulgari Eloquentia"* (Viscusi 1981) and his search for a master trope, or a koine, that would be reliably identifiable as Italian American. The search brought into relief the importance of representative authors such as Emanuele Carnevale, Pascal D'Angelo, Pietro di Donato, John Fante, and others, thematizing instances of misreading, undue appropriation and transformation of cultural icons, and the legitimization of coercive ideologies. But Viscusi's earlier studies allowed him to situate these and other "ethnic" writers within the larger panorama of what I call Euroamerican modernism, of experimental writing. In this larger panorama, there is a greater array of styles, references, and personalities that broaden the reach of the issues to be dealt with. Being able to write from both within literature as a poet and outside of literature as a critic or cultural historian does offer some hermeneutical advantages. In any case, often the literary constructions become the only means of access to earlier articulations of one's past.[1]

Of course, in one's past several languages are spoken, several poetics are articulated, diverse accents and symbolisms punctuate a story, and long silences may be made to speak through the magic of allegory contained already in the very essence of language (see Carravetta 1991, 17–89). We just have to learn how to read them, how to decode them first, and integrate them afterward into a broader quilt of lives and dreams. In the *Oration*, there is no doubting the historical fact that "the Italians went to America in steerage" (Carravetta 2017, 198), but the possibility is aired, right in those contested celebrations of the 500th anniversary of Columbus's colossal "discovery," that "Columbus day will go the way of the dinosaur" (Viscusi 1993, stanza 4). Whether that will actually happen is uncertain, but until it does, we have to acknowledge as a fact that, no matter what we think of the official holiday now, Columbus served as a *mythological figura* to orient the cultural landscape of the immigrants and that for several generations—the 1892 Chicago Universal Exposition highlighted "the spirit of Columbus," the fearless explorer—anchored annual cultural events in most of the United States of America (actually, in all the Americas) well into the 1990s.

The *Oration*, however, is hardly an identity-affirming panegyric to Italian American ideals, unless those ideals are subjected first to some radical reframing, showing how these icons can be manipulated and turned against one's own often naïve sense of identity. The poem represented the United States' dream of being the

New Jerusalem, in essence "a theoretical country," an "outer space /where people come from other places /to try out dangerous ideas" (Viscusi 2013, 202). Thus, Columbus became a founding symbol, a sun god coming from the east, spun into so many histories and epics and novels and plays and names of cities and roads and institutions that we may safely conclude he is more important to the self-definition of the United States than of Italy. The reason, as I have written, is that "Columbus is also the museum of iconographic, pictographic, allegorized figures, the philology of its textual representations, over a period of time, through many social groups, and in terms of effective symbolic power. ... [What would be the motivations behind the efforts aimed] to kill Columbus yet again, five centuries later, especially in North America?" (Caravetta 1991, 205). A provisional response, to which I will return below, sounds something like this: The United States is turning inward, wants to eat its own parents or progeny in a self-destructive tantrum sweeping the entire country as it straddles the millennium. Similar symptoms have been registered in other countries, especially in Europe: resurgent nationalistic movements, refugee crises, central banks' unbridled control, and effective manipulation of minorities' claims and possibilities. And given the role and impact of the United States in the world, we can fairly see how now we are talking about general or world history.

1. SPLAYING OF IDENTITIES

The question of history gains a different coloration in Viscusi's novel *Astoria* (1995), which continues the search into multiple textualities that, inevitably, speak to diverse constituencies. But here we have two new perspectives. The first is the unsettling hypothesis that the Italian American writer as such does not exist, as there is no one type that stands for all the rest; the characterization would be too broad and imprecise and suspiciously aligned with conservative, racist ideologies, which in granting an idealized group identity in effect quells dissent and voids any rewriting of the past (Bernstein 1990, 199–200). What we have are writers, a plurality of experiences and voices that may be grouped under a specific *topica*, where some overlap, some have little in common with one another besides the claim to this literary label. For we have writers who negate their ethnic background, those who foreground it, those who link it to other concerns like folklore or religion, and finally others who go beyond the dualism, the binary, Italy–America. The main setting for *Astoria*, which tells of an epic immigration from the Matese mountains in the Molise region to the basement of the narrator's house in Sunnyside, Queens, is Paris, France. The triangulation of cultures allows for a revisiting of past events large and small, personal and national, as if played against a giant film screen that included Europe, the North Atlantic, the Americas. The novel thus also disclosed a Viconian axiom: that it is we humans who make nations, create history, devise symbols, reckon with social forces (Vico 1999, par. 331) — all through language. Nature has nothing to do with it: "Nature does not reveal nations to themselves. Nations are made through language and through war. One does not touch a nation. One lives in it, as in a language, completely subject to its effects as to the laws and to the value of money" (Viscusi 1995, 50).

Viscusi here returns to the question of class and the structural, metaphysical divide between the immigrant who had no voice and no past and the integrated homogenized individual whose history is made up of financial success and calcified icons. Again, we run into the question of how to articulate a sense of history that would explain somehow the co-presence of many divergent, contradictory pictures of the faces of Italians, Americans, and Italian Americans. There is no single category, no single history, no single stylistic trait, no single complaint. Moreover, through this novel Viscusi discovers that there are silences in the cultural memory he is trying to (re)construct, spaces unnarratable that beckon the reader, the mind. It is a silence that cannot be terminated by a barrage of words; it is more like an "ontological precondition for the very emergence of an as yet unspoken … work/world" (Carravetta 2017, 218).

I could continue with Viscusi's *Buried Caesars* (2006), another of his original and incisive cultural histories of Italy's presence in America and of the complex cultural unconscious of Italian Americans of all stripes. It is, like *Max Beerbohm, or the Dandy Dante* (Viscusi 1986), an exploration of the subterranean links in this palimpsest, a topography of cultural memes and often perverse interconnections in our social history. Again there is a vocation, an obsession almost, with trying to say, as much as to tell anyone in particular, what it is that needs figuring out, who or what someone is in the continuum of societies, in life-as-lived-with-others, the course of things. Except that instead of the high culture now we range from aristocracy to populist politics, to sites where the silence can be given word through its echoes while speaking about other things (as in the etymon of allegory; the ancient Greek *allo-augurai* means *other-speaking*).

2. TRANSITION TO AND THROUGH *ELLIS ISLAND*

In retrospect, all of the above publications seem to be but preparatory exercises, test runs, for the creation of the magnum opus, *Ellis Island* (Viscusi 2013). If the *Oration* is his *Howl* and *Astoria* his *Ulysses*, then *Ellis Island* is definitely Viscusi's *Divine Comedy*. It is a total poem, a colossal work.[2] History as fundamentally a mythical construct that dominates for a certain time is here deprived of any possible claim to universality. In *Ellis Island*, history reveals its web of relations, its essential *anima* as the voice of a shifting fluid community, but no more. The rest would be abstraction, or ideology. Or maybe an underlying dynamic of course and recourse, with the aggravating fact, both effectively and theoretically, that the histories of groups and of nations in general are not always in synchrony. More than any of his previous books, the sweep is greater, global, transnational, a multiverse. This is the epic poem, containing more multitudes, à la Walt Whitman, than any of his previous works. However, Viscusi here operates like Dante—both author and character—in a relentless probing of self, self-and-other, the self of others, and their way of speaking and of being, much like the tapestry of humanity that unfurls before the pilgrim traveling, *this* time, in *this here world made by humans*.[3] For Viscusi, there is no world made by God but at best one made in part by the church, which played a profound role, especially among Italians.

Robert Viscusi's *Ellis Island* and the Sense of History

Pick up *Ellis Island* and you are in for the journey of your life, as the narrating persona guides you through personal, social, historical experiences, speaks in turn in the first, the second, the third person, uses plural pronouns. Yet we can almost identify when the speaking persona is the author: disarming if not brutally honest about his fears and dreams and hypothetical roads not taken and pricking deep scars and furrows carved in the soul and visible only now, later, when looking back, while ahead there is no trace of land, no dove carrying the olive branch, no angel to disband the (d)evils that pop up unexpectedly to block his march. What emerges is a plural voice, a true chorus of the lives that do make up the bulk of History but that can best be gleaned, and hopefully understood, through specific *topoi* that yield powerful figures of the *res gestae* that make up our historical existence. As with a poetic encyclopedia, the best preliminary (and very tentative) approach is to point out the recurrence of some of these *topoi*.

In Book 1 "the stories disintegrate you like waves"[4] announcing that there will be much shifting and tipping and instability and a breakdown of known entities. "I was reading the story of stories / they tell you on the walls of ellis island" (1.3), a place designed "as a ritual entrance into the imaginary universe" (1.6). After an almost predictable list of all the ethnicities and nationalities under which the migrants gather (1.4) there follows a quick reiteration of the us-versus-them dynamic established upon arrival (1.9; 1.10), and then, while on the "isle of possibilities," "the stories howl through me like storms" (1.11). In 2.3 we find a compelling presentation of the emigrant caught in various situations and a progressive identification of the narrating persona with events, clips, souvenirs, shards of memory re-enacted with a crescendo of voices. Some sound like personal memories until we realize that they are the memories of the poet's father, and further along how the father related to the grandfather, and along the way entire prairies and valleys of cultural history are traversed, nailed to their irreversibility as facts but afloat in the ether of signification as linguistic utterances: Meaning requires a listener, an audience, someone who agrees or disagrees, who entertains the traveler or bluntly (when not viciously) rebukes him. One first consequence is the loss of personal identity (2.7), which prompts the self to seek a narrative, being selective, so to speak; "you came to ellis island to leave your thousand dried out selves /at ellis island you forswear the personal past /the entire ritual consists of dismissing objections" (2.8). Like the pilgrim Dante at the entrance to purgatory, the narrator has to start clean and then go through all the terraces to see the evils and violence people can unleash on other people. To do so he must re-enact, re-live, and then refashion, synthesize key experiences of his childhood, when the self was being formed. Sonnet 2.9 is about this personal self-introspection and where, after a collection of the most disparate thoughts, you realize that "they had turned all the words in the book inside out /all the evidence as you read it became folksong." This strains the imagination of our modern-day pilgrim, who takes off into a metaphysical fancy. From early on, music and dance recur as key elements in this sea of history.

Book 3 explicitly names a vast expanse of exploration—"you are seeking an italian in you that nobody sees"—which can lead to a rediscovered Italianness that is unique but that must inevitably acquire its meaning, its validation, when confronted with that of others. Making a generalization is dangerous: It levels the personalities; it prunes the radical wing; it creates a sociological category. History and existence are much greater than this (Carravetta 2017, 3–37). Our pilgrim does not want to change the histories, just to record them, but he is aware that they permeate the present life; "so the golden god of naples whom you carried west /brightens walls and altars simply by suggestion" (3.2). It gets more complicated as we navigate when we read that even of the gods there are different histories (perhaps that's what the Ellis Island experience teaches first of all?) because "when we say Europe we speak of a manifestation of god /one among many" (3.4). In this context, the only thing one knows for sure is one's own body (3.11), and one comes away with the sober realization that "you are a broken statue of the future /no one cares how you got there." The crossing and weaving of possibilities continue through the many Americas (4.2 and 4.3), but the third rail of consciousness keeps tunneling between History and histories, and only the latter seem to have a reality, not necessarily endowed with a sure sense of things or greater symbolic meaning.

One recurring *topos* in the narrative is the figure and different manifestations of the father. I am leaving all the times a sonnet is dedicated to the role and figure of the father but I am resisting the temptation of making that a paradigm of sorts, when the relentless excavations lead to an understanding of the limits of such a master trope: There is one father, but what does that mean to all the fathers in time? To all the families associated with such a driving figure in our past? Look at role models: Are they exemplars of a genealogy or examples of a variety of often wildly different ways of telling the (hi)story? Viscusi recounts in 4.9 an exchange he has with Pietro di Donato in 1991 in San Francisco, at which I was present because we were on the same panel:

> when i say us of course i do not mean us but old men
> pietro di donato the genius poet novelist laid brick for a living
> you have soft hands he said to us younger writers with long hair

As befits the epic style, this kind of personal memory is also an allegory for something else. But there is no ready-made tabula of vices and virtues, with attendant iconographies, as was possible for Dante and the great majority of allegorists up to the nineteenth century. The something else to which the critical imagination is rebounded is itself unstable, at the mercy of the waves of human social interaction. As the word *allegory* implies, it calls for an *other-speaking*, to which must be matched a capacity and willingness to hear the turmoil beneath the surface (see 5.7). The poet thus decides to dig deeper (see 4.10). In this context, one finds a collection of sonnets dedicated to work, to the mechanics of learning, to appreciation for the humble but persistent struggles as per the implied family credo to advance to a respectable profession. Except becoming a professor, and a writer to boot. The narrator's father, much like di Donato, does not appreciate the sons becoming intellectuals; their hands are soft! That spells trouble, the breaking of a vessel stitched up with great effort by the previous generation. But the only thing the narrator can say, defensively, is that one builds houses with bricks *and* with words (4.10; 6.4).

Let me touch upon a few other places that I cannot take up in detail here but that need to be mentioned to people the constellation of topics. There are sonnets dedicated to migration in general (5.3) and to the growing necessity of the poetic persona to reinvent itself from all the fragments strewn in sociocultural memory (see 5.11; 5.12; and most of Book 6). The perturbing factor here is that there exists no original; "anything once known returns as a memory before you first see it" (6.4). In this new context, the (re)writing of history is made possible only through the varied histories, some dominant, some irrelevant, that the actors on the collective scene recount (6.3) over and over (see 6.9; 8.11).

Occasionally the pilgrim sketches imaginative worlds (7.3), returning to dance as a master trope to personify the steps that mark actual experience. The katabasis continues with stirring hypotheses about commitment, an ideology of change, with the growing realization that there is no stable metaphysical foundation, no well-cut anthropological arche. The discovery is terrifying.

In 7.7 we read that people can forget and forgive, but at other times they do not. In any case, forgetting is the greater quantity; "such forgetting underlies the foundations of your project / remember the pattern and memories you need return on their own will." After this point in the poem, the reader pretty much must forget any association of the first-person singular with the author (as should be the case in any reading of literature in general). What I want to underscore now is that, from here on, *Ellis Island* will generate a near interminable procession of *I* and *you* and *us* and *them*, and from their intertwined dynamics that emerge any moment the poet connects the amorphous and endless continuum of history with some trigger situation, a trip, a lecture, a journal note, an exchange with someone, a recollection of adolescence, the love for music and for literature, the constant and often self-flogging analyses of this singularity called the *I* ever and always fluctuating from crest to crest, subject to immense forces from below, subject to punishing adventures from above.

The retelling and reframing of so many experiences do not necessarily lead to an atomistic cynicism or a nihilist, defeatist worldview. Creativity is the ultimate resource in the poem. Listening to and relaunching heard melodies constitutes in itself a life-affirming principle. Storytelling since ancient times has been prized and cultivated for many concomitant reasons, among which is disclosing a different kind of temporality than the chronic one, or the psychological one. The intermingling of different temporalities would require a separate careful study. But it plays right into what constitutes an often-unthematized aspect of identity: How long does it last? Who and what sanction it? Perhaps identity is ultimately made up of a plethora of differences, some vis-à-vis our past, some vis-à-vis our many selves, or personae either imposed or devised (25.3). When feeling lost, "remember a tree rooted in the beginning of time gives you strength" (13.2) and "contrive your world anyway" (13.1), as doubts are followed by projections (13.3; 13.11).

Allegories of travel return, foregrounding the ever-present sense of discovery, of self-awareness required to stay on an even keel during the voyage, to face the host at each port, to negotiate the journey over land, to greet the strangers at each bivouac. But moving on, staying in the journey itself, is the underlying or overarching pulsion. Meeting other groups, relating to strangers as to ancient compatriots, the feeling grows that history and myth are cut from the same cloth. The Other, the foreigner, is slowly amalgamated into a generic *us*, he or she as traveling companions, they merely get off at a different port. Symbolically, in a diachronic scale, the Mohicans came and went (15.3), the "migracani [who] look like moors" are variously labeled (17.3), personal retrieval just another stroll through old notebooks, "down the cellar trying to shift my story's foundations" (17.7). Eventually, the theory of relativity looms as a master trope now, "even a slight change in spelling a name can make a big difference" (17.5).

If we insist on reading some lines in a literal way, there is plenty to analyze as well, "making the new italians is hard because everyone wants the old ones" (18.3; 18.4; but see also 30.1; 30.2), which is a reflection not just on the passing of generations but on the apparently universal tendency to fall back upon the established, imprinted values and habits. Shockingly, that is a foolish belief, as the poet continually unearths cases where such a mentality turned out to be disappointing, painful, or necessarily retrograde and in need of either being discarded or being rewritten. With the new word comes a new reality, so although "we inherit each a box of broken pieces of the past" we also use these pieces: Elevated to ambivalent *figuras*, the poet feels like Mars, who "interprets vulcan's theory of venus to the pizzaiolo" (18.5). The status of the writer, which recurs through a substantial number of sonnets, is explored at various levels, as we saw, from his having to invent new words/worlds, to the reinventing of the past by rewriting it, which does not mean out of nothing but precisely out of an ocean of effective, real possibilities.

The poet originally wanted to write his *Leaves of Grass*, the "colossal" poem, as Emerson had desired in the 1840s,[5] and although many metapoetic lines courageously deal with the ultimate question—why write?—at other points in the text it appears that Viscusi's project is deemed *necessary*, as in: It must come to be written! But he excuses himself for feeling, at times, like an eagle roaming over the jagged terrain, like Zarathustra on top of the mountain; "on these heights if you stand still the ice will speak to you" (13.6). In this perspective, at times Italians are glorified (18.8) at times vilified (18.9). Then follows the inevitable comparison/contrast of the great cultural world systems called Italy and the United States, indelibly framed "italy is tragic, america is magic" (18.11).

3. SWERVES TO NOWHERE

Eventually in *Ellis Island* the reader is more and more drawn into considerations greater than identity, ethnicity, ideology, gender, and race as these are understood in the critical idioms of the past twenty to thirty years. Viscusi's persona enters another ocean; he can no longer be the pilgrim as there is no earthly paradise at the end of the journey, nor is he comparable to Ulysses, for whom there always existed a home to which he always yearned to return. Nor is

Robert Viscusi's *Ellis Island* and the Sense of History

this Aeneas, for he is not journeying to a new land to found an empire and start a new dynasty. The immigrant brings the labor, not the rule nor the capital. The earlier song to the threat of extinguishing the iconographic memory of Columbus in the United States—as we saw in *Oration*—has taught the pilgrim that there is a certain circularity to history, for now it is common knowledge, but neither an ontological *Grund*, nor an epistemological axiom, that "empire subsumes kingdom as kingdom presupposes heaven authorizing kingdom /attempting to understand the topology seems itself un po' esagerato our epics say" (24.10). Note the ending in light irony, almost an invitation to stop attributing so much importance to this pattern. The question remains whether this unchanging law is also cyclical, for that would compel strong reflection about the future. But to call, by contrast, *Ellis Island* the story of Everyman on the other hand makes it an abstraction, a type perhaps useful methodologically within specific disciplines, like sociology or folklore.

But the gist of the poem, despite the often ruminated-upon fact that every story turns into alibis, is to bring into relief the very blood, sweat, pain, and at times momentary relief or joy experienced by hundreds upon thousands of real people who never made it to a footnote in the grand narrative of the national history. The challenge is enormous. It becomes a problem of language, of a need to dig deeper in order to reach some broadly understood sense of being human even before we attach labels to ourselves and act a part for a given extension of time. In this sense the second half of the poem can be read as an inquiry into the nature of migration, of freedom, of justice, of creativity, of love, of the omnipresence of rituals in family and social aspects of life, and an apparently decades-old Oedipal struggle with the father/Father.

At an even higher level of critical abstraction, we can say that *Ellis Island* sketches the outline of what we might call *power in history*, as we read tens of snapshots where the conclusion is that money makes the world go around (see 50.7; "one of the main things about freedom is it's hard to enjoy without money"). It is a realistic and bitter realization, and a detailed study of it would show that it can be read on at least three levels. First, as a force in history, money here is less a Marxian (quantitative: freedom minus property) value and more of a Hegelian self-consciousness, a cultural dynamic that entire communities share (freedom and property). Second, money can be understood as a complex social force in the way Georg Simmel, in *The Philosophy of Money* (1900), recovers and describes the modes in which money *both* liberates the agent to entertain exchanges previously incommensurable *and* yet depersonalizes the individual, transforming her into a fungible value. From a third perspective, historian William McNeill (1980) sees the rise of modernity—and, within that, the rise both of the United States and of Italy—as the consequence of the shift from an "urban transmutation" to the "commercial transmutation":

> Wealth increased as more massive and more mobile capital allowed new technologies, economies of scale, and interregional specialization to reinforce one another. In short, between the fourteenth and the twentieth centuries, acceleration of Europe's capacity to produce wealth became autocatalytic—a self-sustaining process. (65)

The pilgrim records that "ellis island is one focus of an elliptical journey whose other is naples or rome" (51.2) but also that "Whitman compared himself with the grass and planned to return to the grass /…/but other poets resemble magnolia trees elms sycamores oleander bushes." The struggle to avoid being churned and discarded or buried by the self-replicating monster called *capital* requires foisting refurbished myths ("after dinner grandpa sat me on his knee and told me how dante invented italy" [51.10]).

For the rest, there is an endless recurrence of personal memoirs that want to reach out to a superior value or axiom or God, with no success. In fact, all immutable values are doomed, untenable, permutable. There is only seawater under our feet. Viscusi's well-known gift for irony and humor surfaces here and there; it helps to tone down whatever achievement of his the pilgrim has (re)visited during the voyage. And we do not find the poetic persona deprecatory and self-victimizing; rather, it is more like experiencing a super-awareness of the present-at-hand, a realist take that needs not blow things out of proportion. But together, the shiftless wandering and the wisdom splayed through irony are like the songs the sailors sing at night as the ship sails silently through the dark waves, a different one each night, like a medley, a rosary. Perhaps also an endless orchestra rehearsal. The important thing is that it is not a calvary.

4. PROVISIONAL CONCLUSIONS

I would like to conclude by going back to the earlier reference to the avant-garde. *Ellis Island*, according to its author, is made up of sonnets each of whose lines are independent from what precedes and what follows. Each line, in other words, is a coherent grammatical unit, made up of one or more syntagms, but also just as often a complete period, or a sentence (in the ancient Latin sense of *sententia*) understood as a judgment; other times they sound like aphorisms, self-contained pearls of cold rationality, and at still other times just an observation, which, in the allegorical context, still resounds with other possible meanings. It is very hard to read the poems without naturally slipping into a search for a logic, a sense of syntactical *consecutio*, as in standard discursive practice. It is, after all, what I tried above when it came to identifying certain *topoi*: Except in a few cases, it is relatively easy to lift out the verses that express what a given reader wishes to foreground.

This rhetorical dimension of *Ellis Island* acquires dramatic value when we learn that Viscusi has also produced a version that transports the Gutenbergian text to a digital platform where the combinatorial powers of an algorithm can generate basically unlimited combinations of verses. Without getting into the fascinating mathematics of the project, I want to draw attention to the fact that this epic poem is concerned with self and identity and history and change; the very format it has to assume in the digital age speaks to a broader conundrum: Is change, metamorphosis, the ultimate nature of existence? Is history then a cluster of possible narratives floating in the ever-shifting power dynamics of our culture and within which one dominates for a while and then is followed by another? If so, as we are capable of making and remaking the journey by rearranging ad infinitum the utterances or statements of the epic, does that mean that history itself is doomed, that what remains is just a chance alignment of a bunch of sentences? And what happens to human determination? To free will? To the possibility of constructing one's destiny? A certain streak of skepticism alternates with a deeply rooted vein of stoicism. It is a strange combination. The impression arises that in *Ellis Island* the old world and the new are actually not so different. Perhaps. But that apparent similarity would blow the entire discourse of national or ethnic identity out of the water. The issues, the forces, the myths, *are* of a different nature. They concern humanity tout court. By this optic, the world is flat and time is merely a question of keystrokes, everything is available all at once, memory itself leaves the human and rearranges itself in the cybersphere. Continually. It can be playful, no doubt, and suitable to performances, as in a jazz ensemble. But it can also remind one at every moment of the foundationlessness of our existence, of the lability of identities, and the limited shelf life of countries and ethnic enclaves. It is not a reassuring perspective.

The avant-gardistic, experimental aspect of *Ellis Island*—that makes it into a tremendous signifying machine—can support an interpretation whereby no discourse, no logical, consequential narrative is possible, or possible as being the only true version, short of imposing one through whatever institutional or personal/public means one has to effect it. It seems that from History we moved to history, then to a number of histories, finally we end up with a story that reconnects with all previous incarnations. It traces a Viconian pattern, updated to the twenty-first century: The sense of history as we understood it in recent cultural memory is going in several directions at once. One can say that *Ellis Island* represents an "end of history." Or can also say: This is the time for a new beginning, a recourse. But from the whirlwind that is now history (however conceived), we return back to basic life, to biopower.

In the *mare magnum* of existence, we seem to be, allegorically, forever aboard a ship heading for always different ports, some strange or unreachable and prone to become mythic, others realistic and destined to accept the foreigner but at the cost of changing them forever. New lives, new territories, new texts. Infinite reproducibility. Marked by tireless returns and repetition at the ontic, material level, the poem does not fashion and hoist a corresponding difference at the ontological level. The sense of history is not having one that transcends the actor on the stage. Though meanings can be stitched into colorful quilts for a while, the horizons and possible paths before us are innumerable. They require we engage with them, actively. But the sense, understood as direction, is unknown. The gods have fled, and the myths are down to competing life stories. Deprived of our footing, we are destined to move on, as the etymology of *migrare* makes clear. The conclusion: *navigare necesse est*. Beyond Ellis Island.

NOTES

[1] This was the gist of my thesis "The Silence of the Subalterns" in Carravetta, (2017, 107–139); published also in Connell and Pugliese (2017, 132–151).

[2] We read on pages 321–322 of *Ellis Island* that the poem is composed of fifty-two books of twelve fourteen-line sonnets each. At 8,376 lines, *Ellis Island* corresponds to or duplicates the hours in fifty-two weeks. In the end, it can be recited, a sonnet a day, in perpetuity.

[3] See Vico (1999, par. 349): "The world of nations is clearly a human creation, and its nature reflected in the human mind. ... For there can be no more certain history than that which is recounted by its creator." See also par. 331 and 374.

[4] Book 1, sonnet number 3. All subsequent references to *Ellis Island* (Viscusi 2013) are incorporated in this text by book number followed by the sonnet number in that book.

[5] "Time and nature yield us many gifts, but not yet the timely man, the new religion, the reconciler, whom all things await. Dante's praise is that he dared to write his autobiography in colossal cipher, or into universality. We have yet had no genius in America, with tyrannous eye, which knew the value of our incomparable materials, and saw, in the barbarism and materialism of the times, another carnival of the same gods whose picture he so much admires in Homer; then in the Middle Age; then in Calvinism. ... Yet America is a poem in our eyes; its ample geography dazzles the imagination, and it will not wait long for meters" (Whicher 1960, 238).

WORKS CITED

Bernstein, Charles, ed. 1991. *The Politics of Poetic Form*. New York: Roof.

Carravetta, Peter. 1991. *Prefaces to the Diaphora. Rhetorics, Allegory, and the Interpretation of Postmodernity*. West Lafayette, IN: Purdue University Press.

Carravetta, Peter. 1994. "An Other Columbiad." *DIFFERENTIA: Review of Italian Thought* Vol. 6 (Spring/Autumn): 311-320.

Carravetta, Peter. 2017. *After Identity. Migration, Critique, Italian American Culture*. New York: Bordighera.

Connelly, William J., and Stanislao G. Pugliese, eds. 2017. *The Routledge Guide to Italian American Culture*. New York: Routledge.

McNeill, William. 1980. *The Human Condition. An Ecological and Historical View*. Princeton, NJ: Princeton University Press.

Vico, Giambattista. 1999 [1725]. *The New Science*, translated by D. Marsh. New York: Penguin.

Viscusi, Robert. 1981. "*De Vulgari Eloquentia*: An Approach to the Language of Italian American Fiction." *Yale Italian Studies* 1 (Winter): 21-38.

Viscusi, Robert. 1986. *Max Beerbohm, or the Dandy Dante. Re-Reading with Mirrors*. Baltimore: Johns Hopkins University Press.

Viscusi, Robert. 1993. *An Oration upon the Recent Death of Cristopher Columbus*. New York: Bordighera.

Viscusi, Robert. 1995. *Astoria: A Novel*. Montreal: Guernica.

Viscusi, Robert. 2006. *Buried Caesars and Other Secrets of Italian American Writing*. Albany, NY: SUNY Press

Viscusi, Robert. 2010. *Ellis Island*. Libri 1.1-4.12. Edited by qmbretta diaferia. Milan: abrigliasciolta.

Viscusi, Robert. 2013. *Ellis Island*. New York: Bordighera Press.

Whicher, Stephen E., ed. 1960. *Selections from Ralph Waldo Emerson*. Boston: Houghton Mifflin.

Alternative Modernisms: A Contrapuntal Reading of *The Great Gatsby* and *Christ in Concrete*

Donatella Izzo

PROLOGUE

When I first read Pietro di Donato's 1939 *Christ in Concrete*, in the early 1980s, I was an unemployed graduate and aspiring scholar, earnestly at work on the intensive reading and studying needed to pass the selection process that would eventually earn me my first academic position. No one had ever directed me to that book: Educated on the American Renaissance and high modernist canon, I had been trained to seek literary excellence in the terms defined and prescribed by excellent literary works, according to the canon's familiar tautology. But I was curious and I was thorough, and since I had embarked on a systematic reconnoitering of the (to me then) largely unfamiliar expanse of U.S. literature, I tried to read widely and to cover as much ground as I could. I was aware that the Faulkner I had read for my degree and the Hemingway, Caldwell, and Steinbeck I had read as a teenager did not represent the whole range of 1930s American fiction. My choice of *Christ in Concrete* was pragmatic and somewhat perfunctory: I had learned from my study of literary history that it was listed under the rubric of "immigrant and proletarian literature," and the author's name testified to his Italian American origin, allowing me to checkmark both categories with one book.

The book was a genuine surprise: Nothing had prepared me for a novel whose reading effect was much closer to Faulkner and Dos Passos than to Steinbeck or Farrell. Interior monologue and stream of consciousness rather than social realism, lyrical language and oneiric sequences rather than documentary description, linguistic experiment rather than political propaganda—how did this book qualify as the kind of realistic social protest or thesis novel that handbooks associated with the notion of working-class literature? And conversely, how could such a novel *not* have been canonized as a major experimental text of American modernism?

In its more naïve form, the latter question would of course find plenty of answers in my subsequent critical and theoretical readings. But it was not until many years later, when I first read Robert Viscusi's (2006) *Buried Caesars, and Other Secrets of Italian American Writing*, that the question of *Christ in Concrete* came back to me with a different force. In that book, Viscusi gathers a series of dazzling critical analyses, connected by an effort to unearth the complex historical, linguistic, and symbolic substratum of the "Italian American story" (x) — the "Buried Caesars" of the Italian heritage, functioning "as an unconscious imperialist faith" (x) in the face of a twofold marginality, both as peasants in Italy and as immigrants in the United States. Some of these superb readings — originally published in the 1980s — deal with *Christ in Concrete*:[1] These were, as far as I know, the first interpretations to do justice to the significance of this novel's linguistic experimentalism and to the complexity of its sustained symbolism, addressing the novel (especially its unforgettable first section) with a critical engagement commensurate with its literary power. But what takes place in Viscusi's analyses is not just brilliant critical reading. By unapologetically placing it in dialogue with *Moby-Dick* and *The Sound and the Fury*, Viscusi confers on *Christ in Concrete* a comparable status, recognizing in it "that combination of popular appeal and artistic originality that characterizes what used to be called a Great American Novel" (95). This claim, he argues, is based on these novels' capacity to confer epic scope to the exploration of a localized social or geographical position: in this case "the immigrant Italian world as a vision of the worker's destiny in the empire of industrial capitalism" (96). A few pages later, in a similarly bold critical move, Viscusi compares di Donato's "interlinguistic flicker" between English and Italian to Shakespeare's "sprinkling his Warwickshire proverbs with sesquipedalian coinages out of Latin, French, and Italian" (101) and comments on the terrible scene of Geremio's death ("in the old Italian sense of *terribile*, that it displays and makes us feel the absolute terror of terror"), observing that "next to this scene, even *Macbeth* reads like polite literature" (103). Finally, Viscusi assumes di Donato's familiarity with "the leading themes of modernism in arts and letters," affirming that its fruits "are evident throughout *Christ in Concrete*, where one sees what di Donato has assimilated from his exposure to the lessons of modern experimentation in the arts. Clearly he has been a student of futurism, of Joycean stream-of-consciousness, of collage and montage" (172).[2]

Viscusi's peremptory act of canonization—comparable in ambition and method to Matthiessen's *American Renaissance*[3]—may well be read as proof of his own "unconscious imperialist faith" (x): a critical bid for Italian American literary power, meant to effect the crossover of Italian American classics from the marginal niche of ethnic specificity to the universal relevance of capitalized Classics. What concerns me here, however, is not Viscusi's landmark role in the rethinking of Italian American literary studies as a field, but the way in which his readings of *Christ in Concrete* (and of the other Italian American narratives he addresses) are cast in the guise of a sustained dialogue with both the Italian *and* the U.S. literary tradition, whose most canonical classics—from Poe to Hawthorne, from Melville to Emerson and Whitman, from James to Eliot, Faulkner, and Frost—are evoked time and again in his critical discourse. Through this dialogue, *Buried Caesars* does not simply claim an equally canonical status for the works it explores. By dissolving the ghettoization of "the ethnic" as a separate, particular, "special interest" tradition, the book implicitly invites us to rethink the U.S. literary tradition through the lens of the "Italian American story." If the Italian immigrant is in many ways the representative figure of the clash between the traditional ways on one hand and the accelerated, alienated, machine-like tempo of capitalism on the other, what would it mean to reconfigure American modernism, and American modernity itself, by placing the Italian American experience at its center? What would it mean to define the American Dream and the great American novel taking *Christ in Concrete* rather than *The Great Gatsby* as their paradigmatic literary rendering? The pages that follow are a thought experiment inspired by Robert Viscusi's work and meant to pursue some of these counterfactual speculations.

SHORT CIRCUITS, SYLLOGISMS, AND SPECULATIONS

Why choose *The Great Gatsby* as a counterpart to *Christ in Concrete*? The unimpeachable canonical status of Fitzgerald's novel as a classic rendering of the American Dream theme and my longstanding critical devotion to it are certainly a good justification for using it as a touchstone in my experiment. But the true reason is at once more specific and more serendipitous. Precisely because of the prominence of *The Great Gatsby* in my interiorized canon, Viscusi's ongoing contestation and re-inscription, in *Buried Caesars*, of the myth of the gangster as the quintessential Italian American figure created for me an instant short circuit. If what really took place as a flash can be unpacked as reasoning, that reasoning would be a syllogism of sorts—the gangster is *the* Italian American character; Gatsby is a gangster; *The Great Gatsby* is an Italian American story. A faulty syllogism, of course—not all literary gangsters are Italian American, not all literary Italian Americans are gangsters, to say nothing of the presumably non-Italian origin of a character named James Gatz—but still one that, by creating a mental association, suddenly sheds light on formerly ignored parallels.[4]

While admittedly subjective, the juxtaposition of *Christ in Concrete* with *The Great Gatsby* is not, in fact, entirely arbitrary. Though published at a considerable chronological distance (respectively 1939 and 1925), both novels belong within the intellectual and aesthetic project of American modernism. Both engage the conditions of American modernity, albeit from different angles, and both do so resorting to comparable literary devices: formal and narrative fragmentation, diegetic discontinuity, narrative perspectivism, metaliterary moments, thematically fraught imagery operating as a symbolic connective texture, and a version of the "mythical method" based, in both cases, on the sacrifice of a Christ figure and on the use of the seasonal cycle.[5] Both novels take place in roughly the

A Contrapuntal Reading of *The Great Gatsby* and *Christ in Concrete*

same time period—di Donato's story begins in 1923, Fitzgerald's in 1922—in an eastern urban setting (West Hoboken, New Jersey for *Christ in Concrete*; Long Island and New York City for *The Great Gatsby*). Uncannily, in spite of the wide discrepancy of their plots and social milieus, both novels offer chapters crucially hinging on party sequences and funeral scenes, and in both the action is accompanied by a pervasive soundtrack that includes the urban cacophony of work and traffic as well as music: in one case ranging from opera to popular Italian songs to tarantella and in the other case mostly jazz. More important, both novels feature aspiring second-generation immigrants as protagonists[6] and set their personal trajectories against the backdrop of turbulent economic, demographic, and social processes marking metropolitan modernity; and both share those evocative keywords—hope, dream, America—that have installed *The Great Gatsby* as the quintessential novel about the American Dream.

These (apparently critically unrecognized) similarities between the two novels are, to my mind, sufficiently numerous and important to make a comparison heuristically significant. Let me state at once that this comparison is not meant to suggest any direct influence of the earlier on the later novel: As far as I can tell, di Donato never mentioned Fitzgerald's book as one of his formative readings at the Communist Party of America summer camps.[7] But apart from being difficult to document, such an influence would be beside the point. What the comparison may yield, instead, is a sense of *the nature* of the differences between the two novels. It is the nature of those differences, I believe, that has eclipsed the perception of the similarities and impacted the different memorialization and reputation of the two novels: one, though initially underrated, an undisputed classic that no one can afford not to know, whose status is endlessly reproduced by school curricula, college syllabi, and scholarly research; the other, a once acclaimed but now relatively obscure "minor classic," mainly of sectional interest to students of Italian American, working-class, or 1930s literature. And yet, in many ways each novel offers an alternative unfolding of the same basic trajectory: the immigrant's bid for economic survival and progress in the metropolitan space of capitalist modernity. The vast differential in cultural capital and canonical status between these two in other respects comparable novels arguably mirrors the hegemonic relations between the social groups that the two novels primarily represent and address. By focusing on a few relevant metaphorical and thematic clusters of *Christ in Concrete* and comparing them to the parallel clusters in *The Great Gatsby*, I am hoping to do three things: one, provide a small contribution to the interpretative work on *Christ in Concrete*; two, highlight by contrast some of the textual and ideological features that have made *The Great Gatsby* such a perfect and perfectly canonizable classic; three, elucidate the two novels' mutual position as one the shadow image or inverted mirror of the other: two complementary sides of the same narrative, outlining different trajectories against the shared backdrop of a metropolitan space marked by ethnic and class divisions, transnational flows of capital and labor, and internal imperial practices. What I propose, then, is a contrapuntal reading of discrepant experiences in the spirit of Edward Said (1993), one that attempts to restore—in Said's words—"a simultaneous awareness both of the metropolitan history that is narrated and of those other histories against which (and together with which) the dominating discourse acts" (59).

CONCRETE

An ominous God-like personification presides over the world of *Christ in Concrete* (di Donato 1939): "Job," the omnipotent arbiter of the characters' destiny, the deity demanding the sweat and the blood of each immigrant, the authentic—but far from idealized—"melting pot" transforming both the dead and the living, regardless of their national origin and religion, into as many versions of "Comrade-worker Christ" (131): from Geremio, the original "Christ in concrete," (215) crucified on timber and rods of steel and crushed and choked by wet concrete, to each *povero cristo*[8] toiling on the construction site, or immigrant living in the tenements: "Did they not all live one atop the other and feel and taste and smell each other? Did not Job claim them all? ... They, like me, are children of Christ" (100). Work is all pervasive in *Christ in Concrete*. It is the crucial determinant of the plot, whose turning points (Geremio's death, Luigi's accident, Paul's need to leave school and become a bricklayer, Nazone's death) are all work related. It occupies the characters' minds, appears in their dreams,⁹ grounds their sense of self, and simultaneously sustains and threatens their lives. Construction sites are featured in scene after scene. Their function is not simply to illustrate the young protagonist's *Bildung*—in a striking literalization of the notion of "self-construction"—or to allow the description and exploration of a social milieu: Through them, "Job" is made tangible everywhere in the book, in every one of its tactile and bodily details—the feel of brick and mortar, the merciless weather, the weight of tools, the gestures and motions, the bodily effort, the excruciating toil:

> The wet rub of mortar on tender skin ... the first fleshly sense of Job. (69)

> Stab into tub—scoop—swing around—up—swish down—press and push, with bricks and pieces of brick underfoot, stumbling, fighting to keep balance, bobbing, hooking, curving, and praying like a soldier. (135)

> Paul was blue and stupefied with cold. His head and limbs felt artificial, breathing pinched his lungs, and his marrow was coursed with needling shocks. The mortar iced and clung encrusted to his trowel, and when he dumped it on the wall it crumbled. The wet mortar in the wall froze hard. (149)

> This sultry week in July the men moved as though clubbed. The mouth of every little pore distended helplessly. ... Perspiration oozed from Paul's palms and oiled the trowel handle. When rubbing his wet palms on his work trousers the glassy brick dust abrased harshly. (158–159)

The sheer physicality of labor is also occasionally described as producing a dizzying sense of pride and bodily power:

> He was proud that God had given him hand, back, and eye to bring home food, proud that he earned almost as much as the thick-wristed men, proud that he studied blueprints and construction, proud that he felt beauty in his form and soul, proud of his wonderful family. (157)

> Day's richness surged him with feel of trowel brick and mortar along wall, and he gloried in his body's labor. Building took his effort but gave reality. Building possessed his mind, but gave Divinity. He played the instrument of his growing power. (163)

This celebration of the "timed wasteless grace" (68) of the worker's body openly connects modern Italian American construction workers with the classical representations of the body in the ancient Greek and Roman world, implicitly reclaimed as the workers' ancestral heritage: "Old Santos ... was an ancient mighty athlete of Job" (68), "men seeming all alike in olympic contest for living with Job" (171). And yet, the novel never allows us to forget that this display of physical prowess cannot be aestheticized as a classical sporting competition, since its stake is life itself. Even when it offers moments of pride and beauty, Job is primarily about survival: the workers' survival among the dangers of the construction site, and their families' survival, which depends on their pay—"Brick and mortar was to become for Paul as stuff he could eat" (136). It is significant that, when the Depression sets in, Paul's way of encouraging his unemployed godfather is by telling him, "Soon, perhaps, there may be more work than we ever dreamed of" (203). Work is the stuff of the characters' lives and the grimly realistic limit of the horizon of possibility they can dream of; none of the characters ever thinks in terms of easy money or becoming instantly rich. Their life is an unceasing act of "chopping stone into bread" (46), an ongoing struggle whose life-and-death quality is repeatedly metaphorized as a war: "[I]n a few hours pay-check would sign short-short armistice. It was war for living, and Paul was a soldier.... [I]t was men's siege against a hunger that traveled swiftly, against an enemy inherited" (82).

Under conditions of mere survival, as the novel shows us again and again, regarding Job as an opportunity for emancipation and social progress can be a dangerous delusion.[10] In the first chapter of the book, Geremio happily thinks of the house he is going to buy as a result of his hard work: "Twenty years he had helped to mold the New World. And now he was to have a house of his own!" (6) — a moment of fulfillment immediately voided by death, which diverts his house money to the payment of his tombstone and funeral. When Paul first attempts to be hired as a bricklayer and anxiously asks his elders to look at the drywall he has painstakingly built to demonstrate his ability, "there was nothing to be seen. ... A truck had dumped its four thousand bricks there" (70). On Paul's first payday, eagerly anticipated as "the day when Job would first give its holy communion of freedom" (82), his pay turns out to be a scanty five dollars for a week's toil, a sum dramatically inadequate to secure his family's food. Even though he replies to Louis's appeals for him not to quit school that "Job is freedom ... for us" (134), Paul will subsequently dream of his dead father who warns him that "I was cheated, my children also will be crushed, cheated" (215), in words that he will himself echo shortly thereafter: "I only know that I am cheated" (220). But even more than the disappointment of dreams and expectations, it is the pervasive foregrounding of labor in its pure facticity, its harsh physical reality, that acts as the most effective antidote forestalling any possibility of idealization. Translated into a relentless display of flesh and blood, sweat and vomit,[11] aching backs and bruised fingers, the American Dream is itself gutted and crushed, buried under a heap of mortar and brick. The concrete in the title, while immediately alluding to the wet cement that chokes Geremio, congealing him into a Christ image, also evokes the physical hardness and unyielding materiality of a narrative world that stubbornly refuses to be abstracted into any hopeful idealization.

Economic Miracles

Work is virtually nonexistent in *The Great Gatsby*; of all the main characters, only Nick Carraway and George Wilson work, and only the latter appears to actually work for his living. As for Nick, though his move east is officially motivated by his choice of a job, the way in which this decision is presented makes it immediately evident that it has nothing to do with making a living: "Everybody I knew was in the bond business, so I supposed it could support one more single man. All my aunts and uncles talked it over as if they were choosing a prep school for me. ... Father agreed to finance me for a year" (Fitzgerald 1925, 9). Infantilized by his family circle and paradoxically dependent on his father's money for the move that should enable him to support himself, Nick actually seems to embrace his job less as a transition to adulthood than as an extension of his college years: "I took dinner usually at the Yale Club ... and then I went upstairs to the library and studied investments and securities for a conscientious hour. There were generally a few rioters around, but they never came into the library, so it was a good place to work" (63). Nick's work life as such is bracketed, briefly mentioned in a short miscellaneous section at the end of chapter 3 that, while ostensibly meant to reclaim its importance, actually manifests it as utterly incidental:

> Reading over what I have written so far, I see I have given the impression that the events of three nights several weeks apart were all that absorbed me. On the contrary ...
> Most of the time I worked. In the early morning the sun threw my shadow westward as I hurried down the white chasms of lower New York to the Probity Trust. I knew the other clerks and young bond-salesmen by their first names, and lunched with them in dark, crowded restaurants on little pig sausages and mashed potatoes and coffee. (62–63)

Even as he seems intent on providing an account of his work life, Carraway elides it, focusing instead on the moments before and after, on the lunch breaks with his co-workers. The ironically named Probity Trust operates as a synecdoche of his job—much as Job in *Christ in Concrete*, but with quite opposite effects. Here even Nick is literally dematerialized as a worker, his body reduced to a shadow. Nor is George B. Wilson's garage and repair shop rendered in much more material detail. A gray and dusty extension of the surreal, symbolic Valley of Ashes that surrounds it, Wilson's shop is equally shadowy and immediately romanticized by Nick's imagination, as if nothing so squalidly prosaic as this "unprosperous and bare" (30) interior could actually exist in real life: "It had occurred to me that this shadow of a garage must be a blind, and that sumptuous and romantic apartments were concealed overhead" (31).

Wealth—be it old or new money—is equally disconnected from any real-life or material origin and simply rendered as a dazzling display of purchase power and conspicuous consumption. Daisy's romantic appeal for Gatsby, we are told, lies in the "ripe mystery" of her house, the "hint of bedrooms upstairs more beautiful and cool than any other bedrooms, of gay and radiant activities taking place through its corridors, and of romances that were ... fresh and breathing and redolent of this year's shining motor-cars and of dances whose flowers were scarcely withered" (154). As for Tom Buchanan, this is how Nick introduces him: "His family were enormously wealthy—even in college his freedom with money was a matter for reproach—but now he'd left Chicago and come east in a fashion that rather took your breath away: for instance, he'd brought down a string of polo ponies from Lake Forest" (12). Jordan Baker's account of his wedding with Daisy is equally measured in terms of magnificent expenditure: "He came down with a hundred people in four private cars, and hired a whole floor of the Muhlbach Hotel, and the day before the wedding he gave her a string of pearls valued at three hundred and fifty thousand dollars" (82).

The same emphasis on sensational consumption, as is well known, is apparent in the garish excess of Gatsby's parties, his fabulous mansion ("a colossal affair by any standard ... a factual imitation of some Hôtel de Ville in Normandy" [11]), his "toilet set of pure dull gold" (98), and the shirts "piled like bricks in stacks a dozen high" (99) whose colorful display breaks Daisy's composure. Gatsby at first curtly refuses to specify the origin of such an exorbitant purchasing power—"when I asked him what business he was in he answered: 'That's my affair'" (97)—and then vaguely qualifies: "I was in the drug business and then I was in the oil business. But I'm not in either one now" (97). The topic is immediately dropped, like the rest of the many indications of Gatsby's ties with organized crime that are openly offered in the novel, only to be immediately downplayed or romantically transfigured through the narrative legerdemain of Carraway's focus and voice. Even Tom Buchanan's vehement list of Gatsby's shady transactions and connections during the confrontation at the Plaza Hotel in the seventh chapter of the novel comes across as being uttered out of jealousy and class contempt ("a common swindler who'd have to steal the ring he put on her finger" [140]) and is left without comment, immediately superseded in dramatic importance by the collapse of Gatsby's hope—"only the dead dream fought on as the afternoon slipped away, trying to touch what was no longer tangible, struggling unhappily, undespairingly, toward that lost voice across the room" (141)—and shortly after that the death of Myrtle Wilson. The gangster story is thus simultaneously evoked *and* discounted as inessential: the mere means to a romantic end.[12] A similar erasure takes place as regards Gatsby's likely status as a second-generation immigrant. As several critics have observed over the last couple of decades, Gatsby's original name, James Gatz, clearly bespeaks an immigrant background and a Central or Eastern European, quite possibly Jewish, origin. Always punctilious in his ascription of race and ethnicity to secondary characters—the Finnish woman who cleans and cooks for him, the "three negroes" and the "tragic eyes and short upper lips of south-eastern Europe" (75) of the mourners he meets on his way to Manhattan, Wolfshiem as a "flat-nosed Jew" (75), "[t]he young Greek, Michaelis" (142)—Nick Carraway never alludes to Gatsby's immigrant background and never questions his ethnicity. Mimicking Gatsby's own Anglicization, Nick's narrative performs an erasure of ethnicity that exactly parallels his erasure of the illegal sources of Gatsby's wealth. This systematic repression, universalization, and idealization are the necessary condition underlying *The Great Gatsby*'s celebration of the promise and wonder of the New World. The American Dream is thus rendered as an unfulfilled but endlessly renewed promise of social inclusiveness: a promise of whitewashing predicated on the miracle of wealth.

ECONOMIES OF DESIRE, ECONOMIES OF DEBT

The economy of *The Great Gatsby* is an economy of desire, in which romance and upward social mobility, a single object of love and a thousand objects of consumption repeatedly overlap and become mutually instrumental.[13] While ostensibly redeemed (or camouflaged) by his passion for Daisy, Gatsby's path follows a well-rehearsed script: the immigrant's shortcut to assimilation and success through organized crime, which students of Italian American culture such as Viscusi and Fred Gardaphé have taught us to understand in all its historical and cultural complexity. The gangster subverts the Protestant work ethic, unveils the compensatory will to power inherent in any quest for social success, mimics (and in so doing, both endorses and lays bare) the essence of corporate capitalism as the ruthless extraction of financial profit, and enhances the consumption-driven logic of contemporary culture, in which "access to stylish consumption through fancy dress and cars blurred the earlier lines that separated the social classes," operating as "a means of transgressing the social boundaries set up by definitions of class" (Gardaphé 2006, xv, 13).

If James Gatz/Jay Gatsby thus embodies, regardless of his individual ethnicity, the familiar Italian American myth of the gangster, the story of hard labor told in *Christ in Concrete* is the flip side of this myth. It is infinitely evocative that the most memorable scene capturing Gatsby's opulence should revolve around shirts "piled like bricks in stacks a dozen high" (Fitzgerald 1925, 99). In their colorful weightlessness, these metaphorical bricks—one of several images alluding to Gatsby's self-construction from a "Platonic conception of himself" (105)[14]—measure the distance between *The Great Gatsby*'s impalpable world and the hard materiality of *Christ in Concrete*. The clash of worlds is epitomized even more stridently in a line from the celebrated passage in chapter 4 of the novel in which Gatsby and Nick drive Gatsby's car, "with fenders spread like wings," toward Manhattan, "the city rising up across the river in white heaps and sugar lumps all built with a wish out of non-olfactory money" (74). When read contrapuntally with di Donato's implacable descriptions of construction work, this moment fully manifests itself—in a quite literal demonstration of Marx's theories—as a self-aware magic trick of materialization (of the abstract potential of capital) and dematerialization (of the physical actuality of labor), in which a sweet phantasmagoria in white successfully sublimates and elides both labor and capital, the former totally hidden from view and the latter explicitly sanitized by its proverbial capacity to purify itself: *pecunia non olet*. Thus, the wonderful conversion of capital into concrete and of concrete into sugar—the capitalist legerdemain of the endless mutual conversion between the concrete and the abstract—exactly parallels the bracketing of work and of every other actual economic process in the story, rendering both wealth and cities as the instant fulfilling of a magically granted wish.

But *whose* wish is it that has the power to magically transmogrify both sweat and money into a glittering sugarlike surface? If *The Great Gatsby* lends transient credit to the financial magic of capital as infinite creative potentiality through its portrayal of a glamourous milieu thriving on a fragile, soon-to-be-shattered promise of indefinite economic expansion, *Christ in Concrete*, though set in the same years, offers instead a quite different sense of futurity (di Donato 1939):

> The Lean as he fought his burden on looked forward to only one goal, the end. The barrow he pushed, he did not love. The stones that brutalized his palms, he did not love. ... When, when and where would the last stone be? Never... A voice within him spoke in wordless language.
>
> The language of worn oppression and the despair of realizing that his life had been left on brick piles. And always, there had been hunger and her bastard, the fear of hunger. (8)

A Contrapuntal Reading of *The Great Gatsby* and *Christ in Concrete*

> With the beginning of each job men, though knowing one another and having raised Job for years, wed themselves to Job with the same new ceremony, the same new energy and fear, the same fierce silence and loss of consciousness, and the perpetual sense of their wrongness ... struggling to fulfill a destiny of never-ending debt. These men were the hardness that would bruise Paul many times. They were the bodies to whom he would be joined in bondage to Job. ... Life would never be a dear music, a festival, a gift of Nature. Life would be the torque of Wall's battle that distorted straight limbs. (136)

These passages are indicative not just of the obviously different class settings and perspectives of the two novels but more deeply of the way in which this social difference produces totally different temporal regimes and libidinal economies. On one hand, an inexhaustible romantic/economic pursuit fueled by the endlessly renewed dynamic of desire; on the other hand, a relentless iteration of ineluctable acts of subjection, in which desire is preempted by the consciousness of doom.

This grim sense of doom that pervades most of *Christ in Concrete* marks its fundamental economy as a debt economy. Di Donato's insight is thus strikingly aligned with Walter Benjamin's note on "Capitalism as Religion," in which—elaborating on Max Weber's *Protestant Ethic and the Spirit of Capitalism* and on Nietzsche's *On the Genealogy of Morality*, and in dialogue with Ernst Bloch—he famously describes capitalism as a merciless religion, "the first instance of a cult that creates guilt, not atonement" (Benjamin 1996, 288), as shown in "the demonic ambiguity" (289) of the word *Schuld*, which in German means both "debt" and "guilt." This is exactly what the passage from *Christ in Concrete* quoted above describes, with amazing lexical and conceptual precision, as the bricklayers' "perpetual sense of their wrongness ... struggling to fulfill a destiny of never-ending debt" (136): a ubiquitous condition not just of financial insolvency but of foredoomed social bankruptcy. Thus transposed from an economic liability to a pervasive existential one, debt is shown to haunt Paul's feverish and delirious dreams—"'I can't do it!—I can't pay—I can't pay it—' ... 'But mama,' said Paul holding her hand tightly to his heart, 'someone *was* chasing me—like I owed someone a billion dollars and only had a penny—oh mama'" (94)—no less than the various characters' waking life.[15] Strikingly at variance with the immense but never otherwise quantified patrimonies evoked in *The Great Gatsby*, in *Christ in Concrete* figures, repeated in endless additions, multiplications, and divisions of dollars and cents, pervade the characters' interior monologues, rendering their inner life as a constant, anxious reckoning of survival:

> Fifty cents the hour, nine hours the day, brings four dollars and fifty cents. With six days the week brings—six by four brings twenty-four. One-half by six makes three. Twenty-four add three brings the final count twenty-seven dollars. ... Six by four add three brings twenty-seven ...? Yes, twenty-seven it does bring. Say that three dollars shall be expense—leaving twenty-four. Say perhaps four—no, better three. The eight little ones, Annunziata and myself are eight—nine—ten. Ten Christians at twenty-four dollars. (45)

> Two onions. Four potatoes. One-two-three-four-five-six large crumbs   one-two-three-four-five-six-seven-eight-nine-ten-eleven small crumbs. Paul Annina Lucia Giorgio Joseph Adela Johnny Geremio two onions four potatoes. (51)

While someone might want to trace this sense of doom to the fatalistic legacy of the Southern Italian *paesani*'s Catholic quietism vis-à-vis the inherent dynamism traditionally ascribed to the Protestant capitalist bourgeoisie, debt can in fact be seen as a constitutive element of capitalist modernity, if not of human society itself, as argued in Nietzsche's *Genealogy of Morality*. For Nietzsche, the economic relation between creditor and debtor is the oldest and most personal one, which generates measure, evaluation, promise, obligation, guilt, and all the subsequent moral categories. Building on Nietzsche, Marx, and Deleuze and Guattari, Maurizio Lazzarato (2012) notes that debt is a means of ethico-political subjectivization: "Debt breeds, subdues, manufactures, adapts, and shapes subjectivity," producing the individual subject as "a subject answerable and indebted to his creditor" (42). Always inscribed within an asymmetry of power, the debtor, no less than the creditor, is exposed to the radical uncertainty of time and made answerable for his own future. Therefore, Lazzarato continues, "The system of debt must ... neutralize time, that is, the risk inherent to it. It must anticipate and ward off every potential 'deviation' in the behavior of the debtor the future might hold.... The effects of the power of debt on subjectivity (guilt and responsibility) allow capitalism to bridge the gap between present and future" (45–46). Debt thus "appropriates not only the present labor-time of wage earners and of the population in general, it also preempts ... each person's future as well as the future of society as a whole" (46–47).

In different fashions and on different levels, both *The Great Gatsby* and *Christ in Concrete* are narratives of modern capitalism, which they render in ways that are the flip side of each other: hyperbolic purchasing power and flamboyant consumption on one hand; crushing oppression and bare survival on the other. Driven by a future-oriented economy of speculation, *The Great Gatsby* magnificently stages the unsaturable dynamics of desire associated with a rising financial and consumer culture, revealing it as the implicit engine of the American Dream's lure: "the green light, the orgastic future that year by year recedes before us ... to-morrow we will run faster, stretch out our arms further.... And one fine morning—" (Fitzgerald 1925, 188). Ruled by an anxiety-ridden economy of debt, *Christ in Concrete* gives narrative embodiment to the indissociable mutual relation between labor, debt, and guilt that undergirds that self-perpetuating wonder. If Gatsby's thematic keyword is, famously, *hope*, *Christ in Concrete* might be viewed as an apt narrative illustration of Benjamin's idea that capitalism is not a religion of hope, but really has despair as its end: "It is the expansion of despair, until despair becomes a religious state of the world in the hope that this will lead to salvation" (Benjamin 1996, 289).

GETTING CREDIT, GIVING CREDIT

Written from the two opposite sides of both the class divide and the historical and economic watershed of 1929, *The Great Gatsby* and *Christ in Concrete* stage two different cultures, respectively predicated on unlimited credit and on presupposed insolvency:[16] two opposite (though in fact complementary) attitudes that are not just economic positions but worldviews in their own right. Hope versus despair, confidence versus fear, trust versus mistrust in what the future may bring. In the question of credit and debt, an economic relation is conflated with an affective attitude and a system of belief: "It is through debt that capital is able to appropriate not only the physical and intellectual abilities the poor man employs in his labor, but also his social and existential forces" (Lazzarato, 59).[17] There is hardly any need to emphasize that the whole ideological construction of the American Dream is predicated exactly on the same conflation and that while *The Great Gatsby* offers a celebration of the American Dream—albeit one that is paradoxically effected at once *in spite of* and *by virtue of* its exposure as a fantasy—*Christ in Concrete* systematically dismantles the dream through a punctilious re-materialization that challenges the dream's euphemistic, universalizing, and idealizing thrust by foregrounding the actual conditions of existence of its supposed actors and beneficiaries.

Read in this key, the first section of *Christ in Concrete* might allow of a further interpretation, which I offer as a way of both paying homage to and parasitically building upon Viscusi's (2006) memorable reading of the sequence as di Donato's "thin fictional allegory about his own imaginings of his own father's death," in which the author "makes himself guilty of that death" by resorting to a whole Freudian repertoire of "castration, burial alive, splintering of teeth, loss of breath, and suffocation" (103). I would suggest that the "irrepressible anger" (103) that, as Viscusi argues, fuels the gruesome power of the scene is not driven only by the son's resentment for his father's death and abandonment of his

A Contrapuntal Reading of *The Great Gatsby* and *Christ in Concrete*

family but also by a need to punish him symbolically. What Geremio is being punished for, I would argue, is his role as the one character in the story who explicitly embraces the promise of upward social mobility through hard labor that is associated with the notion of the American Dream.

In sharp contrast with the bitter sense of the future conveyed from the very first page of the novel by the Lean's furious words—"Work! Sure! For America beautiful will eat you and spit your bones into the earth's hole! Work!" (3)—and even in spite of his own misgivings about the unsafety of the construction site, Geremio's words and thoughts are constantly marked by an obstinately sought sense of hopeful futurity: "I tell you that all my kids must be boys so that they someday will be big American builders. And then I'll help them to put the gold away in the basements!" (4); "That night was a crowning point in the life of Geremio. He bought a house! Twenty years he had helped to mold the New World. And now he was to have a house of his own!" (6); "I tell you, son of Geremio will never lay bricks! Paulie mine will study from books—he will be the great builder! This very moment I can see him … How proud he!" (10). It is probably no accident that the word "dream," variously inflected, recurs with remarkable frequency in Geremio's section:[18] Its meaning ranges from the quiet warmth of the family at night ("life breathed heavily, and dreams entertained in far, far worlds, the nationbuilder's brood" [6]) and the joyful expectation that is most closely associated with the American Dream ("Geremio was dreaming of the new house and the joys he could almost taste" [9]) to the uncanny sense of unreality ("all appeared unreal, a dream pungent and nostalgic"; "Life, dream, reality, unreality, spiraling ever about each other" [11, 12]) that accompanies the fateful "dreamy afternoon" (13) of the building's collapse and Geremio's excruciating death, which in his incredulous horror he repeatedly tries to exorcize as a dream: "He wiped his eyes in subconscious despair. Where was he? What kind of a dream was he having? … Ah yes, he's dreaming in bed … he must do his utmost to break out of this dream!" (14). Creating a lexical continuity between Geremio's optimistic predictions, his sense of foreboding, and his final, waking nightmare, this terrible scene stages the cruel reversal of his dreams, operating as a stern rebuke of Geremio's reliance on them and of the submissiveness induced by his very hopes, which will actually cost him his life:

> His train of thought quickly took in his family, home and hopes. And with hope came fear. Something within asked, "Is it possible to breathe God's air without fear dominating with the pall of unemployment? And the terror of production for Boss. Boss and Job? To rebel is to lose all the very little. To be obedient is to choke. O dear Lord, guide my path." (12–13)

If his pursuit of the American Dream ends up literally choking and crushing Geremio, it is perhaps his credulity that the author intends to sanction in inflicting on him the physical and symbolic torture mercilessly described in the text. Geremio's faith in the rewards of hard work thus becomes one with his and Annunziata's Catholic faith, constantly evoked in their words and thoughts: Both are exposed as equally groundless. Similarly, the scene of the séance with the Cripple can be read as a staging and a *mise en abyme* not only of the fraudulent emptiness of beliefs but also of the willing suspension of disbelief that undergirds them and of the inherent structure of deferral that sustains alike the Christian faith in the afterlife, the ideological promise of the American Dream, and the medium's vague and conventional assurances, whose efficacy depends entirely on a complicit self-deception on the part of its addressees. While unable to *get* credit, poor people, as it turns out, can nevertheless *give* credit: Credulity is, in fact, their only patrimony and the only form of credit available to them. Lending credit to those future-oriented deceptions that are actually meant to keep them in their state of subjugation is, the novel seems to suggest, their self-delusional and ultimately self-defeating form of speculation.[19]

The rewards of the American dream are thus exposed as a dangerous delusion and denounced as partaking of that debt economy that seals the workers' destiny by binding them to an obligation

A Contrapuntal Reading of *The Great Gatsby* and *Christ in Concrete*

that even death can never fulfill, and that—as in Geremio and Paul's case—becomes their children's legacy. Only after witnessing Nazone's death does Paul realize the true import of this legacy, which seals his sense of the temporality of debt by projecting his memories as a prefiguration of his ineluctable fate—"the world ... would crumple him like his father and Nazone!" (210)—thus making him quite literally *answerable for his own future*:

> Somewhere in the countless bendings and twistings he would lose his balance, a derrick would collapse and blot him out, a sledge would hurtle from above and crumple him, a brick would smash through his skull.
> Ah no, today's Job had choked him—but let him live. Tomorrow he would die. He will have died without having raised his head and shouted defiance! And would be left with stiff outstretched fingers and gummy stilled mouth. (218)

It is certainly appropriate that this fierce indictment of Job as a random dealer of death rather than economic emancipation should come as a result of a literal dream, in which his father, Geremio, abjures his former belief: "I was cheated, my children also will be crushed, cheated. His father begins to absolve and sighs faintly, Ahhh, not even the Death can free us, for we are ... Christ in concrete" (215). This is the critical legacy of disillusion that Paul finally makes his own, denouncing the Cripple's reassuring lies ("Mother ... Papa is not coming back—we shall never meet again" [216]) as much as the comforts of religion ("He pointed to the crucifix. 'That's a lie.' ... '—Our Dio?' 'What Dio and Dio!'" [219]) and the equally deceptive dream of a better life:

> I only know that I am cheated. ... Papa's life has been used against me. My toil has been used against me. ... We have only one life! One life! ... Here where we are is our only life! ... I want justice here! I want happiness here! I want life here! ... Mama, mama, I know so terribly this our only life—... Now! Now! I want salvation now! For I know oh I know we cannot live forever. (220)

The realization of having been "cheated" denounces the whole future-oriented system of the debt economy on one hand and of ideological and religious credit on the other hand as a fraud and ushers in a new emphasis on the possibilities of the present. If, as Lazzarato suggests, the debt economy operates by "possessing the future in advance by objectivizing it," thus "subordinating all possibility of choice and decision which the future holds to the reproduction of capitalist power relations" (46), Paul's insistence on "Now!" rejects the objectivization of the future as both endless debt and endlessly deferred reward and reconfigures the present as a site of rebellion rather than submission, opening up possibilities of choice and decision that might not be entirely contained within and preempted by the capitalist logic and the imaginary it produces.

A WRONG STORY?

"Dear mother, is not all this a wrong story?" (di Donato 1939, 32), Paul wonders as the neighborhood mourners mutter words of conventional piety after his father's funeral. And if we take *The Great Gatsby* as the canonical modernist rendition of the American Dream and the Great American Novel, *Christ in Concrete* is, indeed, a wrong story. Even di Donato seems to be implying as much when, describing the men at work, he paradoxically denies the very possibility of his own novel:

> No poet would be there to intone meter of soul's sentence to stone, no artist upon scaffold to paint the vinegary sweat of Christian in correspondence with red brick and gray mortar, no composer attuned to the screaming movement of Job and voiceless cry in overalls.
> Sugar and shine would ride high in state and wave a wand
> ...
> And blood and stone would go on creating the World.
> Unseen would be the pushing hands and driving shoulders, the ripple-strained stomachs, and gripping feet.

A Contrapuntal Reading of *The Great Gatsby* and *Christ in Concrete*

Unsmelled and untasted would be Tenement and manger of worker. (136)

This metafictional manifesto simultaneously amounts to a statement of personal poetics—the stones, the brick and mortar, the sweat and cries, the smell and taste, the active bodies that make up di Donato's narrative—and to a critique of the lacks, repressions, and evasions in the choice of topics and representational strategies of the coeval literary world. I cannot help wondering, however, about that striking moment "Sugar and shine would ride high in state and wave a wand," which surprisingly encapsulates each one of the key elements of the Manhattan skyline scene in *The Great Gatsby* that I commented on above, contrasting them overtly with a material world of blood and stone that is doomed to remain unseen, unnoticed, and unsung. Indeed, this sentence seems to encrypt a covert dialogue with *The Great Gatsby* that while predating the latter's revival and canonization in the 1940s, anticipates the different positions that the two novels would respectively come to occupy in collective literary memory. Accident or design? Whatever the case, it can be read as a clear-eyed proleptic indictment of prospective processes of literary mythmaking, canonization, and collective memorialization.

NOTES

[1] Original publication dates of the chapters included in *Buried Caesars, and Other Secrets of Italian American Writing*, are as follows: "*De vulgari eloquentia*" (1981); "The Semiology of Semen" (1986). The chapter on "The Italian American Sign," also dealing with *Christ in Concrete*, appeared in the volume for the first time. Tamburri (2014) builds and refines on Viscusi's analysis of the novel.

[2] This may of course be considered obvious on the mere strength of textual evidence; and yet, the critical studies of the novel have never spelled it out explicitly, and di Donato himself, in his interviews, constantly refrained from mentioning such influences, preferring to emphasize his personal trauma as the authentic autobiographical source of his original story, rather than any formative readings.

[3] Matthiessen's book (1941) is discussed by Viscusi in a long endnote, in full awareness of the significance of Matthiessen's deployment of the term "Renaissance" in his act of canonization (Viscusi 2006, 242).

[4] In his survey of non-Italian American literary gangsters, Gardaphé (2006) mentions *The Great Gatsby* without further pursuing the association. Just as *Christ in*

Concrete has seldom been tackled by modernist studies scholars, the insights provided by Viscusi (2006) and Gardaphé (2006) on the cultural and historical significance of the Italian American gangster, to the best of my knowledge, have never been brought to bear on *The Great Gatsby*.

5 Let me note in passing three major modernist features of *Christ in Concrete* that lie outside of the scope of the analysis that follows. The first is the emphasis on the shock of the urban experience as epitomized by jarring sounds, such as the construction site's "inferno of sense-pounding cacophony" (di Donato 1939, 46) or the experimentally rendered city noise: "Noise! Noise O noise O noise and sounds swelling in from the sea of city life without of pushing scurrying purring motors and horns and bells and cries and sirens and whistles and padded stream of real feet O noise O noise O noi—se" (172). The second is the pervasive mechanization of human bodies, along the lines of the "body-machine complex" discussed by Mark Seltzer (1992) in *Bodies and Machines*: "no longer Geremio, but a machinelike entity" (9); "a human metronome" (22); "a Christian thermometer of meat and bone" (142). The third is an insistence on fragmentation that renders this familiar modernist device as the stylistic and structural equivalent of the literal fragmentation of bodies and selves, the crushing of the characters' lives and their lack of control over their existence. Apart from the obvious example of Geremio, Luigi is a literally fragmented self, his loss of a leg a bodily equivalent of the metaphorical breaking up of unity so pervasive in modernist writing, and his split self-perception both a consequence and a metaphor of his job-related dismemberment: "What do you thus? Who separated us? Where go you now without leg where leg should be? ... I, man disjoined" (139).

6 Long ignored by critics, the ethnic quality of Gatsby's story has been recognized by twenty-first-century readers. Among other contributions see: Joe Kraus (2006), Charles Lewis (2007), and Benjamin Schreier (2007).

7 See Dorothée von Huene-Greenberg (1987) and the interviews published as appendixes A and B Diomede (1995).

8 The term *povero cristo* literally translates as "poor Christ," but in this context it means "poor guy" or even "poor wretch," according to colloquial Italian usage.

9 In addition to Paul's final dream in the "Annunziata" section, see Luigi's dream at the hospital in chapter 5 of the "Job" section, entirely pervaded by the actions and objects—brick, hammer, stone—of the construction site.

10 I will return to the novel's treatment of the future and to its exposure of religious and ideological delusions in the sections that follow.

11 On the symbolic value of vomit, see Fazio (2007). It is worth noting that if work is the testing ground of masculinity, the women's lives are rendered in equally and possibly even more strikingly physical details, as witnessed in the protracted scene of Annunziata giving birth. Indeed, the sense of women's corporeality is pervasive in *Christ in Concrete*, foregrounded not just in the birth scene but also from the very opening pages, in the constant mention of women's breasts, bellies, and flesh in the verbal exchanges between the workers. This is in sharp contrast with the stylized silhouettes of Daisy Buchanan and Jordan Baker in *The Great Gatsby*, as well as with Daisy's report of coming to from anesthesia after her daughter's birth. This sanitization and abstraction of the body are also evident in

Gatsby's incredulous look when the appearance of Daisy and Tom's daughter faces him with the fleshy evidence of Daisy's motherhood and the couple's sexual relationship.

[12] On the significance of the act of erasure in the novel, see Barbara Will (2005).

[13] On the relationship the novel establishes between ethnicity, democratic inclusiveness, desire, and consumer capitalism, see Donatella Izzo (2015).

[14] The brick metaphor is also used in chapter 3 in a comment on the real but unused books in Gatsby's bookcases, seen as stage props in a realistic mise-en-scène: "[I]f one brick was removed the whole library was liable to collapse" (52). After Gatsby's death, his father comments that "If he'd of lived, he'd ... of helped build up the country" (175), thus highlighting the underlying symbolic relationship between Gatsby's self-fashioning and America's.

[15] See also the Christmas episode: "The Donovans, the Farabuttis, the Lobans, the shabby, the debtors, will gather at the right of the altar and kneel with gentle tremulous touch to the Child Jesus in manger with outstretched baby arms" (156).

[16] See the scene in which, after his father's death, Paul tries to get food on credit: "'... Perhaps? you could? give us credit? until I went to work ...? The Sisters at school say that I am smart and shall someday —' No no no no no no no no no no. 'I would like to do that, but I can not'" (52). Immediately after that, Paul goes to a shop displaying "a cardboard poster [which] said in gilt letters on black that: IN GOD WE TRUST ... OTHERS PAY CASH" (52).

[17] On the affective operation of capitalism, see also Frédéric Lordon (2013). Within this affective operation, the episode of the wedding festa, with its overflowing abundance of food, laughter, dance, song, and physical enjoyment, amounts to a veritable moment of Carnivalistic suspension of the capitalist economy and logic.

[18] I have counted ten occurrences in the fourteen pages of the section.

[19] It is no accident that the novel most overtly takes stock of the American Dream in Nazone's disillusioned speech immediately after the 1929 stock market crash (chapter 2 of the final section), thus marking the simultaneous crisis of both systems of speculation, the financial and the ideological: "The career of builder in this land is done. This land has become a soil that has contradicted itself, a country of Babel where Christians are beginning to wander about in hungry distress cursing each other in strange tongues, ripping their hearts, and possessing no longer even fingernails with which to scratch their desperation. ... Discovered by an Italian—named from Italian—But oh, that I may leave this land of disillusion!" (203).

WORKS CITED

Benjamin, Walter. 1996 [1921]. "Capitalism as Religion." In *Selected Writings*, Vol. 1, edited by Marcus Bullock and Michael W. Jennings, 288-291. Cambridge, MA: Belknap Press of Harvard University Press.

Di Donato, Pietro. 2004 [1939]. *Christ in Concrete*. New York: New American Library.

Diomede, Matthew. 1995. *Pietro DiDonato, the Master Builder*. Lewisburg: Bucknell University Press; London: Associated University Presses.

Fazio, Michele. 2007. "'Vomit your Poison': Violence, Hunger, and Symbolism in Pietro di Donato's *Christ in Concrete*." *MELUS* 32 (4, Winter): 115–137.

Fitzgerald, Francis Scott. 1975 [1925]. *The Great Gatsby*. Harmondsworth: Penguin.

Gardaphé, Fred. 2006. *From Wiseguys to Wise Men. The Gangster and Italian American Masculinities*. New York: Routledge.

Huene-Greenberg, Dorothée von. 1987. "A MELUS Interview: Pietro di Donato." *MELUS* 14 (3-4, Autumn-Winter): 33–52.

Izzo, Donatella. 2015. "Imparare a desiderare: il capitalismo affettivo in *The Great Gatsby*." *Ácoma* 8 (Spring-Summer): 65–79.

Kraus, Joe. 2006. "De-centering the Canon: Understanding *The Great Gatsby* as an Ethnic Novel." In *Multiethnic Literature and Canon Debates*, edited by Mary Jo Bona and Irma Maini, 127–144. New York: State University of New York Press.

Lazzarato, Maurizio. 2012. *The Making of the Indebted Man: An Essay on the Neoliberal Condition*. Los Angeles: Semiotext(e).

Lewis, Charles. 2007. "Babbled Slander Where the Paler Shades Dwell: Reading Race in *The Great Gatsby* and *Passing*." *LIT: Literature Interpretation Theory* 18 (2): 173–191.

Lordon, Frédéric. 2013. *La Société des affects*, Paris: Seuil.

Matthiessen, Francis Otto. 1941. *American Renaissance. Art and Expression in the Age of Emerson and Whitman*. Oxford and New York, Oxford University Press.

Said, Edward. 1993. *Culture and Imperialism*. London: Chatto and Windus.

Schreier, Benjamin. 2007. "Desire's Second Act: 'Race' and *The Great Gatsby*'s Cynical Americanism." *Twentieth Century Literature* 53 (2), (Summer): 153–181.

Seltzer, Mark. 1992. *Bodies and Machines*. New York: Routledge.

Tamburri, Anthony Julian. 2014. "Pietro di Donato's *Christ in Concrete*: An Italian/American Novel Not Set in Stone." *LIT: Literature Interpretation Theory* 14 (1): 3–16; now in *Re-Reading Italian Americana*.

Specificities and Generalities on Literature and Criticism, 2013. Madison: Fairleigh Dickinson University Press.

Will, Barbara. 2005. *The Great Gatsby* and the Obscene Word." *College Literature* 32 (4, Fall): 125–144.

Viscusi, Robert. 2006. *Buried Caesars, and Other Secrets of Italian American Writing*. New York: State University of New York Press.

Augusto Bassetti and the First English Grammar for Italian Speakers Written and Published in the United States (1885)

James J. Periconi

Around the time of the great wave of European migration, Italian-language books had long been available in the United States, imported by the Italian-language newspaper *L'Eco d'Italia* since at least January 1862, and probably earlier.[1] It was not until 1876, however, that English grammar books in Italian and Italian-English dictionaries were first advertised in *L'Eco* in New York City and imported from Italy, and just a few years later by *L'Eco*'s upstart rival, *Il Progresso Italo-Americano*, which was established in 1880.[2]

Then in 1885 Augusto Bassetti, an Italian American living in New York City, self-published and widely distributed his *Manuale per imparare gli elementi e la retta pronunzia della Lingua Inglese senza maestro per uso principalmente degli emigranti Italiani del Prof. Augusto Bassetti* (Manual for Learning the Elements and Correct Pronunciation of the English Language without a Teacher, for Use Principally by Italian Immigrants by Prof. Augusto Bassetti). This book, designed in the United States by an Italian specifically for Italian immigrants, was a new kind of primer, different from previous imported English grammar books for Italian speakers. It would be the first of several such publications over the next couple of decades. This essay sets out to suggest that some combination of social, linguistic, pedagogic, and historical needs justified this book's creation.[3]

How does this work—the first American-produced grammar by an Italian American developed specifically to teach English to Italian immigrants who knew little standard Italian—reflect those specific needs?[4] What inroads did its publication make, if any, into the business that appears to have started in 1876 of importing as many as a half-dozen different competing grammars from Italy? But above all, why might Italian immigrants to the United States by the 1880s need a new kind of grammar book to learn English when so many were already available in New York City?[5]

I propose to answer these questions principally by looking at works from the mid-1880s: two English grammars for native Italian speakers; a bilingual Italian–English dictionary; and the first novel (of two) by Bassetti, who was the first of a half-dozen U.S.-based writers of English grammar books for Italian speakers and Italian–English dictionaries. How exactly were these books structured differently from previous offerings, if indeed they were, toward attracting a new class of readers, namely, marginally literate Italian immigrants?

Besides the evidence in the texts themselves, I look at the paratextual evidence in Bassetti's advertisements for those works in local Italian newspapers, appearing virtually daily for about five years from August 1885 through June 1890. During this period, we see Bassetti's explanation of what was new in these volumes, including their special utility for Italian immigrants. I further explore how the print advertisements reveal Italian immigrants' special needs and the response of the marketplace, in particular how they attracted the kind of new book-buyers Bassetti sought.

A Brief Biography of Augusto Bassetti

Census and death records tell us Bassetti was born in Italy in 1830 or 1832.[6] He arrived in New York in about 1855 and became a citizen on October 19, 1874. He died in a home for the poor in Manhattan on September 27, 1901.

In 1858, he had a brief but intense backstage relationship in New York, reflected in extensive correspondence with a Torinese soprano, one Marietta Piccolomini, while she was on tour in America in October and November of that year, not long before her marriage to another back in Siena in 1860.[7]

On April 6, 1867, we also know, Professor Augusto Bassetti "gave a concert and lecture [that 'dwelt upon the history of music']" at Irving Hall, as reported in a local paper (*New York Sun* 1867, 4).[8] The review also notes, mentioning Piccolomini by name, that there was a "prima donna whom [Bassetti] once knew" whom he mentioned in his lecture (*New York Sun* 1867, 4). He is referred to in these newspaper articles as "Professor" Bassetti, and he uses that title in his first grammar book, but his university or place of origin in Italy, which sometimes appears in American imprints about a European author to give some credibility to the author and his or her opinions, is not given. The quality of the Italian used in his books is suggestive of someone with more than a few years of schooling, but it lacks the sophistication of, say, prefatory remarks made in grammars produced in Italy in the middle and late nineteenth century.

Finally, we note that the advertisements in *Il Progresso Italo-Americano* and *L'Eco d'Italia* for his books cease in 1894; one appearance in an Italian American directory (*Guida italiana* 1894) suggests that he was still active a year before: Bassetti is listed in the New York City section under the heading "Editori Librai" (Publishers/Booksellers), at Post Office Box 3813, along with Carlo Barsotti, the publisher of *Il Progresso Italo-Americano* from its inception in 1880; Francesco Zanolini, whose bookstore ads were frequent in the late 1890s; and Giovanni Cereghino, whose ads first appear in the Italian newspapers in 1889 and continue through 1905; these were all listed at Manhattan street addresses.

MARKETING THE *MANUALE*

In the August 26, 1885, issue of New York City's *L'Eco d'Italia* there appeared an advertisement in Italian for a book written by Bassetti in Italian that, based on my bibliographical review, was the first in Italian published in the United States during the Great Emigration:

ATTENTI ITALIANI
LIBRO per imparare gli elementi e la retta pronunzia della lingua inglese SENZA MAESTRO.

Ogni parola inglese porta scritto sotto come si pronunzia con ortografia italiana; dimodochè, ognuno, che sa leggere e scrivere un poco l'italiano, può imparare da se stesso, a scrivere l'inglese come si scrive, e parlarlo come si parla; oltrecciò può perfezionarsi nella retta scrittura dell'italiano. Libro di genere affatto uuovo [sic] e di somma utilità per tutti gli italiani, ma particolarmente per quei poveri emigranti, che approdano a questi lidi senza sapere una parola di quella lingua che deve dare loro il pane e la fortuna. (*L'Eco d'Italia* 1885, 4)

(ATTENTION ITALIANS
A BOOK for learning the elements of the correct pronunciation of the English language WITHOUT A TEACHER.
Each English word has printed under it how it is pronounced, with Italian orthography; by this means, *everyone who can read and write a little Italian* can learn by himself how to write English as it is written, and speak it as it is spoken; beyond this, *he can improve himself in properly writing Italian*. This book is *of a completely new type* and of the *greatest utility* for all Italians, but particularly *for those poor immigrants who reach these shores without knowing a word of that language* that should provide them with their bread and their fortune.) (Emphasis added and all translations mine.)

The advertisement also listed the book's price at 50 cents per copy and indicated it could be bought in bulk (minimum one dozen) for a 25 percent discount for $4.50. It further stated that one could obtain copies from the author at certain hours and locations on MacDougal and Spring Streets and at the café or pastry shop near the Bowery at all hours of the day. The ad lists several other locations where the book was sold, such as "respectable Italian stores." Bassetti suggests that Italian stores could buy the books wholesale and then resell them for a profit in addition to "il tirare nuovi avventori, e dar voga e rispetto ai loro negozi" (drawing new customers, and bestowing a fashionableness and respectability on their stores). Customers could also write or come directly to

Bassetti at his home address on "Vendom" (in later ads corrected to "Vandam") Street at certain hours.

Bassetti's distribution was new because it allowed Italian immigrants who were too busy to go to the offices of either of the two newspapers where imported books were sold or unable to mail payment to those offices an easy way to buy them. Moreover, it was evident from the advertisement that Bassetti grasped that making books available in places where people would meet as part of normal social intercourse (along with the accompanying cordiality) was conducive to selling and profits. In addition, he emphasized the "respectable" character of participating Italian stores that carried "fashionable" books and with his book available drew "new customers."[9]

His book was "of a completely new type" and was designed to be of the "greatest utility" for all Italians "but particularly for those poor immigrants" who arrived in the United States not knowing a word of English. Above all, these poor immigrants, needing to know only "un poco l'italiano" (a little Italian) in order to find Bassetti's grammar to be useful, could learn English "without a teacher." The phrase "senza maestro" would also be a major selling point in the advertising copy and on the covers and title pages of each of the U.S.-composed English-grammar books for Italians that were published in the twenty years following Bassetti's (1885) publication: that of Francesco Zanolini, Francesco Frugone, and Angelo de Gaudenzi in the 1890s; and one produced by Alfonso Arbib-Costa and Alberto Pecorini in the first decade of the twentieth century. Bassetti's methodology of writing as a teacher speaking directly to the reader of the book, however, was unique to him.

Bassetti's creation of a new kind of grammar is on par in significance, in language-learning circles, with Noah Webster's 1828 creation of an American dictionary. Webster gave the United States its own dictionary distinct from Samuel Johnson's original 1755 publication;[10] Bassetti's grammar did the same for Italian students of English.

Most significant was the fact that the immigrant Italian who knew only "un poco l'italiano" could "improve himself in the correct writing of Italian" at the same time he was learning how to write English "come si scrive" (as it is written) and speak English "come si parla" (as it is spoken). For Italians who arrived in the United States mostly speaking their local dialect and who may have only briefly studied standard Italian language in Italy,[11] Bassetti's grammar must have been a godsend, truly a way for them to improve their Italian as much as to learn the new language that would help "to give them their bread and their fortune" (Bassetti 1885). Bassetti's potentially doubly empowering pedagogical act makes the publication all the more remarkable.

Why would this have been important? At least in early twentieth-century New York City, teachers and others have long seen original-language retention as a hindrance to assimilation. Speaking—and, worse, reading and writing in—the language of one's origins retards the acquisition of the language of the adopted country and thus impedes assimilation.

On a practical level, learning Italian may actually have been as important for the process of becoming American as learning English—maybe even more so. Robert Viscusi (2006) addresses the matter of language and identity for early Italian immigrants in this way:

> This was the age of nations, and before Calabrian and Sicilian immigrants could become Americans, they needed to understand their place in that age. They needed to find a way of becoming Italians. The task was more demanding than one might at first suppose. ... The immigrants recognized that other Americans thought of them as *Italians*, and they sought ways to make sense of that in their lives. The paradox of their situation was that they could not safely become Americans until they had found a way of knowing what it meant to be Italians. (19)

Bassetti's 1885 grammar is deceptively simple. It is a brief work, only thirty-one pages of text, each one followed by a blank page.

Bassetti gives detailed "OSSERVAZIONI SULLA PRONUNZIA" (observations on pronunciation) followed by some examples, and then, on page 5, "DIREZIONI PER L'USO DEL LIBRETTO" (directions for the use of this little book), he indicates what the blank pages are intended for:

> Ogni studente più [sic] usarlo a suo modo, ma il meglio sarebbe di copiare attentamente nel foglio bianco, a lato alla pagina stampata; prima, la frase Italiano, poi ancor più attentamente l'Inglese come si scrive. Non più. La pronunzia segnata non si deve mai copiare ma solo leggere e ripetere finchè si abbia acquistato il vero suono. Copiandola si confouderebbe coll'Inglese come deve essere scritto e farebbe più male che bene. Lo studente non deve lasciarsi trasportare dalla voglia di imparare tutto in un momento. Le parole e frasi di questo libretto sono tutte di prima necessità. Epperciò non si può dire, come è il caso di tante grammatiche, che le parole e frasi che avete avanti gli occhi, non vi fanno per l'uso presente, e così saltarle per andar avanti. Qui tutto vi fa e vi è necessario per ogni momento; epperciò impossessatevi bene di quello che avete per le mani prima di passare ad altro. Il dire che questo manuale può insegnarvi tutto e far miracoli, sarebbe certo grave follia. Ma un libro più utile e più necessario ad ogni Italiano che approdi a questi lidi non è ancor mai venuto alla luce del mondo. Istruitevi e farete fortuna. (Bassetti 1885, 5)

> (Each student can use it [the book] in his own way, but the best would be to copy attentively on the blank page alongside the printed page; first, the Italian sentence, then still more attentively, the English as it is written. Nothing more. The signed pronunciation ought never be copied but only read and repeated until it has acquired its true sound. Copying it would confuse one with English as it ought to be written and would cause more harm than good. The student ought not to be carried away by the wish to learn everything at once. The words and sentences of this book are all of primary necessity. Thus, one can't say, as is the case with so many grammars, that the words and sentences

that you have before your eyes won't be sufficient for you for the present moment, and so you'll jump ahead. Here everything will be sufficient for you and is necessary for you for each moment. Thus, hold tightly to what you have in your hands before moving on to another page. It would be grave folly to tell you that this manual can teach you everything and work great miracles. But a book more useful and more necessary for each Italian who approaches these shores has never seen the light of day. Find out about it yourself and you'll make your fortune.)

Thus, the book that claims to be designed to help readers learn English "senza maestro" actually provides a teacher within the book itself. After an initial tip of the hat to each reader's ability to make one's own decision on the subject, Bassetti provides precise instructions on what to do and what not to do in using the book. The reader is encouraged to make his/her reading become his/her writing on those blank pages in this, in effect, workbook. He cautions not to turn the *oral* signs provided in the pronunciation guide into *written* ones: Oral and written serve two distinct functions. The oral transcriptions are to help one be understood by Americans and to develop a better ear for understanding native English speakers. Bassetti warns students not to jump ahead out of impatience. In effect, he's saying: I'm with you each step of the way; so, stay with me if you know what's good for you!

The blank pages served another, equally important, function besides repeating the phrases or sentences from the grammar as a teaching aid: They were there to provide space for the intersection of the largely oral culture from which the immigrants came with a written culture that they would encounter.

SALES AND REPRINTS

On December 22, 1885, Bassetti announced with great excitement that "the utility of this [first] book, confirmed by experience, has caused such a rapid sale as to require a SECOND EDITION of it, now ready, much better executed and with important additions, which make the work complete of its type" (*L'Eco d'Italia* 1885).

The success of Bassetti's *Manuale* can be deduced from the fact that it was advertised almost without interruption for a five-year span from August 1885 to June 1890.[12] During this period it had been joined in advertisements by *Secondo libro...* (Bassetti 1986a), which contained some short stories and sample letters, a *Nuovo dizionario...* (Bassetti (1886b), a pronunciation dictionary, and two novels (Bassetti 1887, 1889).

The ads for Bassetti's *Manuale* of 1885 are similar over time, but there is an advance of the attention-grabbing sort: "ATTENTI ITALIANI" soon becomes a strident "ATTENTI ITALIANI!" or "ATTENTI ITALIANI!!!" which seems appropriate especially when the ad appeared, as it sometimes did, right next to a far larger, longer multicolumn ad for the offering of 100 or more imported books. And when his ad appears right next to these longer ads, the imported grammars and Italian–English dictionaries are not advertised. Soon, "ATTENTI ITALIANI" is followed or replaced by the name of a bookstore, Libro D'Oro or Tre Libri D'Oro; this happens by the time Bassetti (1886a) has published a second volume of grammar with stories (*Secondo libro...*) and a dictionary (1886b). Bassetti is thereby transformed from a voice crying in the wilderness with his one "libretto" into a real *libraio* (bookseller). Finally, he adds a novel and then, in 1889, as noted, a second novel.

The "second edition" of the *Manuale*, published in 1886, is titled *Secondo libro del manuale per imparare la lingua inglese senza maestro, contenente storiette amene ed il segretario spedito di Augusto Bassetti* (Second volume of the instruction book for learning English without a teacher, including pleasant short stories and a guide to letter writing by Augusto Bassetti). Bassetti calls the instructions of the *Secondo libro* "osservazioni sulla pronuncia ed uso di questo libro" (observations on pronunciation and the use of this book). No longer a mere "libretto," it is a distinctly different book, a more advanced one, with a few short and easy stories followed by model letters. His instructions or "observations" are as follows:

> La pronunzia sotto le parole inglesi si deve leggere come se fosse in Italiano.... Le pagine bianche debbono servire per note ed esercizii: scritti sempre colla mattita; perchè così si possono corregere, alterare o togliere del tutto, e preservare il foglio netto da cancellature. Queste pagine sono più utile di quello che si crede, per tutti.... (Bassetti 1886a, 1)
>
> (The pronunciation under the English words ought to be read as if they were Italian.... The blank pages ought to serve for notes and exercises; write always with a pencil; so that you can correct, alter or remove everything; keep the page clean and clear of strikeouts. These pages are more useful than you might think, for everyone....)

There follow two stories, *Il re e il contadino* and *Il lupo e la volpe*, each about four pages long, and every line appears in Italian, English as it is written, and the English pronunciation guide, with ample space between each set of three lines, resulting in very little text on each page, and the stories—already pared-down versions of Aesop's fables—are even more simplified.

The book's second part, *il segretario spedito*, offers about twenty "model" letters, on each of the last twenty pages of this thirty-four-page book. "Segretari" had a long history in Italy and were published on their own in addition to becoming a staple of each of the U.S.-issued Italian grammars (Trasciati 2009).

LIBRO TERZO

Bassetti (1886b) also published his dictionary, a slim work containing perhaps 20 percent of the words found in contemporary dictionaries; it is more like a slightly larger pocket dictionary for the business tourist to use. The translations are simple bordering on simplistic: All or nearly all are one-word translations, and few words are given the multiple translations that so many words in any language possess. The preface to the "libro terzo," which is his *Nuovo dizionario italiano ed inglese*, includes Bassetti's claim to having created an entirely "new" kind of dictionary:

> I dizionari al giorno d'oggi sono tanti che sembrerebbe cosa la più facile al mondo, di farne uno nuovo, copiando dagli altri.
> Per fare un dizionario inutile questo sarebbe il caso; ma per farne uno utile, e da servir meglio degli altri, la cosa è differente! – Senza perder tempo in chiacchiere inutili, diremo solo che questo piccolo dizionario è stato compilato in un modo tutto nuovo, o perfettamente adatto, per aiutare gli italiani in America, ad imparare la lingu del loro paese adottivo.
> Altri simili dizionari, sebben buoni e più copiosi, hanno la pronunzia segnata a numeri, che a gente di poca istruzione sono misteri incomprensibili. Di più; trovata che si è la parola italiana ed il corrispondente in inglese come si scrive; bisogna cercar la pronunzia nella parte inglese del dizionario, e colà oltre di essere numerata, spesso si trova anche dimezzata – altro mistero per le persone semplici — In questo dizionarietto al contrario si trova la pronunzia tutta in disteso, all'italiana, come volgarmente si dice; – immediatamente sotto la parola inglese – cosa del tutto nuova.
> Ci fermiano qui! – Lodar le cose proprie è un debole di natura. Epperciò lasciamo la cosa intieramente al giudizio del pubblico! (Bassetti 1886b, 3)

(Dictionaries nowadays are so many that it would seem to be the easiest thing in the world to make a new one of them, copying from the others. To make an unhelpful [useless] one, that would be the case. But to make a useful one of them, and to better serve others, is a different matter! Without losing time in chattering uselessly, we'll say only that this little dictionary has been compiled in an entirely new way, or perfectly adapted to help Italians in America learn the language of their adopted country. Other similar dictionaries, even if good and more copious, have pronunciation signed in numbers, that for people of little [prior] school instruction are incomprehensible mysteries. What's more, having found how the Italian word and its corresponding English word are written, you have to look for the pronunciation in the English part of the dictionary; and there, beyond being numbered, often is found cut in half—another mystery for simple people; in this little dictionary, on the other hand, the pronunciation is to be found all laid out, in the Italian manner, as commonly spoken—immediately under the English word—rather a new thing. Let's stop here! To praise one's own things is a natural weakness. So let's leave the thing entirely to the judgment of the public.)

As we will see, this boast is repeated in Bassetti's first novel (1887), *Amor focoso*, discussed below. There Bassetti as narrator answers the question of whether his own dictionary contains enough words:

> Il Calabrese capì dal nome che voleva dire il Cuculo, e chiamò all'autore se anche quel nome si trovava nel suo Dizionario! Avutane risposta affermativa disse:
> —Dunque c'è tutto là dentro!
> —C'è tutto quello che fa bisogno per gli emigranti italiani in America. Non una parola di più, nè di meno—rispose l'autore! (Bassetti 1887, 35)

> (The Calabrese understood from the name ["cuckoo"] that he meant the "Cuculo," and he asked the author whether that name was found in his Dictionary!
> He responded affirmatively, saying:
> —So, that's all there inside [the dictionary]!
> —It's all that is needed for immigrant Italians in America. Not a word more nor a word less—answers the author!)

First Novel (1887)

Bassetti's first novel, self-published, in which he advertises his own dictionary, is titled *Romanzotto Storico Contemporaneo intitolato Amor Focoso, Ossia Avventure di un Ex-Brigante Calabrese in America* (Historical Contemporary Novellette entitled Fiery Love, or the Adventures of an Ax-Bandit Calabrese in America).[13] It helps us understand why Bassetti's deceptively basic approach to learning English was maybe just what the doctor—or at least the gatekeepers to entry to American life—had ordered. The novel embodies these two principles: that this is how to learn English so as to enable you to "make your bread and your fortune" in America, while at the same time improving your Italian (though no reason is given as to why improving one's Italian while trying to learn English is desirable).

Bassetti wrote of *Amor Focoso* in early, pre-publication advertising that it was a "History of a bandit leader" (*Il Progresso Italo-Americano* 1886, 4). It could be labeled a didactic novel, but it is mostly a fantastic tale full of improbable events. The best student of early Italian American writing in Italian, the late Francesco Durante, characterized the author of *Amor Focoso*, based on his initial review of the novel, as "something mysterious … the book seems like the work of a crazy person" (Durante 2018). That description seems apt, as the book features characters whose existence at first appears designed mostly to spur book sales. But upon further examination, the novel is much more significant. In fact, *Amor Focoso* is a parable of the mechanism by which gaining access to the English language and its culture gives one entrée to life in the United States and, ironically, the fact that it accomplishes this also for the children of immigrants by giving them access back to the Italian language (and thus culture) of their ancestors.

The novel's hero is an unnamed Calabrian, a former bandit who emigrates to the United States, deciding to turn over a new leaf and leave behind the world of brigandage. He dreams just after disembarking in New York City that he can be a success by finding a good wife, raising strong children, and supporting them all. He finds the good wife, an Irish American woman, within days, and twelve years on, he is selling fruit on the street to support a growing family, including four strong sons.

In the story's narrative the former bandit has just been persuaded to buy Bassetti's dictionary. It is interesting to note how several matters that were either explicitly stated in the ads for the grammars and especially the dictionary (for instance, how the dictionary could be used, that it followed two earlier works using "the same method already published before," and the way Bassetti organized it, with Italian phrases, equivalent English phrases, and phonetic English pronunciation) are reflected in the "romanzetto storico contemporaneo" that *Amor focoso* claims to be:

> Lo stesso giorno che si mise in vendita il nuovo Dizionario italiano ed inglese, colla pronunzia segnata chiara ed in pieno, all'*italiana*, sotto ogni parola, pubblicato per uso speciale degli italiani in America di AUGUSTO BASSETTI:—un ragazzo di parenti italiani, ma nato in New York, che era andato attorno a vendere questo, cogli altri due libri sullo stesso metodo gia prima pubblicati;— verso la sera, avendoli venduti, tutti meno un dizionario;— passando vicino ad un banchino di frutta, si mise a dire al venditore, gridando come quando da piccolino vendeva giornali per la strada:
>
> —Ecco un libro che t'insegna in un momento, tutte le parole inglesi che tu non sai ancora!—Settantacinque soldi!—Vattene, vattene, disse il venditore, non mi seccare; son dodici anni che io son in America, e so l'inglese tutto quanto!—V'ingannate, disse il ragazzo,—secondo le istruzioni che aveva ricevuto dall'autore;—Non sapete ancor tutto!—Ecco, come si dice in inglese, il pipistrello, la lodola, l'usignuolo? —Vattene, non vendo uccelli io; vendo frutta, disse il Calabrese: — poichè tale era il venditore.— Bene, soggiunse il ragazzo; come si chiama la melagrana, la nespola, l'uva spina? — Non ho mai venduto di queste frutta, rispose il Calabrese, raddolcito e pensieroso!— Se non si dovessero sapere che le parole delle cose che si vendono, disse il ragazzo, come si potrebbe parlar di amore, di politica, ed altre cose del mondo? — Hai ragione, hai ragione, mio buon ragazzotto, disse il Calabrese:—comprerò quel

libro; ma bisogna che tu m'insegni come si fa a trovare le parole che uno vuole. (Bassetti 1887, 9-10)

(The same day that the new Italian English dictionary is put on sale, with the pronunciation clear and fully laid out in Italian under each word, published for the especial use of Italians in America by AUGUSTO BASSETTI, a boy from an Italian family but born in New York, who had gone around selling this dictionary, along with the two other books on the same method already published before, toward evening, having sold all the books save one dictionary, passing near a fruit stand, he began to tell the seller, calling out like he used to when at a young age he sold newspapers on the street, "Here's a book that teaches you in a moment all the English words that you don't yet know! Seventy-five *soldi*! "Get lost, get lost," said the vendor, "don't annoy me; it's twelve years I am in America, and I know as much English as I need to know!"

"You deceive yourself," said the boy, according to the instructions that he had received from the author. "You do not yet know all the words! Look, how it's said in English, il *pipistrello* [bat], the *lodola* [skylark], the *usignuolo* [nightingale]? "Get lost, I don't sell birds, me; I sell fruit," said the Calabrese, since that's who it was. "Well, added the boy," what do you call in English the *melangrana* [pomegranate], the *nespola* [medlar], the *spina uva* [gooseberry]? "I've never sold these fruits," responded the Calabrese, softening and getting thoughtful! "Even if you didn't have to know the words of things that are sold," said the boy, "how could you speak of love, of politics and of other things of the world?" "You're right, you're right, my good little boy," said the Calabrese. "I will buy this book, but I need you to teach me how it's done, to find words that one wishes to know.")

The boy proceeds to teach the Calabrese how to look up a word — if one is searching for *usignolo*, for example, they begin by finding "U" and then find the column for *USI* and proceed down the page with a finger until the word is found. "Usignolo — You see how I do it—Here it is." After this lesson, the Calabrese speaks, praising the Bassetti method over those of the dictionaries and grammars one could buy in Italy, the books that were Bassetti's competition:

> Bravo, bravo; esclamò il Calabrese; ora capisco, perchè quando leggeva un libro inglese che mi fecero comprare a Napoli prima di partire, e che lo pagai cinque lire, nessuno mi capiva! —Appunto, disse il ragazzo; quel libro là v'insegnava l'inglese come si scrive, ma non ti diceva come si deve pronunziare.—Eccoti settantacinque soldi: disse il Calabrese; e prendi frutta dal mio banco quanta ne vuoi; tu mi hai fatto bene il Maestro! —Ci sono due altri libri di questo metodo, soggiunse il ragazzo; oggi; li ho venduti tutti; ma domani ne avrò degli altri. — Portameli qui; domani; disse il Calabrese: io, stasera mostrerò questo libro qui, alla mia moglie, che s'intende bene dei libri inglesi; e vedrò quel che mi dice!—Come può la vostra moglie, aver imparato l'inglese meglio di voi? domandò il ragazzo.—Ma lei non è italiana, rispose il Calabrese; io l'ho sposata in New York tre giorni dopo il mio arrivo. Ora abbiamo quattro bei figliuolini; e forse questi libri possono anche servire a far loro imparare bene l'italiano; che nessuno ce lo mostra quì in America; ed io non voglio che i miei figli non sappiano la lingua del bel paese dove è nato e cresciuto il loro padre. (Bassetti 1887, 10–11)

> ("Bravo, bravo, now I understand why when you read an English grammar book that they made me buy in Naples before leaving, and I paid 5 lire for it, no one could understand me!" "Exactly," says the boy, "that book will teach you English as it is written but not as it's pronounced." Here you go, here's your 75 soldi," says the Calabrese. "And take as much fruit from my stand as you like, you have made me the teacher!" There are two other books of this method," added the boy, "today I sold them all; but tomorrow I will have some more of them." Bring me them here tomorrow," said the Calabrese. "I will this evening show this book to my wife, who understands well English-language books, and I will see what she has to say to me! *and perhaps these books can also*

serve to make my four sons learn Italian well; that's something that no one has shown them here in America and I don't want my sons not to know the language of the beautiful village where their father was born and raised." [Emphasis added.])

He is happy to have a book with which in a moment he can find English words that he previously had not known and that includes pronunciation that empowers him to read by himself, without the help of anyone. Note how Bassetti also fuels consumer fears of scarcity, of missing out if people don't buy his books now—the boy has sold out his stock of the grammars for the day. Most of all, the Calabrian feels confident now that he can communicate orally with others, a feeling the imported Italian grammars evidently did not allow him ("now I understand why when you read an English grammar book that they made me buy in Naples before leaving . . . no one could understand me!") (Bassetti 1887, 10).

The Calabrese teaches himself some words in English that are not exactly casual English: "My dear, my dear, how do you do this evening?" The hero's wife is so "surprised and pleased" when her heretofore non-English-speaking husband of twelve years speaks English; she asks to be shown the grammar book:

> La moglie in estasi per la sorpresa ed il piacere, si fece mostrare quel libro che aveva comprato; e da donna istruita come era vide subito che era un dizionario, grandemente utile per gli italiani, per lo più poco istruiti, per imparare da loro stessi le parole inglesi come si scrivono, e come si devono pronunziare, e chiamò al marito chi ne era l'autore.—Non lo so—disse il Calabrese — ma credo che sia un mio paesano.—E vi sono italiani in New York che sappiano scrivere libri, come questo?—chiamò la moglie. (Bassetti 1887, 12)

> (The wife, in ecstasy for the surprise and the pleasure, makes him show her the book that he had bought; and the woman, cultured as she was, sees suddenly that it was a dictionary, greatly

useful for Italians, for the least schooled, to learn the English words by themselves as they are written, and as they ought to be pronounced, and asked her husband who was its author: "I don't know," responds the Calabrese, "but I believe it is one of my countrymen." "And there are Italians in New York who know how to write books like this?" exclaimed his wife.)

His wife looks at the book that has given her husband his newfound articulation and wonders, "Are there Italians in New York who know how to write books like this one?" (12). "I think so," says the Calabrian, "Italians are hardly all so ignorant as am I and all those whom you knew at the Five Points." She replies:

> Hai ragione! ... —Dopo che sposai te, non vidi mai altri italiani, che quelli che hanno dimorato intorno a noi. Onesti, buoni sì; ma semplice e poco istruiti. Ma durante i primi anni dopo che arrivai in America, ne ho veduti degli altri tutto differenti. (Bassetti 1887, 12)

> (You're right ... after I married you, I never saw other Italians other than those who lived around us. Honest, good, yes; but simple and little schooled. But during the first years after I arrived in America, I saw some others of them completely different.)

She looks at the name of the author and is amazed, saying, "This is one of the Italians I first knew in New York when I was fourteen years old, that is, two years after I had arrived, impoverished, from Ireland." As a young servant girl in the house of wealthy New Yorkers, she met Bassetti, who was giving language lessons to an aspiring opera singer.[14] The young lady of the house was studying music hoping to become the prima donna in New York, so "she was taking [in addition to music lessons] lessons in Italian language from another Italian," a friend of the music teacher. Because the boy who sold Bassetti's dictionary gets copies of them from the author to sell, the boy knows how to find him, and so

Bassetti himself appears in the following chapter of the book, somewhat improbably coming the very next night to the house.

The author speaks in Italian to the eldest of the Calabrese's sons, eleven years old, asking him if and where he went to school. Our hero's son understands everything Bassetti says "but responds promptly in English perfectly correct in grammar and in pronunciation. ...[T]he Calabrian for his part immediately responds, in pretend severity":

> —Il Signore ti parla in Italiano, e tu gli rispondi in inglese! Ti farò io studiare la lingua del tuo *papá,* e ti farò io stesso il maestro. Copierai ogni giorno una pagina dell'italiano, che c'è in quei due libretti scritti da questo signore e lo studierai a memoria. Dell'inglese e della pronunzia che c'è sotto tu non ne hai bisogno; ma fan per me, che non so ancora bene l'inglese. Quando tu avrai copiato e studiato a memoria l'italiano che c'è in que due libretti, tu saprai parlare e scrivere l'italiano tanto bene quanto l'inglese. Perchè tu sai già molto dell'italiano, ma non lo sai bene, e resti impicciato a parlarlo! (Bassetti 1887, 16)

> (The gentleman [i.e., Bassetti] speaks to you in Italian, and you respond to him in English! I will make you study the language of your *papa,* and I will make you yourself be the teacher. Copy, every day, a page of Italian that is in these two little books, written by this man, and you will commit it to memory. You needn't write the English and the pronunciation that is under [each Italian sentence] for yourself; but do it for me who does not know English very well yet. When you will have copied and committed to memory what is in these two little books, you will know how to speak and write Italian as well as you do English. Because you already know much Italian, but you don't know it well, you remain hampered in speaking it.)

What preceded this discussion of the impact of Bassetti's books was the revelation by the Calabrese's wife of her bitterly hard life in Ireland and as a servant girl before her marriage. What follows it is an extended tale about the Calabrese as a bandit and how his life of adventure ended. With Bassetti's dictionary in hand, our hero is miraculously enabled to speak in English to his wife so that she understands him, apparently for the first time in twelve years. The nameless ex-bandit tells this story to those assembled in his house. We are given to understand that the couple's love and their marriage are deepened and enriched by his ability to speak English.

Bassetti is assuring the reader that those who gain access to language because of his books will have an almost incalculable gain for their efforts; this applies both to the poor Italian immigrant who has thought for twelve years he could get away without learning English and to his Irish wife, whose husband's first English words produce a tremendous outpouring of her own history.

What is clearly one of Bassetti's major selling points for his grammars and dictionary is proposed in his first novel: that access to language—both one's own language and that of their adopted country—enables one to open up the past as never before. Husband and wife declare that they never heard these stories of each other's past lives. Access to language equals access to the past as well as the practical benefits of an improved work life—the Calabrian can now sell less-common fruits like the pomegranate and the gooseberry, and he also has the ability to learn the language he can use for love and politics, as the persuasive boy salesman explains to him.

Nor do the benefits of such access accrue only to the married couple: their sons, steeped in English, but with only a hearing (not speaking or writing) knowledge of Italian, will now get to know Italian far better if they follow Bassetti's instructions and copy his sentences in longhand on the blank pages that his grammars so conveniently provide.

Finally, implicitly if not explicitly, access to language makes possible not only access to one's history but also a release from the burdens of the past. There is no obvious connection between the Calabrian's utterance, "My dear—how do you do this evening?" and his telling the story of his bandit life. Yet the first thing leads to the next. Access to language provides perspective about life; we cannot know why this former bandit decides to lead a quiet life selling fruit after such an exciting early career until we hear how his bandit's existence began to lose its glow when the political climate in Calabria changed as the Risorgimento took hold. Similarly, there's nothing in our hero's awkward English sentence that should obviously lead to the wife telling the story of her life in Ireland and as a poor servant girl in New York City. The coincidence is brought to light, rather, by her husband's recently acquired facility with his adopted language.

CONCLUSION

Bassetti's new works did not dominate the market for long. He is listed as a bookseller in the *Guida italiana e calendario universale del Progresso Italo-Americano* (*Guida italiana* 1893), with a P.O. box in place of an address (indeed, in the 1890 New York Police Census, he is no longer among those living at 20 Vandam Street in Manhattan); and the *Catalogo generale della biblioteca gratuita* (General catalog of the free library) (*Catalogo* 1896) reveals no trace of his grammars or dictionary (or novels), though it does show the grammar of one of his successors, Francesco Frugone, the *Nuovo libro per imparare l'Inglese*; but the listings are mostly made up of some old standard imports, like the Ollendorff *Gramatica Inglese*.

It is also clear from advertisements that Bassetti's new kind of grammar and dictionary did not totally supplant the more traditional ones: Even after nearly five years of his seemingly productive advertisements for his own works, the same imported grammars and bilingual dictionaries for Italian speakers wanting to learn English were still being advertised. Indeed, perhaps to draw readers' attention as was not previously necessary, such works have their own sections in an ad in *L'Eco d'Italia* on April 6, 1889, a day when Bassetti's ad does not appear. And as if to suggest that by the middle of 1890 Bassetti had learned that if you can't beat 'em, join 'em, his own ad announced, in addition to his two grammars, the dictionary and his two novels, the availability of

James J. Periconi

"*[a]nche gran varietà di libri Italiani — Catalogo Gratis,*" (also a great variety of Italian books — free catalog).

Much work needs to be done to further analyze the evidence from advertisements and otherwise of both imported and U.S.-produced grammars and dictionaries and their social impetus and impact. So, too, more bibliographical analysis of these works is necessary. But it is clear that Bassetti's grammars, dictionary, and novels, though they seemed to be at their height for only five years, provide new insights into how Italians learned Italian to connect to their country of origin while learning English to connect to their adopted country. Bassetti's work spawned imitators in the half-dozen or so such grammars and dictionaries that appeared over the next couple of decades, all works that enabled Italian immigrants to create their own culture as they learned both English and Italian.

NOTES

[1] Paolo Bossange of 49 Walker Street in New York City was selling them by April 19, 1862.

[2] Though *L'Eco* commenced publication in 1850, microfilm copies of it at the New York Public Library (NYPL) begin at 1862 and contain only seven years of issues of *L'Eco* before 1876. Note that as early as the 1820s in New York City, an Italian émigré (and former librettist for Mozart) named Lorenzo da Ponte had imported Italian books, but the bookstore established by him and his brother did not survive the 1830s. And here I must thank the NYPL for its generous appointment of me as a Wertheim Research Scholar from September 1, 2018, through the present, because it gave me the space, time, and privileges of perusing its extraordinary collection of U.S. Italian newspapers and books in a private reading room and without restriction.

[3] This essay is offered in loving homage to my two best teachers about Italian American literature and history in all their manifestations: first, Robert Viscusi, my earliest and, until his death on January 19, 2020, still the best teacher; and, second, the late Francesco Durante, whose recent and premature death (August 3, 2019, at age sixty-six) leaves me more personally bereft than I can say, as well as being a very great blow for Italian American studies. Even while the Italian American Writers Association (IAWA), which Bob co-founded, rightly promoted new Italian American writing, Bob also doggedly reminded us about Italian language's beginnings that we must study our Italian-language history if we are to adequately understand how Italian American literature defined and shaped the culture of Italian Americans and Americans generally. That work with Bob led to my meeting and developing a deep friendship with Francesco, starting with the latter's gracious permission for me to mine his spectacular draft bibliography in

1999 to include many of his bibliographic entries of U.S. Italian-language imprints he would first publish in 2001, the year after publication of the IAWA *Bibliography of the Italian American Book* (Gardaphé and Periconi 2000). If there is anything useful in what I have to say here, it is due to the tutelage of Bob and Francesco.

4 Readers may know of other attempts to address this and other questions raised here, but I have found none. Neither Bassetti himself nor any of his works referenced in this essay are to be found in either the text or bibliography of the "bible" of early Italian American literature in Italian, namely, Durante (2005).

5 *L'Eco d'Italia*, August 30, 1876 (J. P. Roberts's *Dizionario*), was the first I found, to which was added on September 16 of that year John Millhouse's *Nuovo dizionario italiano ed inglese*. I found neither these nor any other such dictionary in any advertisement with lists of books available for sale before this time, between 1862 and 1876, even when the printed list in newspaper ads approached 200 works.

6 Thanks to Stefano Morello, Assistant Director for Digital Projects (American Social History Project, CUNY) for finding this biographical information.

7 This correspondence between Bassetti and the opera singer can be found in the Archivio di Stato di Siena (busta 106), as referenced at the SIUSA (*Sistema Informativo Unificato per le Soprointendenze Archivistiche*); https://siusa.archivi.beniculturali.it/cgibin/pagina.pl?TipoPag=comparc&Chiave=325194&RicProgetto =personalita (accessed December 2019). Thanks to Professor Sergio Luzzatto, University of Connecticut, for finding this. Piccolomini's U.S. tour is recounted in Richard Grant White's *Opera in New York* (1882, 203). Thanks to fellow Grolier Club member Mark Tomasko for finding this.

8 See *New York Sun* for these quotations; see, also, *New York Herald* and *New-York Daily Tribune*. All three of these reviews of the opera and Bassetti's lecture are presented at some length in https://www.musicingotham.org/event/98681 (accessed December 2019).

9 See Adam Smith (1813) for an explanation of how modern capitalism reflected such behavior. The availability of Italian books in New York before that primarily at the offices of the newspapers (*Il Progresso* and *L'Eco d'Italia*) represented an older way of selling that would soon be completely displaced by Italian books being hawked on the streets and sold by outdoor vendors. See also Periconi (2018).

10 See Peter Martin (2019), for a discussion of why Webster and others felt in the 1820s America that Americans needed to have their own home-grown dictionary to replace later editions of Samuel Johnson's, *A Dictionary of the English Language* (1755).

11 For the gradual rise in literacy in Southern Italy in this era, see Carlo M. Cipolla (1969).

12 At first Bassetti's ads appear in the both rival newspapers. By September 1, 1885, the book becomes available for purchase at the offices of *Il Progresso* itself, at 2-4 Centre Street, Figure 2. Naturally, this outlet does not appear in ads in the *L'Eco*.

13 This first novel of Bassetti's (1887) is a work purporting to be one of a series or library of books titled "Romanzo Storico Contemporaneo," similar to the series titles that Italian publishers who exported books to the United States conventionally used, such as the "Biblioteca Amena" of Treves or the "Biblioteca Romantica

Illustrata" of Sonzogno. Bassetti's two novels were reprinted in 2018 by Facsimile Publisher in Delhi, India, www.facsimilepublisher.com (Gyan Books).

[14] Though this seems to come out of left field, in fact it does not, given Bassetti's background, discussed in the biographical section.

WORKS CITED

Bassetti, Augusto. 1885. *Manuale per imparare gli elementi e la retta pronunzia della lingua inglese senza maestro per uso principalmente degli emigranti italiani, di Augusto Bassetti*. New York: n.p.; tipi di H.W. Ormsby, National Union Catalogue Pre-1956 Imprints, Vol. 38, 480, item 0175426.

Bassetti, Augusto. 1886a. *Secondo libro del manuale per imperare la lingua inglese senza maestro, contenente storiette amene ed il segretario spedito di Augusto Bassetti*. New York: n.p. Hathi Trust. http://hdl.handle.net/2027/uiuc.6772818 (accessed October 30, 2019).

Bassetti, Augusto. 1886b. *Nuovo dizionario Italiano ed inglese, colla pronuzia segnata chiara ed in pieno, con ortografia italiana sotto ogni parola, per uso speciale degli italiani in America, di Augusto Bassetti*. New York: n.p. NUC Pre-1956 Imprints, Vol. 38, 480, item 0175427.

Bassetti, Augusto. 1887. *Romanzetto storico contemporaneo intitolato Amor focoso: ossia avventure di un ex-brigante Calabrese in America*. New York: n.p.; tipi di J.H. Carbone & Company, Reprint 2018. Facsimile Publisher/Gyan Books, Delhi, India. NUC Pre-1956 Imprints, Vol. 38, 480, item 0175428.

Bassetti, Augusto. 1889. *Il mago delle Alpi: ossia l'anello incantato*. New York: n.p. Reprint 2018. Facsimile Publisher, Delhi, India. Library of Congress control number 16014220.

Cipolla, Carlo M. 1969. *Literacy and Development in the West*. Baltimore: Johns Hopkins University Press, 19, 94–97, 127.

Durante, Francesco. 2005. *Italoamericana: Storia e letteratura degli italiani negli Stati Uniti d'America*. Milan: Arnoldo Mondadori. In English as *Italoamericana: The Literature of the Great Migration, 1880-1943*. Robert Viscusi, Anthony Julian Tamburri, James J. Periconi. New York: Fordham University Press, 2014.

Durante, Francesco. 2018. Letter to the author, October 30.

Gardaphé, Fred, and James J. Periconi. 2000. *The Italian American Writers Association (IAWA) Bibliography of the Italian American Book*. New

York: Shea and Haarman Publishing and the Italian American Writers Association.

Guida italiana e calendario universale del Progresso Italo-American per gli Stati Uniti, il Canada, il Mexico, etc. [sic] *Dono ai suoi abbonati per l'anno 1893*. 1893. New York: Tipografia del Progresso Italo-Americano, HathiTrust Digital Library. https://babel.hathitrust.org/cgi/pt?id=mdp.39015027783607&view=1up&seq=5 (accessed December 15, 2019).

Il Progresso Italo-Americano. 1886. February 20, 4.

L'Eco d'Italia. 1885. December 22, 4.

Martin, Peter. 2019. *The Dictionary Wars*. Princeton, NJ: Princeton University Press.

Millhouse, John. 1853. *Nuovo dizionario inglese-italiano e italiano-inglese con la pronuncia segnata a norma della grammatica analitica*. Milan: F. Bracciforti.

New York Sun. 1867. "Amusements: Interesting Concerts," April 8, 4.

Periconi, James J. 2018. "Italian American Book Publishing and Bookselling." In *The Routledge History of Italian Americans*, edited by William J. Connell and Stanislao G. Pugliese. New York and London: Routledge.

Roberts, J. P. 1867. *Dizionario italiano-inglese e inglese–italiano ad uso di ambedue le nazioni*. Florence: G. Barbera Ed.

Smith, Adam. 1813. *The Theory of Moral Sentiments*. Edinburgh: J. Hay.

Trasciati, Mary Ann. 2009. "Letter Writing in an Italian Immigrant Community: A Transatlantic Tradition." *Rhetoric Society Quarterly* 39.1(January): 73–94.

Viscusi, Robert. 2006. *Buried Caesars and other Secrets of Italian American Writing*. Albany: State University of New York Press, 19.

White, Richard Grant. 1882. *Opera in New York*. New York: The Century Company.

The Life and Poetry of Simplicio Righi

Francesco Durante

> *Editors' Note:* The late Francesco Durante, an enthusiastic contributor to this volume, submitted this essay to the editors shortly before his death on August 3, 2019, a circumstance that necessitated our preparation of it for publication without the benefit of his partnership in the editing process.

Simplicio Righi—or "Rosina Vieni," as he used to sign some poems published in *Il Proletario*, the official paper of the Italian branch of the Socialist Labor Party—is well known by Italian American literature scholars. This is almost exclusively because of his sonnet "Vennero i bricchellieri a cento a cento," which Henry Louis Mencken (1947) included in his famous book *The American Language* as an important example of the contribution of Italians to the development of a new American language independent from the original British English. "Vennero i bricchellieri" is, in a way, a masterpiece and an almost unique example of using an Italian American hybrid idiom outside of a comedic context. Nevertheless, until recently scholars have not been much interested in exploring Righi's work apart from looking for more gems like "Vennero." To my knowledge, my edited collection of Italian-immigrant writing *Italoamericana* (Durante 2014) is the only book where one can find more than one of his poems.[1]

Righi was born in Carpi (Modena province, Emilia-Romagna) on December 27, 1869. Engaged in the socialist movement, he was among the founders of the Circolo Socialista Carpigiano, which he served as secretary, and in 1895 he was elected city counselor for the Socialist Party. Along with some comrades, he was accused and tried, beginning in September 1893, for inciting class hate and disobeying the associated laws; while he was acquitted in his first trial, on the appeal he was condemned to five months' incarceration and fined 85 lire, although Carpi municipal leaders testified that the Socialist League had not been responsible for any disorder in the city (Pecoraro 1983, 26–31).

After graduating in 1897 with a medical degree from the University of Bologna with a dissertation on *La sintomatologia del neurastenico* (The neurasthenic's symptomatology), Righi emigrated to the United States in 1898, the same crucial year that food riots in Milan drove so many radicals out of Italy (many of them to the United States). We do not know if he was personally involved in the Milan protests; what seems certain is that he emigrated as a socialist, an antimonarchist, and probably as a political refugee. Shortly before leaving Italy, Righi's wife Giuseppina gave birth to their son Arrigo; the two of them would join Righi in New York City six years later in 1904, when Arrigo was seven years old. For forty-four years Righi practiced general medicine from his Manhattan office at 82 Washington Place.

As soon as Righi reached New York City, he joined the Socialist Labor Party (SLP) and quickly became a contributor to *Il Proletario*, then based in Paterson, New Jersey (later in New York City). A young journalist from the Abruzzi named Camillo Cianfarra was editor in chief of the official SLP paper in those days, and Righi became one of his most important collaborators, contributing articles as well as poetry. Righi stayed on after Cianfarra left the position and was replaced by Dino Rondani. Later, when Cianfarra returned to the editorship in July1900, after Rondani went to Italy to serve in parliament, Righi made the speech at his farewell party. As an important contributor, he endured the harsh debates with Paterson's anarchists, whose journal *L'Aurora*, directed by Giuseppe Ciancabilla, was their radical organ. A controversy arose between Cianfarra and Righi about the way *Il Proletario* was dealing with the continuous attacks coming from *L'Aurora*, especially when, during a party meeting of the Barre, Vermont, socialist granite cutters in December 1900, a policeman was shot while trying to break up a fight started by a group of anarchists. Righi was irritated because he thought Cianfarra dedicated too much space to this particular "accident." He wrote a letter to the editor saying that the paper should have more strenuously deplored "the wickedness of the murder and the duplicity of the anarchists" and ignored the insults coming from the anarchist scoundrels via their publications: Righi thought that *Il Proletario* should be entirely devoted to socialist propaganda. Cianfarra, who published the letter, replied, admitting that sometimes it was very hard not to answer Ciancabilla's accusations: "From now on," Cianfarra wrote, "I will let the anarchist ravens croak till depletion" (Righi 1901).[2]

When Cianfarra, after strong, sometimes violent, internal opposition from the social democratic wing, resigned in 1901, Righi succeeded him for a short time at the head of the paper until the new editor, Giacinto Menotti Serrati, nominated directly by the Italian Socialist Party, arrived from Italy. Righi kept the paper on the same political line as his predecessor and, among other things, was engaged in the usual dialectical skirmishes with the *stampa coloniale* (literally colonial press), i.e., the Italian American press, in particular *Il Progresso Italo-Americano*, *L'Araldo Italiano*, and the *Bollettino della Sera*, New York City dailies that were objects of ridicule because of their imperfect Italian and their often absurd political lucubrations.

As was the case for not a few Italian American radicals of that time, Righi's active political militancy came to an end with the outbreak of the World War I. His son Arrigo, having earned a degree from Columbia University, was sent to the Italian front on the Isonzo River as a lieutenant of the grenadiers, and there he was awarded a military decoration. Later, he was stationed at the Italian garrison in Fiume (Rijeka, Croatia) before Gabriele D'Annunzio and Italian army irregulars took over the city in September 1919. Doctor Righi traveled to Italy that same year and visited the region, stopping to see his son in Fiume. Once back in New York City, Righi wrote an article for Agostino De Biasi, editor of the New York City monthly *Il Carroccio*, relating his impressions of the trip. Righi said that he had spent "fifteen days of most intense joy" in Fiume, calling it "una città italianissima" (a most Italian city). He added that he recognized the need to reunite Fiume definitively with Italy, otherwise "we should remove the word *justice* from our vocabulary." He told of coming across a child desperately weeping on the doorstep of a house; he tried to console him by giving him a coin, an Austrian *corona*. The child looked at the coin but refused it because it was Croatian (*la xe croata*, in the dialect of Trieste) (Righi 1920, 475–476).

Righi was a prominent figure in the New York City's Italian immigrant community: Looking through the Italian American press, we discover he attended many meetings, dinners, and celebrations at a number of Italian organizations together with personalities like the poet Riccardo Cordiferro, the journalist Agostino De Blasi, sculptors Attilio Piccirilli and Onorio Ruotolo, and even future mayor Fiorello La Guardia. He still wrote verse, but now he was publishing his poems in a totally different variety of journals, for instance *Zarathustra*, founded in New York City by the journalist Ernesto Valentini (Cianfarra's friend who had served in the Labor Information Office for Italians in 1906), and particularly in the Italian American monthly *Il Carroccio*, a fiercely nationalist paper that later became resolutely Fascist. In 1928 the doctor returned to Italy accompanied by his wife.

Italian writer Mario Soldati in his book *Addio diletta Amelia* (1979) mentions a "Saverio Righi," but doubtless he is speaking of Simplicio. It is likely that Soldati did not know that Righi had died. Soldati's *Addio diletta Amelia* represents his return to the United States forty years after publishing his first important book, *America primo amore*, in 1935, when Soldati was considering emigrating to the United States. Initially, as we know from his manuscript notes and other archival materials, Soldati had planned to discuss Righi in *America primo amore*, but he did not. Instead, in this new book he sketches an affectionate portrait of Righi as someone who, sitting in his old-fashioned home in Greenwich Village, might not have seemed out of place in the nineteenth century: "Portly, rosy, with sparkling blue eyes, blond hair streaked with grey, a blond mustache and a constant smile that is half witty and half mocking. Usually dressed in an elegant grisaille, with a snow-white piqué waistcoat, and a watch with a gold chain" (Soldati 1979, 153). Significantly, Soldati describes him as a man who, even in the mid-1930s, when the majority of Italian Americans had become staunch Fascists, remained "un diamante dell'antifascismo" (a diamond of antifascism). Soldati added that Righi was a very pleasant conversationalist and was fond of talking U.S. politics. He spoke "with disdain" about the Irish Americans overrunning Tammany Hall[3] and also about President Herbert Hoover, and he was sure that U.S. political life was on the verge of a radical change, "as he foretold Roosevelt and the *New Deal.*" Righi exemplified a strange mix: deeply American, but also typically *emiliano*, a champion of that region, and a socialist who had stayed as faithful to his ideals as he had been in the years of Andrea Costa (1851–1910). Righi never tired of telling Soldati how advanced the United States was in any field, compared to Italy's backwardness. But his was not the ordinary Italian American point of view: "Now I know that Righi was American also because he was antifascist, because he had decided to be American in order to free himself from all that was Fascist in Italy even before the word *Fascism* existed" (Soldati 1979, 155). Soldati writes of Righi that he was a man who could be "modern" while preserving "the oldest and noblest heart of Europe" (Soldati 1979, 157).

Simplicio Righi died at age seventy-three, after a short illness, on October 16, 1943, leaving behind his wife and son. All sources say that Righi was a kind-hearted man and a very popular and generous doctor, the kind who would treat low-income workers for free (Obituary of Semplicio Righi 1943a, 1943b).

From a literary point of view, Righi's production is deeply rooted in the tradition of Italian *poesia sociale*, a genre that had flourished in the second half of the nineteenth century among the great authors of the Risorgimento, including Nobel-prize-winning poet Giosuè Carducci and the father of modern Italian verse, socialist Giovanni Pascoli, as well as their many imitators. Blending social themes with bohemian inspiration, *poesia sociale* had found in the new and subversive political movements, including the Socialist Party and the anarchists, a natural, if not exclusive, habitat. This was almost the standard poetry practiced in the Little Italies, and we can clearly see its influence on other early Italian American poets, such as Riccardo Cordiferro or other more politicized authors, like anarchists Giuseppe Ciancabilla and Umberto Postiglione as well as socialists Giusto Calvi, Giuseppe Bertelli, Giuseppina Martinuzzi, and Efrem Bartoletti. The most famous of these, Arturo Giovannitti, represents something completely different: His poems seem both "older" in the sense that they re-elaborate themes and motifs of traditional Southern Italian folk culture, and also more "modern" if we consider his love of American verse (particularly that of Walt Whitman), his religious inclinations (Giovannitti was a Protestant as well as a socialist, whereas Italian socialists were generally atheists), and his interest in the European avant-garde movements of the early twentieth century.

Over the years we can see a radical change in Righi's work: Although he never completely abandoned his early subversive muse, his poems written and published in the 1920s bear the mark of an elderly man's pessimism that is very distant from the boldness of his youthful compositions. And they reveal a resurgence of affection for his old roots, for the beauty of the simple and quiet life in the old country compared to the chaos and the noise of the big metropolis.

Righi's poetry touches on many subjects and uses a variety of tones. In general, when he writes about "serious" subjects (particularly in the *Primo Maggio* or Labor Day issues of *Il Proletario*) he signs the poems with his real name, but when he produces satirical verse he employs the pen name Rosina Vieni. In both cases, he uses regular verse, with stanzas, rhymes, and codified prosodic structures (*forme chiuse*) — mostly the *sonetto* (sonnet), the *canzone*, the ode, or, in the more light-hearted compositions, popular forms like the *stornello*. In this way, he appears to be intimately linked to the Italian tradition: His poems exhibit an excellent knowledge of the poetical tradition (and almost a veneration for Dante) and techniques, and a sophisticated richness in his use of rhetorical elements, such as metaphors, synesthesia, enjambements, and elaborate and often unusual lexical choices.

Simplicio Righi, "Maggio sobillatore"
(*Il Proletario*, Paterson, 1 maggio 1899)

  Redimito di fronde e di verzura,
ne l'amplesso del sole,
ecco ritorna, de la dea natura
Maggio, superba prole.

  Ecco: sui campi gli occhi sitibondi
Figge il lavoratore,
e nella calda fantasia giocondi
pampini e tutta in fiore

  vede la terra. E pensa: - Eccolo il sangue
mio che laggiù scintilla,
ecco il sudor del misero che langue
in perle auree sfavilla!

  Dai solchi arati sorgerete, opime
messi di fulve spiche,
e voi, sudati grappoli, o sublime
fior de le mie fatiche;

  e narrerete agli uomini: ogni zolla
dove un fil d'erba è nato,
ogni stelo che spunta, ogni corolla
di giardino o di prato,

  cela la punta di una spina, asconde
di tormenti una storia...
Brindate, o sommi, a l'armonie gioconde
del mondo e della gloria!

  Ma tu vieni, bel maggio. Oh, almen la spene
reca al lavoratore,
e nerbo audace a scuoter le catene,
Maggio sobillatore!

New York, 26 aprile

("Instigator May"
Crowned with fronds and green leaves
in the embrace of the sun
here May returns,
the superb offspring of Mother Nature.

Look: the worker turns his thirsty eyes on the fields
and in the warm carefree reverie
vine leafs, and everything blossoming

he sees the earth. And he thinks: - There my blood
down there is glittering
there's the sweat of the wretched who fades away
shining like golden pearls!

From the ploughed furrows you will rise, plentiful
harvests of blond spikes
and you, sweaty bunches, oh sublime
flower of my labors;

and you will tell the men: every clump
where a blade of grass is born
every stem, every corolla
of garden or meadow,

conceals the tip of a thorn, hides
a story of agony ...
Make a toast, great ones, to the happy harmonies
of the world and of glory!

But come you, fair May. Oh, a hope at least
bring to the worker
and a bold audacity to cast off chains,
May, the instigator!)

Rosina Vieni, "Transvaaleide"
(*Il Proletario*, New York, 25 novembre 1899)

Quando recò il telegrafo
la notizia feral della rovina,[4]
scoppiò in dirotto pianto la regina…
E ben donde n'avea d'essere afflitta!
La regina Vittoria tramutavasi
in regina sconfitta.

("Transvaaleide"
When the telegraph brought
the gloomy news of the failure,
the queen started crying her heart out…
Sure she had a good reason for that!
Queen Victoria was turning
into a defeated queen.)

Rosina Vieni, "Inno dei banchieri"
(*Il Proletario*, New York, 2 dicembre 1899)

 Su, banchieri coloniali,
su, scappiamo in fitta schiera;
questa è l'unica maniera
di goderci l'avvenir.
 Colle pene e coll'insulto
di finirla è giunta l'ora;
vada il mondo alla malora
niun di voi vuol più soffrir.
Al riscatto del lavoro
  qualcun altro penserà;
  noi vivremo col lavoro
  dei cafoni al Canadà.

 La risaia e la miniera
fiacchi gli altri ad ogni stento
come bruti d'un armento

vadan gli altri a lavorar.
  Il cafone a cui rubammo
tante volte sopra l'aggio,
se ci vuol pagare il viaggio
siam dei ciuchi a non andar.
Al riscatto del lavoro *ecc*.

  L'adorato capitale
lo teniam nella bisaccia;
abbiam fatto buona caccia
stando in mezzo agl'italian;
  lo strumento del lavoro
nelle mani dei cafoni,
fece si che i *taccoloni*
ora stanno in nostra man.
Al riscatto del lavoro *ecc*.

  Se divisi siam canaglia;
lo siamo pur se siamo uniti;
siam gli eroi dei cinque diti,
unghie lunghe e pelo in cuor.
  E con quel che non è nostro
noi disfar, rifar possiamo,
la consegna sia: - Partiamo,
che ci attende già il vapor.
Al riscatto del lavoro *ecc*.

  Benedetto chi gavazza
nell'ebbrezza e nei festini,
specialmente coi quattrini
che il cafon depositò;
  benedetto chi sghignazza
sullo scempio dei fratelli,
che si strappano i capelli
pel danaro che sfumò.
Al riscatto del lavoro *ecc*.

I confini scellerati
noi dobbiamo ringraziare;
oltre i monti ed oltre il mare
ci si sta più ben che qui;
  verso libere contrade
ci conduca omai la sorte;
portiam via la cassaforte,
forza, amici, è giunto il dì
Al riscatto del lavoro *ecc.*

  O sorelle di fatica,
o consorti negl'inganni,
care banche, che agli affanni
ci strappaste, ed al soffrir,
  ai ribaldi socialisti
che ci copron di libelli,
deh, tenete gli sportelli
sempre chiusi in avvenir!
Al riscatto del lavoro *ecc.*

  Se uguaglianza non è frode,
fratellanza un'ironia,
se scappar non è follia
per amor di libertà;
  ci sentiam tutti fratelli
se ci son carabinieri;
per gl'italici banchieri
il fuggir non è vilta
Al riscatto del lavoro
  qualcun altro penserà;
  noi vivremo col lavoro
  dei cafoni al Canadà.[5]

("Anthem of the Bankers"

  Go on, colonial bankers,
Go on; let's flee in great numbers;

this is the only way
to enjoy our future.
  It's time to get rid
of punishments and insults;
damn the world,
none of you wants to suffer anymore.

  Someone else
  will think about the liberation of labor;
  we will live with the work
  of poor peasants in Canada.

  The rice paddy and the mine
the others worn down by every effort,
like a herd of beasts,
let them go to work.
  The peasant whom we robbed
of the fee so often,
if he wants to pay our trip
we'd be idiots not to go.
Someone else will think about *etc.*

  To the beloved capital
we carry it in the rucksack;
we had a good hunt
among our fellow Italians;
  the tool of work
in the hands of the peasants
made sure the wedges
are in our hands.
Someone else will think about *etc.*

  If divided, we are scoundrels;
just as we are when we are united;
we are the heroes of five fingers,
long nails and hairy hearts.
  With that which is not ours

we can undo, redo,
no matter what the task: - Let's go,
the steamboat is waiting.
Someone else will think about *etc.*

  Blessed the one who frolics
in drunkenness and at parties,
and especially with the money
that the peasants consigned;
  blessed the one who sneers
over the slaughter of brothers
who are tearing out their hair
for the money they've wasted.
  Someone else will think about *etc.*

  We should thank
heinous confinements;
beyond the mountains and the sea
one is much better off than here;
destiny is leading us
toward free areas now;
we carry along the strongbox,
Let's go, friends, the day has come.
Someone else will think about *etc.*

  Oh sisters of exertion,
oh partners in deceits,
dear banks, that release us from
our grief and sufferings,
  to the villainous socialists
who cover us with libel,
alas, close the counters
and keep them closed in future!
Someone else will think about *etc.*

  If equality is not a fraud,
brotherhood irony,

if running away is not insanity
for the love of liberty;
  we feel we were all brothers
when the police are around;
  to the Italian bankers
escaping is not cowardice
Someone else
  will think about the liberation of labor;
we will live with the work
of poor peasants in Canada.)

Rosina Vieni, "L'amnistia a New York"
(*Il Proletario*, New York, 4 gennaio 1900)

Visto e considerato
che il furto, la rapina e il peculato
perdonati non fur con l'amnistia,
la colonia italiana
resta, né più, né meno, come pria.
Nessun se ne va via,
nessun parte per l'Italia madre;
e per quante amnistie verranno poi,
sempre intatte staran le oneste squadre
dei colonici eroi.[6]

("Amnesty in New York"

Considering
that theft, robbery, and embezzlement
were not remitted with the amnesty,
the Italian colony
stays, more or less, as it was before.
No one goes away,
no one is leaving for Mother Italy;
and for all the forthcoming amnesties
untouched will be the honest squadrons
of our colonial heroes.)

Rosina Vieni, "Stornello"
(*Il Proletario*, New York, 3 febbraio 1900)

Fior d'Amaranti:
Senza che noi andiamo in Louisiana,
C'è Collins che ci lincia tutti quanti![7]

 (Amaranth flower:
Without even going to Louisiana,
Here is Collins who lynches us all!)

Rosina Vieni, "Domani …"
(*Il Proletario*, 9 giugno 1900)

Su l'ardua vetta, affaticato e stanco
giunse il Veggente, e ne la fresca ombria
posò lo sguardo e il fianco;
e nel futuro dell'umanità,
sognando, osando, amando,
lanciò gli strali della fantasia.
E nuovi campi e novelle città
sorrisero al Profeta,
lucenti al sole della libertà.

Non più catene ai polsi ed al pensiero.
Maestra e donna ai popoli, la scienza;
unico nume, il vero,
e, duce, la coscienza.
Non più solcata dal dolor la fronte,
non più dal pianto rigata la faccia;
ma dal pian biondeggiante,
ma dal mar, ma dal monte,
ecco il lavoratore
levar solenne verso il ciel le braccia,
e gridar forte ai secoli:
- Io, io sono il signore.

Il Veggente si scosse,
e vanì il sogno de la fantasia,
il suo bel sogno d'oro.
Ma in fondo a l'orizzonte
fra l'ondeggiar de le bandiere rosse,
da mille gole lamentose uscia
la canzon dei reietti.
Uomini e donne in coro
venian cantando: - Siamo i poveretti,
siamo i tapini, noi, nati a la fame;
naufraghi dell'amor, siam maledetti,
viviam nei cenci e moriam nello strame.
Fiorite, o campi, anche per noi: crescete,
messi, figliuole delle nostre mani,
raggi del sole, tepidi, piovete,
risplendi alfine o sole del domani.

New York, 1 giugno 1900

("Tomorrow ...")

On the steep peak, tired and weary
came the Seer, and in the fresh shade
rested his gaze and his limbs;
and toward the future of humanity,
dreaming, daring, loving,
he shot the arrows of his imagination.
And new fields and new cities
smiled to the Prophet,
shining in the sun of freedom.

No more chains on wrists and on thought.
Teacher and queen to the masses, science;
a single idol, the true,
and, commander, conscience.
No more brow furrowed by pain,
no more face streaked with crying;

but from the blond plains,
but from the sea, from the mountain,
here is the worker
who lifts solemnly to the sky his arms,
and shouts out to the ages:
- I, I am the master.

The Seer shook himself,
and the dream of his imagination vanished,
his fair golden dream.
But down at the horizon
amid the flutter of the red flags,
from a thousand mournful throats issued
the outcasts' song.
Men and women in chorus
came singing: - We are the poor,
the wretched, we, born to starve;
castaways of love, we are doomed,
we live in rags and die in straw.
Bloom oh you fields for us too: grow
harvests, daughters of our hands,
rays of sunshine, you rain down warm,
shine at last oh sun of tomorrow.
New York, June 1, 1900)

Rosina Vieni, "Dopo la parata"
(*Il Proletario*, New York, 29 settembre 1900)

È finita la festa
che sovra l'altre tien la prominenza:
or staremo a veder che cosa resta
per la Beneficenza ...
Dopo tanto armeggio di colonnelli,
di marescialli e di luogotenenti,
bisognerà pensare ai poverelli
ed ai nullatenenti!

Ben venga dunque il resoconto, e i numeri
badate ben che siano sinceri:
mettete bene al posto lor le virgole,
mi raccomando i zeri.[8]

("After the Parade"

The party is over,
the most important of them all:
now we'll see what's left
for charity ...
After all this messing around of colonels,
marshals, and lieutenants,
it'll be time to think about the poor
and the destitute!
So welcome the balance sheet, and make sure
the numbers add up:
put the commas in the right place,
Pay attention to the zeros.)

Rosina Vieni, "Pantalone"
(*Il Proletario*, New York, 10 novembre 1900)

Se vinceva l'argento,
il popolo moria di fame e stento;
ma poi che l'oro vittorioso uscia
il popol creperà d'apoplessia...
Ogni metallo è buono, in conclusione,
per pagare l'esequie a Pantalone.[9]

(If silver won,
people would die of hunger and privation;
but seeing as how gold emerged victorious,
people will die by apoplexy...
Any metal is good, in conclusion,
To pay for the funeral of Pantalone.)

Rosina Vieni, "High Life"
(*Il Proletario*, New York, 8 dicembre 1900)

- Che n'è del vostro cuor, bella signora? -
chiedeva il ganimede:
- Datemi un bacio, andiamo, alla buon'ora,
ché nessun ci vede -.
Ella, soffusa di rossor la fronte,
diè un bacio al giovinotto:
ma un istante di poi, l'ombra del conte
apparve nel salotto.
- Che avete moglie mia? nel viso, parmi,
così rossa, perché? -
- Nulla: è il marchese che volea spiegarmi
la regola del tre -.
New York, 1 dicembre 1900

"High Life"

(What's in your heart, fair lady?–
asked the dandy:
–Give me a kiss, come on, it's OK,
nobody can see us.–
And she, blushing up to her forehead,
gave a kiss to the lad:
but a minute later, the shadow of the count
appeared in the parlor.
–What's happening, my wife? Your face looks
so red; why?–
–No reason: the marquis was just explaining
to me the rule of threes.–)

Rosina Vieni, "A la mia gattina"
(*Il Proletario*, 15 dicembre 1900)

O vergine gattina,
che dormi, onesta e quieta,

sotto la stufa a gas della cucina;
o morbida bestiola
dal collare di seta,
qual sogno mai ti cruccia o ti consola?
Sogni forse le lotte
terribili, cruente,
quando, nell'imo d'una negra notte,
timido passa, in fretta,
un topo impertinente,
e tu corri all'assalto, alla vendetta?
O pur sogni, beata,
le carezze del gatto
che sta al secondo piano, di facciata?
e che ogni tanto appare
e mangia dal tuo piatto,
e insiem ti ruba il cuore e il desinare?
Io, sai?, sono una bella
fanciulla di vent'anni,
e ho la grazia, il sorriso e la favella:
ma il mio brutto destino
mi dié tutti i malanni
quando nascer mi fe' senza un quattrino...
E perciò dal mio cuore
è per sempre bandito
quel che i felici chiamano l'amore;
ogni balda speranza
di correre a marito
nel mio povero cor non ha più stanza...
Te fortunata e lieta,
o mia bella dormiente,
a cui la dote è un collare di seta;
a cui tutto è concesso
che a me non si consente:
e un casto bacio ed un fecondo amplesso!

New York, 9 dicembre 1900

("To My Kitten"

Oh virgin kitten,
you who sleep honest and quiet,
under the gas stove in the kitchen;
oh soft little beast
with your silky collar,
which dream worries or comforts you?
Maybe you dream of quarrels
terrible and bloody,
when, in the deep of the darkest night,
an insolent mouse,
passes timid and impertinent,
and you jump to the assault and to revenge?
Or maybe you dream, content,
Of the caresses of the cat
that lives on the second floor across the street?
and who now and then shows up
and eats from your dish
and steals both your heart and your food?
You know, I am a nice
girl of twenty,
and I have grace, a smile and a way with words:
but my ugly destiny
gave me every misfortune
when it made me be born without any money...
That's why from my heart
is forever banished
what the happy call love;
any bold hope
of finding a husband
no more dwells in my poor heart...
You, lucky and gay,
oh my sleeping beauty,
whose dowry is a silky collar;
you to whom everything is granted

Francesco Durante

that for me is not granted,
a chaste kiss and a fruitful embrace!
New York, December 9, 1900)

Rosina Vieni, "Segno dei tempi"
(*Il Proletario*, New York, 12 gennaio 1901)

Il re della Fraterna, il biondo Vito,
l'han messo a dormire!
Non c'è proprio che dire:
legge fatale, eterna,
è che il mondo cammini e vada innante ...
Il secolo che fu decimonono
esser potea col trono
a dispetto di Bresci e Passannante;
nel secolo ventesimo
non valgon più un centesimo,
né corone di prenci e principesse,
né conti, né contesse!
     A.G. Uzzino[10]

("Sign of the Times"
The king of the Fraterna, Vito the blond,
they put him to sleep!
There is nothing to say:
The fatal and eternal law
Says that the world must continue on ...
The century that was the nineteenth
had power with the throne
despite Bresci and Passannante;
in the twentieth century
neither crowns, nor princes or princesses,
neither counts nor countesses
are worth even a cent!
     A.G. Uzzino)

Simplicio Righi, "Gli emigranti dell'ideale"
(*Il Proletario*, New York, 1 maggio 1901)

Mista al fragor dei flutti, tra il sibilo dei venti,
  prorompe dai navigli la ribelle canzon
  e da la spiaggia applaudono le turbe dei redenti,
  e del riscatto sventola superbo il gonfalon.

Cantano i venienti: - "Noi siamo gli emigranti
  "esuli della vita, transfughi del piacer
  "prodigo a noi fu iddio sol di singhiozzi e pianti,
  e andiam cercando un dio più savio giustizier

"Curvi sotto la ferula del torrido solleone
  "curvi sotto la raffica del verno micidial
  "e sangue, e nervi, e muscoli regalammo al padrone
  "e figli, e spose, e madri donammo all'ospedal

"In grembo alle miniere lasciammo il fior degli anni,
  "nella negra officina lasciammo la beltà;
  "lo scherno dei vigliacchi, la frusta dei tiranni,
  "tutto provammo, e il marchio vil della carità.

"Eccoci qui, ridotti a scheletri viventi,
  "vaganti nell'oceano vasto dell'ideal,
  "ma, tra il clamor dell'onde e la rabbia dei venti,
  "fieri i navigli avanzano nella marcia fatal.

"Noi del dolore umano siam gli eterni emigranti,
  "esuli della vita, trasfughi del piacer:
  "ma una fede gagliarda ci grida – avanti, avanti.
  "e una fiamma vermiglia c'illumina il sentier…

Intanto su la spiaggia, tra le turbe gioconde,
  balza da mille petti l'hurrà liberator
  e al canto dei ribelli un gaio inno risponde,
  il forte inno dei liberi, il santo inno d'amor.

Francesco Durante

E cantano i redenti: - "Deh, venite, o fratelli,
  "scendete a questi lidi sacri a la libertà:
  "d'una catena immensa noi qui siamo gli anelli,
  "noi qui siam l'uguaglianza, siamo la civiltà.

"Come macigni inutili d'una vecchia fortezza
  "caddero ad una ad una le ree divinità,
  "ed or siede sui ruderi, in sua maschia bellezza,
  "audace scolta e vigile, la nova umanità.

"Bella di spighe e grappoli, bella di suoi tesori,
  "per noi tutti è la terra, e splende a tutti il sol;

  "né catene agli schiavi, né ciondoli ai signori,
  "ma il pane a tutti i liberi porgon l'aratro e il suol.

"Deh, qui venite, o misere turbe affamate e scarne
  "scendete qui, o superstiti d'una barbara età;
  "date alla vene e all'ossa vigor di sangue e carne,
  "e ai genuflessi spiriti date la libertà."

("The Immigrants of the Ideal"

Mixed with the din of waves, in the hiss of winds,
  out of the ships gushes the rebel song
  and from the shore applauds the crowd of the redeemed,
  and the banner of redemption proudly flutters.

The newcomers sing: "We are the immigrants
  exiles of life, deserters of pleasure
  God was generous to us only with sobs and tears,
  and we are looking for a wiser avenger God

"Bowed under the staff of scorching summer sun,
  bent under the gust of lethal winter
  and blood, and nerves, and muscles we gave the boss,
  and children, and wives, and mothers we gave to the
                                [hospital.

"In the belly of the mines we left the prime of life,
  and in the black workshop we left our beauty;
  the scorn of cowards, the tyrants' whip,
  all of this we endured, and the vile mark of charity.

"And here we are, reduced to living skeletons,
  wanderers in the great ocean of the Ideal,
  but, amid the clamor of waves and the rage of winds,
  our ships proudly advance on their fatal march.

"We are the eternal immigrants of human pain,
  exiles of life, deserters of pleasure:
  but a strong faith cries out to us: forward, forward,
  and a red flame illuminates our path...

Meanwhile, on the shore, among the joyful crowd,
  bursts out of a thousand hearts a liberating cheer,
  and to the song of rebels replies a happy anthem,
  the strong anthem of the free, the holy anthem of love.

The redeemed are singing: - "Alas, come you oh brothers,
  land on these shores sacred to freedom:
  we are rings of an immense chain,
  here we are equality, we are civilization.

"Just like useless stones of an old fortress
  the divine criminals fall one by one,
  and now on the ruins, in its masculine beauty,
  audacious and vigilant sentry, the new humanity sits.

"Fair with spikes and bunches, fair with its treasures,
  the earth is for us all, and the sun shines on everyone;
  no more chains for slaves, nor jewels for the rich,
  but the plough and the land give bread to all those
                              [who are free.

"Alas, come, oh poor starving, gaunt crowds,
  land here, oh survivors of a barbarous era;

give your veins and bones the energy of blood and flesh,
and to the kneeling spirits give liberty.")

Rosina Vieni, "L'asino e il cammello"
(*Il Proletario*, New York, 16 novembre 1901)

Chiese una volta l'asino al cammello:
- Che cosa è quel fardello
che porti sul groppone? -
Il cammello, che è scaltro e furbacchione,
(tutti i gobbi son furbi)
sapete che rispose?
- Fu la Natura che il fardel mi pose
su la schiena e perciò
fino a la morte mia lo porterò.
Stolto invece è colui che da Natura
ebbe il dorso diritto
ma per pigrizia d'animo e paura
di frusta o di bastone,
porta il fardello che vuole il padrone.
                    New York, 8 novembre 1901

("The Donkey and the Camel"

The donkey once asked the camel:
- What is that burden
you carry on your back? -
The camel, who is crafty and astute
(like all hunchbacks are),
do you know what he said?
- It was Nature that gave me the burden
on my back, and that's why
I'll carry it till death.
Rather a fool he who from Nature
got a straight back
but out of laziness of soul and fear

of whip or cane,
carries the burden the boss wants him to.
>   New York, November 8, 1901)

Rosina Vieni, "La parabola del campanile"
(*Il Proletario*, New York, 30 novembre 1901)

D'un campanile su la vetta altera
tra il Battaglio e la Campana
s'accese un giorno una disputa fiera.
Il Battaglio gridava:
- Son io che picchio ne' tuoi fianchi, e il suono
Ond'è percosso l'aere
È merto mio -. Perdono,
diceva la Campana,
l'opra del tuo picchiar sarebbe vana,
se da l'anima mia
metallica e canora
non vibrasse pel ciel l'onda sonora.
A tai superbi accenti
qualche cosa si mosse
giù dal basso. – Tacete, impertinenti,
(brontolava la Corda)
o mi credete sorda?
le vostre, debbo dirla? son bugie:
ché se non fosser le fatiche mie,
in parola d'onore,
non fareste, voi due, tanto rumore … -
Un'altra voce, a un tratto,
rompe da l'imo fondo:
- Cos'è questo vociar, poffare il mondo?
fate silenzio, io sono il Campanaro,
il Campanaro io sono,
io che tiro la Corda, ed io che suono. –
Seccato dal frastuono
di voci sì diverse,

Francesco Durante

il Cappellano uscì di sagristia,
e gridò forte: - Zitto, o vil genia;
ognuno di voi altri è un servitore;
qui non c'è che un signore,
e son io quello, il direttor d'orchestra. -
E, a un cenno ch'egli fece colla destra,
il Campanaro cominciò a tirare,
la Corda a traballare,
il Battaglio a picchiare,
la Campana a suonare ...

(Morale)
E il Prete a comandare.

New York, 20 novembre 1901

("The Parable of the Bell Tower"

From the bell tower on the lofty summit
between the Clapper and the Bell
arose one day a fierce debate.
Cried the Clapper:
- I am the one that knocks on your sides, and the sound
by which the air is stricken
is thanks to me. - Pardon me,
said the Bell,
the work of your knocking would be vain,
if not for my metallic
and singing soul,
which vibrates up to the sky a sonorous wave.
In reply to these haughty accents
something moved
down below. - Shut up, you insolent ones
[grumbled the Rope]
do you think I'm deaf?
Yours - must I say it? - are lies:
because if it weren't for my efforts,

on my honor,
the two of you wouldn't make so much as a sound … -
Another voice, all of a sudden,
came from the very bottom:
- What is all this chatter, for heaven's sake?
Be quiet, I am the Bell Ringer,
the Bell Ringer am I,
I the one who pulls the Rope, I the one who sounds. -
Annoyed by the clamor
of the various voices,
The chaplain came from the sacristy
And yelled loudly: Quiet, you shoddy bunch;
Each one of you is a servant;
There is only one lord here,
And it is I, the orchestra director.
And, with a signal from his right hand,
and the Bell Ringer started pulling,
the Rope tottering,
the Clapper knocking,
the Bell resounding …

 (Moral)
and the Priest commanding.)

Simplicio Righi, "Oggi e domani"
(*Il Proletario*, 1 maggio 1902)

Oggi …
  Oggi, freni e manette
ai polsi ed ai cervelli
e se gli schiavi diventan ribelli
fucili e baionette.
  Oggi, su l'altrui solco,
curva la fronte e di sudor bagnato,
agonizza il bifolco,
e dentro alle miniere,

nel ventre della terra inesplorata
maledicendo muore il picconiere.
 Oggi, un mondo di schiavi e di padroni,
di pecore e leoni!

Domani ...
 Oh, domani non più le fronti prone,
non più ceppi e catene,
ma dell'umanità dentro le vene
scorrerà il sangue della redenzione!
 Domani, affratellati
saranno tutti i cuori
e sol d'amore canteranno i vati,
e all'anime redente
il maggio nuovo dei lavoratori
riderà eternamente.
 Tutto un mondo di liberi, domani,
che si stringon le mani.

 ("Today and Tomorrow"
Today ...
Today, brakes and throttles
on our wrists and our brains
and if slaves become rebels
rifles and bayonets.
Today, on another's furrow
curves the forehead bathed in sweat,
the yokel agonizes,
and inside the mines,
in the belly of the unexplored earth,
cursing, the laborer dies.
Today, a world of slaves and masters
of lambs and lions!
Tomorrow ...
Oh, tomorrow no more bowed heads
no more chains and fetters,

but from humanity's veins
the blood of redemption will flow.
Tomorrow, our hearts
will become like brothers'
and prophets will sing only of love,
and to the redeemed soul
the new May day of laborers
will laugh eternally.
A whole world of free men, tomorrow
holding hands.
[translation by Peter Covino])

Simplicio Righi, "The Skyscraper (Il grattacielo)"
(*Il Carroccio*, New York, a. IX, n. 10, Ottobre 1923)

Quale sull'erba molle
s'erge l'ippocastano
e al sol, come un titano,
le immense braccia estolle;
e porge alta la testa
alle procelle e al gelo,
sfida proterva al cielo
tra i nuvoli in tempesta;

tale la bieca fronte
il grattacielo innalza,
e l'ombra sua rimbalza
sul tuo grigio orizzonte,
Manhattan, e la faccia,
da mille occhi forata
s'aderge arrovellata
d'orgoglio e di minaccia.

Nelle tenebre fitte
della fatal miniera
scese una bruna schiera
d'anime derelitte,

e a te curve recaro,
o Anteo rimbaldanzito,
muscoli di granito
e tendini d'acciaro.

Dagli antri impervii e cupi
del bosco sterminato,
ove urge ognor l'agguato
dei crotali e dei lupi
trassero a suon di scuri
l'asta e la tua bandiera
che ride e ondeggia e impera
sui templi e sui tuguri.

Nel tuo viscere immane
serpono gli ascensori
turgidi d'acri umori,
gonfi di linfe umane;
e in lor vicenda alterna
l'odio e l'amor traboccano,
baci e saette scoccano
dalla tragedia eterna.

Ah! non per questo il sole
pinge de' suoi colori
le nuvole ed i fiori,
il vespero e le aiole;
e mille e mille brezze
scendono ai monti e ai piani
e allegrano gli umani
di tenere carezze!

No, non vogl'io l'osanna
che libertade accese
librar per te, o borghese,
divinità tiranna;
altri il mio verso adori

numi discreti e cari,
e più sereni altari
il picciol estro infiori.

D'una casetta bianca
sotto il ruvido tetto
celar l'estremo affetto,
posar l'anima stanca,
e, a torno, il cinguettio
dei passeri in amore,
i biancospini in fiore,
e il murmure d'un rio.

O giorni oscuri e cheti,
autunno della vita,
luce vi sian gradita
i miei quattro Poeti:
luce che abbelli ancora
la fin del mio cammino,
pietosa al mio destino
e al dubbio che m'accora.

E tu, Pascoli mio,
postremo italo vate,
tra un'empia e torva etate
surto, silvano Iddio,
fa che il tuo dolce canto
a goccia a goccia cada
come una pia rugiada
sul mio che sa di pianto.

("The Skyscraper"

Like the horse-chestnut
it emerges from the soft grass,
and toward the sun like a titan
extends its immense arms;

and high offers its head
to the storms and the ice,
arrogant challenge to the sky
amid the clouds in a storm;

such its sinister brow
the skyscraper lifts,
and the shadow bounces
on your gray horizon,
Manhattan, and the face,
pierced by thousands of eyes,
rises tormented
by pride and by threat.

Into the deep darkness
of the deadly mine
descended a dark crowd
of derelict souls,
and to you they brought,
oh newly emboldened Antheus,
muscles of granite
and tendons of steel.

From the impassable and gloomy caves
of the endless forest,
where the ambush of the rattlesnake and the wolf
eternally presses
they dragged to the accompaniment of their axes
the pole and your flag
that shines and waves and rules
over the temples and over the slums.

Amid your enormous guts
wind the elevators
swollen with pungent humors,
turgid with human sap;
and in their alternating sequence

overflow hate and love,
kisses and thunderbolts shoot out
from the eternal tragedy.

Alas, it is not for this that the sun
paints with its colors
the clouds and the flowers,
the evening and the flowerbeds;
and thousands upon thousands of breezes
descend to mounts and plains
and cause happiness to people
with tender caresses!

No, I don't want the praise
that freedom ignited
to soar for you, oh bourgeois,
despotic goddess;
other idols my verse
venerates, delicate and dear ones,
and more serene altars
my little whim will deck with flowers.

Under the uneven roof
of a white little house
I'll hide my last feeling,
rest my tired soul,
and all around the twitter
of sparrows in love,
and the hawthorns in blossom
and the whisper of a creek.

Oh humble days and quiet,
autumn of life,
may my four Poets
be for you a welcome light:
light that beautified
the end of my path,

compassionate to my destiny
and to the doubt that stabs in the heart.

And you, my Pascoli,
at last Italy's bard,
in this unholy, menacing age
risen, oh sylvan god,
let your sweet song
fall drop by drop
like a pious dew
on mine, that knows weeping.)

Simplicio Righi, "I sonetti di Manhattan"
(*Il Carroccio*, New York, n. 2, febbraio 1924)

"Broadway"

Corre per l'ampia via, torbido in vista,
il vecchio fiume delle genti umane,
e dalle limacciose onde una trista
nebbia vapora di speranze insane.

A qual meta, a qual gloria, a qual conquista
Muovete, o turbe, e a quai chimere arcane?
e quale audace o stolido Battista
la novella vi dié di un gran dimane?

Lungo è il cammino e poco pane avete,
duro è l'asfalto e son stanche le piote,
e nelle secche gole arde la sete.

Di qua, di là, dagli alti grattacieli
piove un riso crudel che vi percuote,
o nati a naufragar, spiriti aneli!

("Broadway"

The old river of human people
runs down the wide way, murky on sight,
and from the shady waves a sad
mist of insane hopes evaporates.

For what purpose, what glory, what conquest
Do you move, oh crowds, to which arcane delusions?
and which bold or foolish Baptist
gave you the news of a great future?

Long is the path and you have scarce bread,
hard is the pavement and tired are your feet,
and in desiccated throats thirst is burning.

Here, there, from the high skyscrapers
a cruel laugh rains down that pummels you,
oh anxious souls born to founder!)

"The Subway"

Dante, io vorrei che tu scendessi in questa[11]
Bolgia feral che ogni altra bolgia avanza,
ove tace di sole ogni speranza
ed il fragore vince ogni tempesta;

sì che su la fronte ampia ed onesta
cui solcò l'ira e in che fe' il duol sua stanza,
urlasse un'altra fiata in sua possanza
la bufera infernal che mai non resta.

Ahi, la bufera rabida s'abbatte
sovra costoro, e seco li trascina
nella morta vallea del disinganno![12]

Corron costor come pecore matte,
corron costor, di su, di giù, a rovina:
corron costoro, ed il perché non sanno.

("The Subway"

Dante, I wish you would descend into this
frightful ditch, bigger than any ditch,
where any hope of sun ceases
and the din defeats every tempest;

so that on the ample and honest brow
furrowed by rage and where pain dwelt
another period could shriek in its strength
the infernal storm that never ceases.

Alas, the rabid storm falls
over these ones, and drags them along
to the dead valley of disillusion!

They run like a crazy sheep,
they run headlong up and down till they collapse:
they run, and they don't know why.)

"Columbus Circle"

Dal suo marmoreo stelo il Genovese
veglia su la gran piazza brulicante;
donde, come su immense ali distese,
sale il ritmo dell'urbe altisonante.

Rigido, austero, impavido a l'offese
della terra e del ciel sta l'Almirante,
e par che pensi al dì che su le attese
sponde prima stampò l'orma gigante.

E par che dica: - Sol per voi, figliuoli,
con la *Santa Maria* salpai sul nero
vergine mar che un polo e l'altro bagna;

e volli a nuovi lidi e a nuovi soli
recar, superbo e povero nocchiero,
il cuor d'Italia ed il vessil di Spagna.

("Columbus Circle"

From his marble stalk the Genoese
watches over the swarming square;
from which, as though on immense spread wings
climbs the rhythm of the high-flown city.

Stiff, stern, impervious to offense
of the earth and of the sky stands the Admiral,
and it seems he thinks about the day that on his longed-for
shores he made his giant mark.

And it seems he is saying: - Only for you, my sons,
on the *Santa Maria* I sailed on the black
virgin ocean that bathes one pole and the other;

I wanted to bring to new shores and new soils,
proud and humble helmsman,
the heart of Italy and the flag of Spain.)

"Greenwich Village"

Sotto una luce pallida e vermiglia
traballano per via Venere e Bacco:
ella ha nei baci il puzzo del tabacco
ed egli sa di "whiskey" a un par di miglia.

Ella sen va, mostrando la caviglia,
coi pié nelle scarpine senza tacco;
ed egli vien, dinoccolato e stracco
schizzando intorno a sé lazzi e fanghiglia.

Ma da le tane ove la dea lussuria
siede in bigoncia e mesce il fescennino
filtro nei lombi e tra gli amplessi umani;

da le taverne ove la morte infuria
esce un veggente e ascolta il mattutino
canto del gallo. Che sarà, domani?

("Greenwich Village"

Beneath a light soft and red
stagger on the street Venus and Bacchus:
she in her kisses has the stink of tobacco
and he smells of whiskey from a couple of miles away.

She goes, showing her ankles,
her feet in the shoes without heels;
he comes, shambling and weary
splashing around himself jokes and mud.

But from the nests where the goddess lust
sits with legs sprawled and pours her smutty
potion into the loins and amid human embraces;

from the taverns where death ravages
there comes out a seer who listens to the early
cockcrow. What will happen tomorrow?)

"Little Italy"

Occhi in cui brilla il sol di Mergellina
labbra in cui trema il riso di Sorrento,
fiori del mio giardin che il gelo e il vento
divelsero alla gran madre latina;

o fanciullo, che il pianto e lo sgomento
poppasti con la bocca piccolina,
e tu, bella a mirar, bruna bambina
nata e venuta su tra stento e stento;

lo sapete che ovunque il pié sospinga,
tutta la terra a l'esule è noverca,
e dove il giorno sorge e dove scende?

Ah, gran mercé, che nella sua raminga
anima ride un dio che non si merca:
- Amor che a cor gentil ratto s'apprende.[13]

("Little Italy"

Eyes in which the sun of Mergellina shines,
lips on which the laugh of Sorrento trembles,
flowers of my garden that ice and wind
pulled out of their great Latin mother;

oh child, you who nursed with your tiny mouth
weeping and dismay,
and you, pretty little brown girl,
born and grown up amid many hardships;

do you know that wherever the foot falls
the entire earth is a stepmother for the exile,
both where the day rises and where it goes down?

Alas, but in his wandering soul
there laughs a god that money can't buy:
- Love, which quickly arrests the gentle heart.)

Simplicio Righi, "Monna Lisa"
(*Leonardo da Vinci Art School*, special issue 1924–25)

Sovra uno sfondo tragico ove dura
grave il silenzio delle cose morte,
la divina beltà delle tue smorte
mani, o Gioconda, brilla e s'infutura;[14]

ma della bocca tua tenera e pura
e delle maliarde iridi accorte
il sorriso fatal m'agita forte,
mi persegue nel tempo e mi tortura.

Forse sul labbro tuo, pallida sfinge,
forse negli occhi tuoi trema il sorriso
nunzio al Maestro di carnal disio?

O pure al fato che a morir ti spinge
ilare e mesta affacci il dolce viso,
ilare e mesta nell'estremo addio?

("Monna Lisa"

On a tragic background where stands
heavy the silence of dead things,
the divine beauty of your lifeless
hands, oh Gioconda, sparkles and prolongs;

but from your soft and pure mouth
and of your bewitching irises
the fatal smile distresses me so intensely,
pursues me in time and tortures me.

Maybe on your lips, pale sphinx,
maybe in your eyes wavers the smile
that signaled carnal desire to the Maestro?

Or to fate, that pushes you toward death,
cheerful and sad you show your sweet face,
cheerful and sad in the final farewell?)

Rosina Vieni, "Vennero i bricchellieri"
(*Zarathustra*, New York, 15 maggio 1926)

Vennero i *bricchellieri* a cento a cento,
tutta una *ghenga* coi calli alle mani
per far la casa di quaranta piani
senza contare il *ruffo* e il *basamento*.

Adesso par che sfidi il firmamento
a onore e gloria degli americani;

ma chi pensa ai *grinoni*, ai paesani
morti d'un colpo, senza sacramento?

Che val, se per disgrazia o per *mistecca*
ti sfracelli la carne in fondo al *floro* -
povero *ghinni*, disgraziato *dego*?

Davanti a mezzo ponte di *bistecca*
il *bosso* ghigna e mostra i denti d'oro:
- Chi è morto è morto... io vivo e me ne frego.[15]

("The Bricklayers Arrived"

The bricklayers arrived hundreds at a time
a whole gang with callused hands
to build the house of forty stories
not counting the roof or the basement.

Now it seems to challenge the firmament
to the honor and glory of the Americans;
but who cares about the greenhorns, our citizens,
dead by a sudden blow, without sacrament?

What's it worth, if by bad luck or mistake
you shatter your bones on the floor below —
miserable guinea, wretched dago?

In front of a half pound of steak
the boss shows off his gold teeth and sneers:
Who's dead is dead ... I'm alive and jeer.
[translated by Peter Covino])

NOTES
[1] The pen name *Rosina Vieni* comes from a popular song of Northern Italy known by three different titles: "Quelle stradelle," or "E qui comando io," or "Cara Rosina." "Quando la luna la cambia color / Vieni Rosina, vieni Rosina / Quando la luna la cambia color / Vieni Rosina faremo l'amor." On Righi, see Durante (2014), Bencivenni (2011), and Marazzi (2012). The sonnet "Vennero i bricchellieri" is also in Mencken (1947).

Francesco Durante

² See also De Ciampis's (n.d.) huge unpublished typescript "De Ciampis Papers, Immigration History Research Center."
³ Also, in *Il Proletario* Righi took the chance of attacking Tammany Hall, writing that it was the American equivalent of Italian freemasonry, that is, the most powerful enemy of the people (*La Massoneria*, July 7 and 14, 1900).
⁴ This refers to the news of British failure during the first phases of the second Anglo-Boer war against the forces of the republics of Transvaal and Orange Free State.
⁵ Sudden bankruptcies were pretty common in the Little Italies, and at the turn of the century there were many cases of Italian American bankers escaping from the United States, carrying with them all the money that Italian workers (the poor, innocent *cafoni*) had entrusted them. The most typical way of doing this was to cross the northern border and hide in Canada. Among many others who did this in these months was a certain Antonio Pesce, who had a bank in Mulberry Street. He flew to Canada with all the bank's money (see *"La fuga di un altro banchiere"* 1900).
⁶ At the end of 1899, the government of the Kingdom of Italy granted a general amnesty on political crimes, excluding crimes as theft, robbery, and embezzlement.
⁷ This *stornello* says that the popular "Doctor Collins," a typical kind of American charlatan medical doctor who in those years was widely advertising in all Italian American newspapers, had resulted in more victims than the famous New Orleans lynching of 1891.
⁸ The parade to which this poem refers is the annual one of September 20, celebrating the conquest of Rome by the Kingdom of Italy. In *Il Proletario* of one year before (September 23, 1899), Righi—signing himself as *Esse.Erre.*—published an article under the title *"La parata sfila!"* (The parade passes by) in which he underlined that all the Italian generals, all the captains, and all the soldiers parading in New York were complete fakes. It was the first time he saw the parade in New York, and he found it simply embarrassing. Quite the same things, written in a more sarcastic form, Righi repeated on July 21, 1900 (*"In conspetto della breccia,"* Facing the breach, i.e., the breach of Porta Pia through which the *bersaglieri* had entered Rome in 1870). Again in *Il Proletario* Righi signed with his name (June 30, 1900) an article on *"Il militarismo"* (Militarism), inscribing in his argument also the fake militarism of Italian American parades, and saying that militarism was "the most damaging among modern social sores."
⁹ This poem speaks about the U.S. presidential election of 1900, in which William McKinley (Republican) beat William Jennings Bryan (Democratic). From a socialist point of view, it did not make much difference: Republican or Democrat, the people would starve and die anyway, and a general funeral must be paied for with public funds. The name *Pantalone*, as the mask of the *commedia dell'arte*, is an Italian popular idiom to mean "people."
¹⁰ The poem refers to Vito Contessa, chairman of the Fraterna Society, who had been replaced as the head of the powerful Italian American association. Giovanni Passannante was the anarchist who in 1878 tried unsuccessfully to kill King Umberto I, while Gaetano Bresci was the anarchist who traveled from Paterson to

kill the king in 1900. The poem is signed with a pun: *A. G. Guzzino*, that is, *aguzzino* (persecutor).

[11] This incipit is modeled on the famous sonnet "Guido, i' vorrei che tu e Lapo ed io," LII, *Rime*.

[12] The rare term *vallea* comes from Dante, *Inferno*, XVI, 29.

[13] Quotation from the famous verse of Dante in the episode of Paolo and Francesca, *Inferno*, V, 100.

[14] The rare verb *infuturarsi* is a quotation from Dante, *Paradiso*, XVII, 98.

[15] This famous sonnet is almost an *hapax*, one of the very few texts where the typical Italian American pidgin is used in a serious context. In the original, all the words written in italics are Italian American neologisms modeled on American words.

WORKS CITED

Bencivenni, Marcella. 2011. *Italian Immigrant Radical Culture. The Idealism of the* Sovversivi *in the United States, 1890–1940*. New York: New York University Press, 149–150.

De Ciampis, Pasquale Mario. n.d., "De Ciampis Papers, Immigration History Research Center: University of Minnesota." *Il Proletario,* 215–222.

Durante, Francesco. 2014 [2005]. *Italoamericana. The Literature of the Great Migration*. New York: Fordham University Press, 610–612.

"*La fuga di un altro banchiere.*" 1900. *Il Proletario,* August 18.

Marazzi, Martino. 2012. *Voices of Italian America: A History of Early Italian American Literature with a Critical Anthology*. New York: Fordham University Press, 199–200.

Mencken, Henry Louis. 1947. *The American Language. An Inquiry into the Development of English in the United States*, 4th ed. London: Routledge and Kegan, 642.

Obituary of Semplicio Righi. 1943a. *The New York Times,* October 17.

Obituary of Semplicio Righi. 1943b. *Smithtown Star,* Smithtown, NY, October 20.

Pecoraro, Mario. 1983. *Il socialismo carpigiano nelle pagine di "Luce."* Mantova: Arcari, 26–31.

Righi, Semplicius. 1920. "*Istantanea fiumana.*" in *Il Carroccio*, New York, no. 12, 475–476.

Righi, Simplicio. 1901. "*Socialisti e anarchici.*" *Il Proletario,* February 2.

Soldati, Mario. 1979. *Addio diletta Amelia*. Milan: Arnoldo Mondadori, 153–157.

Living on the Hyphen: Two Italian-Born Writers in the United States

Paolo Giordano

> Di tutte le lontananze, l'America è la più vera ed esemplare.
> —Mario Soldati, *America primo amore*

Today several writers born and culturally trained in Italy live in the United States and write in Italian and English.[1] The list is long and their writing has defined itself as a distinctive American voice in Italian literature and/or an Italian voice in American literature and by their form and content recognizes the fact that Italian America is neither monolingual nor monocultural.

On the phenomenon of Italian American culture and its different aspects as manifested through its literature, Paolo Valesio (1989) states the following:

> The confusing codes, registers, genres (be they literary or cultural) often lead to reciprocal misunderstandings. ... It becomes necessary, therefore, to distinguish between the following:
>
> 1. Not strictly literary autobiographical and memorial texts, whose collection and systematic analysis is, nonetheless, important for a dialectical understanding of the various components of literary history.
>
> 2. Novels or short stories written in English by members of the Italo-American community, containing predominance of themes that can be considered characteristic of such a community.
>
> 3. Works by those that I have called writers between two worlds: the Italian expatriates in the United States who write exclusively or largely in Italian. (273)[2]

Valesio's model offers an excellent starting point in trying to navigate both the intricacies of Italian American culture and a literature born out of mixed cultural and linguistic referents.

For this essay I would like to consider Valesio's third distinction, authors whom he calls "writers between two worlds," in particular two writers I consider exemplary to this category: Giovanni Cecchetti and Joseph Tusiani. Cecchetti and Tusiani, like other writers with similar experiences, operate in and from a reality that is "bilingual, bicultural [and] biconceptual" (Hicks 1989, xxv). In Roland Barthes's terms their artistic perceptions are illuminated from two or more sets of referential codes. "Juxtaposed between multiple cultures" (Hicks 1989, xxiii), these poets create literature that explores, is influenced by, and is sensitive to the different cultural and linguistic referents that help mold it. They are "cultural border writers" (Hicks 1989, xxv).[3]

Giovanni Cecchetti, born in the town of Pescia (Pistoia province) in Tuscany, emigrated to the United States in 1948 and, while developing his poetic voice, went on to become a scholar of Italian letters at various U.S. universities. Those who knew Cecchetti know how much he loved his adopted land, but he at the same time was always and unmistakably Italian, more precisely Tuscan, in his way of being and showing himself to others, often rude but always direct (see note 3). Cecchetti always composed in Italian, be it poetry or prose, not because of a lack of skill and mastery of the English language—a quick cursus through his critical studies written in English instantly dismisses such a notion—but because of an unwavering loyalty and devotion to the culture of Italy and a belief that the only true poetry one can write is done in one's native language. In a short essay that appeared in *Forum Italicum*, "Sullo scriver poesia," Cecchetti (1992) writes the following:

> E la lingua? È quella in cui si è nati; è la lingua d'un'infanzia trasfigurata, carica di quei sensi che allora sarebbero stati irraggiungibili. Nessuno può scrivere poesia in un'altra lingua, sovrapposta e quindi fittizia, che non gli può diventare linguaggio, sebbene ci stia dentro quotidianamente. In questa può scrivere

versi, magari dei buoni versi, ma non poesia—la quale non può nascere in chi si trova bloccato nella prigione dell'artificio. Noi che abbiamo avuto un'infanzia in Italia (quell'infanzia che in certo modo include anche l'adolescenza) possiamo scrivere poesia solo in italiano. L'inglese è la lingua della prosa. (251-252)

(And the language? It is the one in which you are born; it is the language of a transfigured childhood, loaded with those senses that would then have been unattainable. No one can write poetry in another language, superimposed and therefore fictitious, which cannot become a language, even though he is in it every day. In this he can write verses, maybe good verses, but not poetry—which cannot be born in those who find themselves stuck in the prison of artifice. We who had a childhood in Italy [that childhood that in a certain way also includes adolescence] can write poetry only in Italian. English is the language of prose.[4])

(All translations mine.)

Cecchetti made his debut in print in 1967 with the poems of *Diario nomade*, and his second collection of poetry, *Impossibile scendere*, appeared in 1978. Fredi Chiappelli, in his 1975 essay "Sulla poesia di Cecchetti," published in *Forum Italicum*, identified exile, memory, the inexorable passage of time, and modern man's existential and spiritual battle among alienated and alienating landscapes and phenomena as the salient thematic elements in Cecchetti's work.

When one considers Cecchetti's (1985) last work of prose, *Danza nel deserto*, the thematic elements identified in his first two volumes of poetry and that Rebecca West put in perspective in her review of *Nel cammino dei monti* (Cecchetti's third collection of poems) are still present and reinforced by his use of the desolate landscape of the California desert as stage and frame for the twelve short stories that comprise this 127-page volume. Cecchetti lived on the margins of the California desert for over forty years. The stories of *Danza nel deserto*,[5] while echoing Dino Buzzati's *Il deserto dei tartari* (1997), strongly reflect Cecchetti's experiences of living and working on the periphery of that American desert landscape for a good part of his life. The desert for Cecchetti is a metaphor for the solitude that envelops humanity in contemporary society and the squalor that solitude represents. In the desert, nature breaks the boundaries that we consider "normal," that is, livable. With the desert as stage and frame, these stories acquire a highly surrealistic quality; they portray a world of fantasy where reality is in constant flux and transfiguration while at the same time remaining real. As he stated in an interview with Michael Lettieri (1989), the stories are nothing more than "immagini del mondo in cui viviamo, quasi forme simboliche, ossia forme quasi allegoriche" (123) (images of the world in which we live, almost symbolic forms, rather, almost allegorical).

The men and women who populate the world of *Danza nel deserto* are individuals who live in solitude, and the more they try to break the wall of solitude, the stronger and more impenetrable that wall becomes. *Danza nel deserto* is a book about *communication* or, better yet, the *lack of communication* in contemporary society:

> È il mondo in cui vivo ancora: un mondo di gente che ride e che piange di là dalle vetrate, che muove serissima le labbra, senza che non ci sia mai un interlocutore. So che tutti cercano parole, dimentichi del nido del grillo canterino, e poi si contentano della risata solitaria o del sussurro di colomba. (Lettieri 1989, 123)

> (It is the world in which I still live: a world of people who laugh and cry from windows, who move their lips very seriously, without an interlocutor. I know everyone is looking for words, forget the nest of the singing cricket, and then they're content with a solitary laugh or the whisper of a dove.)

In the story "Il telefono," the traveler/narrator of *Danza nel deserto* visits an old school chum who lives in a small one-room house away from civilization. Inside the small house the traveler sees statues of men and women that are really telephones:

"Non capisco niente," dissi. M'avvicinai a un uomo con gli occhi tesi.

"Non codesto. È un ventriloquo. Ha il telefono in pancia; ripete solo quel che dicono i vicini." ....

"Prova a parlare con qualcuno," disse; "Forse risponde . . . questo."

M'avvicinai e dissi nel ricevitore: "Come sta?" Mi giunse una risposta monosillabica, un suono agglutinato, come in cinese.

Provai le altre statue; le risposte non cambiarono. A volte i suoni scivolavan via; a volte si gonfiavano in modo da sembrar grida disarticolate da giungla. M'arresi.

"Senti," disse il vecchio compagno di scuola. "Credevo che con un estraneo diventassero normali. Invece ... da principio cominciarono a farmi degli scherzi. Se dicevo qualcosa in un ricevitore, rispondevan con lunghi discorsi in coreano, in persiano, in armeno ... o almeno così credevo, perché spesso non riuscivo nemmeno a riconoscer la lingua.... Pensai che si fossero abituati a questi scherzi perché li avevo collegati alle linee internazionali. Allora li misi sulla rete nazionale. Peggio che peggio: colpi di tosse, abbai, grida, addirittura canzoncine a bocca chiusa. Insomma voci, non parole.... C'è da disperarsi." (Cecchetti 1985, 30–31)

("I don't understand anything," I said. I approached a man with tense eyes.

"Not that one. It's a ventriloquist. He has the phone in his belly; he just repeats what his neighbors say.

"Try talking to someone," he said. "Maybe he'll answer . . . this one."

I approached and said into the receiver, "How are you?" I got a monosyllabic answer, an agglutinated sound, as in Chinese.

I tried the other statues; the answers were always the same. Sometimes sounds slipped away; sometimes they swelled up to sound like disarticulated cries from the jungle. I gave up.

"Listen," said the old schoolmate. "I thought they became normal with a stranger. Instead ... from the beginning they started playing jokes on me. If I said anything in a receiver, they would respond with long speeches in Korean, Persian, Armenian ... or so I thought, because I often couldn't recognize the language.... I thought they got used to these jokes because I connected them to international lines. So I connected them to the national network. It was worse than before: coughing, barking, shouting, even closed-mouthed songs. You know, voices not words.... It's enough to drive you mad.")

The protagonists of *Danza nel deserto* attempt communication but are constantly frustrated, either by their own actions or by events that are outside of their sphere of control. They live as in a dream world. Their need to communicate is so intense that they invent ways of communication that are doomed to failure. Why, then, in this world of instant connectivity through technology, is communication so difficult? Cecchetti offers an answer in the above-mentioned interview with Michael Lettieri:

> Il mondo che sognano, quello in cui poi finiscono per vivere, a volte è molto insolito, come è sempre il caso dei sogni; e quindi non è percepibile dagli altri. È percepibile solo da loro stessi, perché gli altri hanno un loro mondo di sogni che è totalmente diverso. Questo spiega perché la comunicazione è così difficile, anzi direi impossibile. E lo è naturalmente non solo per queste persone, ma per tutti gli altri che io non considero. (Lettieri 1989, 125)

> (The world they dream of, the one they end up living in, is sometimes very unusual, as is always the case with dreams; and, therefore, it is not perceptible to others. It is understandable only to themselves, because others have their own world of dreams that is totally different. This explains why communication is so difficult, indeed I would say impossible. And it is of course not only for these people, but for everyone else that I don't consider.)

The theme of the "impossibility of communication" (Lettieri 1989, 126) is one that ties a number of Cecchetti's works together. In *Il villaggio degli inutili,* a collection of stories written when the author was a young man but published in 1981, the initial story, "La sporta del viandante," clearly explores the themes of the impossibility of communication among men/women and of the continuous flux of reality:

> Ogni tanto aprivo la sporta e ne tiravo fuori una casa o dei brandelli, e mi mettevo a studiarmeli in mano. Non mi ci volle molto ad accorgermi che nella sporta avevo creduto di metter l'infinito, ed invece non avevo depositato altro che una gran quantità di limiti. Continuai lo stesso a raccogliere e conservare. ...
>
> Però troppe eran le cose che avevo e che dovevo portarmi dietro. Un giorno cominciai a tirar fuori quel che ci avevo messo. Ma tutto era incredibilmente cambiato. Ciò che era originariamente bianco s'era fatto rosso, e viceversa. Le cose azzurre eran diventate grigie. Ma che c'era dentro quella sporta per causare simili trasformazioni? Non l'ho mai saputo. (Cecchetti 1981a, 17–18)

> (Every now and then I would open my bag and pull out a house and some rags, and I'd begin to study them. I believed I was putting a universe of things in my bag, but it didn't take long for me to realize that instead I deposited nothing but a great quantity of limitations. Nonetheless, I kept collecting and storing....
>
> But I had too many things to carry with me. One day I started to take out what I had put into it, but everything had changed incredibly. What was originally white was now red, and vice versa. The blue things had turned gray. What was in that bag that caused such transformations? I never knew.)

The American desert returns as a protagonist in the collection of poems *Nel cammino dei monti*. In the poem titled "Las Vegas," Cecchetti takes the reader to that most surrealistic of experiences: Las Vegas, the city of metal, neon, and glass that rises, like a phoenix, out of the Nevada desert—the city where America dreams and plays. When the poet is faced with this surrealistic sight his agony over the faith of society overwhelms him. Las Vegas is a metaphor for contemporary society, a society that has no foundation, a society built on sand:

> Se si stacca una scaglia ecco che crolla
> a briciole la rete, e non c'è più nemmeno
> un'ampolla opaca al chiodo
>   della parete. (Cecchetti 1980, 43)
>
> (If a scale breaks off, the net
> collapses into bits, and there isn't even
> an opaque ampoule attached to the nail
>   on the wall.)

Thus, the desert becomes metaphor for contemporary life and society, for an emptiness that is within us and that we are not able to fill. Contemporary American society, in its endless quest for happiness and material success, is destined to fail, and all it can hope for, according to Cecchetti, is the infertile, arid desert.

Cecchetti's intimate ties with Italy and the American West make him a most original multifaceted poetic voice of Italian literature in America. His cultural border crossings produce a literature that captures "both the concrete and the ephemeral nature of the seen world and of lived experience and concentrates on the struggle of human consciousness to move beyond space and time into an acceptance of the limits of both that might lead to the repatriation of the exiled soul" (West 1981, 98).

Joseph Tusiani, born more than ninety years ago in the town of San Marco in Lamis (Foggia province), Apulia, is the migrant who came to the United States in 1947 at the age of twenty-three, with a university degree in hand, in search of his father, the father who had emigrated when Tusiani's mother was pregnant with him, the father he had never seen.[6] Tusiani became a naturalized U.S. citizen in 1956 and had for more than sixty years been active in the United States as a poet, translator, critic, lecturer, and professor.

With the now relatively famous verses from "Song of the Bicentennial," "Two languages, two lands, perhaps two souls ... / Am I a man or two strange halves of one?" (Tusiani 1978, 7), Tusiani perfectly verbalizes the plight of the migrant. In *Gente Mia and Other Poems* (1978) and in the autobiographical trilogy *La parola difficile* (1988), *La parola nuova* (1991), and *La parola antica* (1992a) (The Difficult Word, The New Word, and The Ancient Word), published thirteen years after *Gente Mia*,[7] Tusiani speaks precisely to that initial impact he had, as an Italian intellectual, with the United States. In these works, Tusiani examines the major themes that are associated with immigration: the spiritually and psychologically violent act of division from one's family and native land (which is the first experience of the new immigrant), the dreams of the migrant, the prejudice he encounters, the process of Americanization, the question of language, the alienation and the realization that the new world is not the "land of hospitality" he believed it was.

When the emigrant, after a long and wearisome crossing, disembarked at Ellis Island he was immediately faced with the first major obstacle: a strange language. Tusiani knew, as do most of those born in another country, that the emigration odyssey takes many forms, first and foremost coming to terms with the actual, physical separation from the country of birth and from family and friends. This most evident element of emigration is initially the most traumatic. When the migrant arrives in the new country, the voyage is not finished; other "voyages" must be undertaken in the quest to assimilate into mainstream U.S. culture. The most important of these voyages is the linguistic/cultural one. By necessity he must immediately begin the journey from one language, Italian or one of the many Italian dialects, to another, American English. Once the process has begun he slowly, imperceptibly really, begins to lose his native language and the ideas and cultural values that the native language transmits. A cultural transformation begins to take place, and he starts to lose a part of himself. The question of language, or rather loss of language, is of primary importance to Tusiani when discussing the experience of emigration. He introduces this line of reasoning in "Song of the Bicentennial," the first composition of *Gente Mia*, by a series of questions:

> Do I regret my origins by speaking
> this language I acquired? Do I renounce,
> by talking now in terms of only dreams,
> the *sogni* of my childhood? What has changed
> that I had thought unchangeable in me? (Tusiani 1978, 5)

Tusiani looks at the language question not only as a sociological problem but also as a spiritual dilemma. The answer to these questions is that something *has* changed and that every phrase, every word uttered in English, separates him a little bit more from his roots:

> Now every thought I think, each word I say
> detaches me a little more from all
> I used to love— (Tusiani 1978, 7)

For Tusiani when *sogni* becomes *dreams*, *cielo* becomes *sky*, and *mamma* is translated to *mother*, much more transpires than the immigrant's process of Americanization and acculturation. Tusiani, cognizant of the fact that words communicate a plethora of memories, images, and emotions, knew that *cielo* elicits mythicized visions of the old world and that *sky* will only remind the immigrant of the ghetto in the immense concrete jungle he now calls home, and when *mamma* is translated to *mother* much of what was his life begins to disintegrate and will eventually be lost as the immigrant moves farther away from Italy and toward American life and culture:

> Mother, I even wonder if I am
> the child I was, the little child you knew,
> for you did not expect your little son
> to grow apart from all that was your world....
> Yet of a sudden he was taught to say
> "mother" for Mamma, and for cielo "sky."
> That very day, we lost each other. (Tusiani 1978, 5)

Loss of the Italian language (or dialect) is for our poet "a betrayal or denial of his original world—indeed his very origin, his very self" (Tusiani 1982, 153–54).

After many years of writing in English, Tusiani returned to Italian in the autobiographical trilogy, where again he takes up the problem of language. In *La parola antica* (The ancient word), the third volume of the trilogy, he discusses it at length:

> Due lingue. La realtà dello sbarbicamento (uso questo termine per indicare lo sradicamento completo) comporta diversi problemi o traumi, prima di tutto quello di un nuovo linguaggio. Progredendo nell'acquisizione della lingua straniera, si corre il rischio, per ragioni di umana vanità, di ritenere inferiore quella materna?
> ...
> Non si cade in questo pericolo se il fenomeno del bilinguismo lo si considera non come conquista ma come rinnegamento forzato delle proprie origini e di se stessi. Il bilingualismo, cioè, diventa sinonimo di disintegrata unità familiare, per cui una madre non è più in grado di comprendere il proprio figlio. Dal giorno in cui il figlio dice "Mother" per "mamma" e "sky" per "cielo," fra madre e figlio c'è già una separazione spirituale che lo studioso di linguistica non può catalogare. Se le parole sono suoni articolati che simboleggiano e comunicano un'idea, il termine "mamma", a differenza di "mother," il nuovo termine acquisito, simboleggia e comunica un intero mondo di sentimenti che nessuna espressione straniera può comprendere e rispettare. Abolirlo significa rigettare l'esistenza di una fanciullezza intimamente legata a tutti gli episodi, piccoli e grandi, e a tutte le emozioni, importanti e non importanti, connessi ed ispirati da quell'unica parola. Non assimilazione o americanizzazzione, dunque, ma ambivalenza, un'ambivalenza di pensiero e sentimento, di dubbio e di certezza, di sogno e realtà.[8] (Tusiani 1992a, 143–144)

> (Two languages. The reality of eradication [I use this term to indicate complete uprooting] involves several problems or traumas, first of all that of a new language. As we progress in the ac-

quisition of the foreign language, do we run the risk, for reasons of human vanity, of believing that the mother tongue is inferior?

One does not fall into this danger if the phenomenon of bilingualism is seen not as a conquest but as a forced denial of one's origins and of oneself. Bilingualism, that is, becomes synonymous with the disintegration of the family unit, whereby a mother is no longer able to understand her child. From the day the child says "mother" for "Mamma" and "sky" for "cielo," there is already a spiritual separation between mother and child that the scholar of linguistics cannot catalogue. If words are articulate sounds that symbolize and communicate an idea, the term "mamma," unlike "mother," the new term acquired, symbolizes and communicates a whole world of feelings that no foreign expression can understand and respect. Abolishing it means rejecting the existence of a childhood intimately linked to all episodes, small and large, and to all emotions, important and not important, connected and inspired by that one word. Neither assimilation or Americanization, therefore, but ambivalence, an ambivalence of thought and feeling, of doubt and certainty, of dream and reality.)

The consequence of this transformation is that the immigrant, by expressing himself/herself in the acquired tongue, translates not only the language but his very soul, and in that process of translation he slowly and unrelentingly begins to change. He now has the language and the culture of two lands: "America and Italy but in what order? Shouldn't we say: Italy and America?" ("America e Italia; in quale ordine, però? Non dovremmo dire: Italia e America?") (Tusiani 1992, 143).[9] Tusiani poses these questions because he believes that the immigrant cannot totally assimilate into the adopted culture:[10]

> Posta in termini diversi la domanda è: fino a qual punto l'emigrato può assimilare la nuova lingua e la nuova civiltà, e in che maniera dimenticare e rinnegare sé stesso in mezzo alle nuove e impellenti esigenze della sua vita? Anche se la risposta sia priva di validità scientifica, il poeta ci dice che non esiste, e non può

esistere, un assorbimento totale, *e che non potrà mai esserci un'accettazione totale, cioè spirituale, delle tradizioni della nuova terra.* (Tusiani 1992, 143: emphasis mine)

(In different terms, the question is: to what extent can the emigrant assimilate the new language and the new civilization, and how can he forget and disavow himself in the midst of the new and urgent demands of his life? Even if the answer is devoid of scientific validity, the poet tells us that there can't be, and cannot exist, a total absorption, and *that there can never be a total spiritual acceptance of the traditions of the new land.*)

Tusiani's continuous feeling of uprootedness lies primarily within this context of never having fully "spiritually" assimilated into American culture. He expressed it best in his "Song of the Bicentennial":

Then who will solve this riddle of my day?
Two languages, two lands, perhaps two souls. ...
Am I a man or two strange halves of one? (Tusiani 1978, 7)

It is precisely the unsolved riddle and the feeling of being suspended between two worlds, of not belonging, and of navigating between two cultural systems that, I believe, pushes Tusiani to return to Italian, the language of his native land, for his autobiography.[11]

The resolution is his awareness of being suspended between two worlds, his acceptance of his biculturalism, for which, instead of seeing himself as not belonging to either one or the other world, he can accept himself as the man of "two languages, two lands ... two [socio-cultural] souls." After forty years the riddle has been solved. The questions posed in "Song of the Bicentennial" have now become statements (Giordano 1994, 82).

As Paolo Valesio wrote in the introduction to the special issue of *Gradiva*, "Italian Poets in America," "Exile is a slinking beast; it bides its time, without hurry, but it gets you in the end. When all the illusions of moderation and equilibrium and normal routine are gone, we find ourselves face to face with a radical choice" (Valesio 1993, 5). The individual can accept his existential condition as "Other," or he can deny this condition and try to assimilate as much as possible in the new reality and "with a constant policing of all his rebellious thoughts, doubts, or bursts of despair—live out his life as an adoptive existence" (Valesio 1993, 5).

The two poets that I have briefly touched upon confronted their situation in radically different ways. For Cecchetti, the literary journey was different, his creative writing is in Italian; English is the language of his academic work and translation. The intimate ties that he had with Italian culture and with the American West made him one of the original voices of Italian literature in the United States. His continuous drifting back and forth across the border of two cultures gave life to literature that captures both the ephemeral nature of American society and the real concrete nature of a lived experience, concentrated in the effort of human consciousness aimed at pushing beyond space and time toward acceptance of the limits of both.

Tusiani is known as a poet who wrote in four languages[12] and who later in life returned to writing in Italian and his native Gargano dialect to somehow find a solution to his psychological state of being a man divided between two lands and two cultures.[13] But try as he might, all the years living and working in the United States had a profound effect on his life and on his work. In the last episode of the *La parola antica* Tusiani recounts that one day, on an airplane returning from a trip to Italy, he dreams that he finds himself with his mother in a long corridor with many doors illuminated by a bright white light. There is a door at each end of the corridor, one marked "Entrance" and the other marked "Exit." Tusiani and his mother begin walking toward the door marked "Exit." When they get to the end of the corridor they realize that now the sign on the door as changed to "Entrance" and that the door at the other end of the corridor says "Exit":

> Arrivai sotto quella scrittura e lessi "Entrata". Mi voltai e vidi, lì dov'era mia madre la parola "Uscita".... Rifeci il cammino,

ma quando raggiunsi mia madre, in alto, al posto di «Uscita» lessi nuovamente «Entrata». ... E per quaranta volte, affannato, ansioso, con la speranza e la disperazione che mi spingevano e guidavano, corsi da un'estremità all'altra di quell'enorme corridoio. (Tusiani 1992a, 308)

(I arrived at the door and the sign read "Entrance." I turned around and saw, where my mother was, the word "Exit." ... I made my way back, but when I reached my mother, at the top, instead of "Exit," I read "Entrance" again. ... Forty times, breathless, anxious, with the hope and despair that drove me, I ran from one end of that enormous corridor to the other.)

In the middle of his dream, Tusiani is awakened by the flight attendant announcing their arrival in New York City. The book ends with this short paragraph:

Andando verso il Bronx, nella limousine della Poten notai un altro particolare: i tergicristalli, strusciando da destra a sinistra, da sinistra a destra, sembravano dire Entrata-Uscita, Uscita-Entrata, ma non sapevo più che cosa significassero quelle due parole, né a chi fossero rivolte. (Tusiani 1992a, 310)

(Heading toward the Bronx, in the Poten limousine [his brother's petroleum company], I noticed another detail: the windshield wipers, rubbing from right to left, from left to right, they seemed to say Entrance-Exit, Exit-Entrance, but I didn't know what those two words meant, nor to whom they were addressed.)

A careful reading of the last pages of Tusiani's trilogy suggests that maybe the poet has come to an understanding of his condition as Other, and it is really very simple. In the motion of the windshield wipers that seemed to say to him Entrance-Exit, Exit-Entrance, Tusiani finally realizes that he is a man suspended between two worlds, that he is a man of two languages and two souls.

Notes

[1] With regard to the title of this essay: Perez-Firmat's (1994) *Life on the Hyphen* explores the "1.5 Generation" of Cubans that lived on the hyphen, neither one or the other but a fertile hybrid of both, while Tamburri's (1991) original and perceptive *To Hyphenate or Not to Hyphenate?* examines the hyphen from a political, social, and philosophical perspective. Also see Tamburri's (1998) other equally suggestive essay "Rethinking Italian/American Studies: From the Hyphen to the Slash and Beyond," in *Beyond the Margin: Readings in Italian Americana*.

[2] It is important to note that Valesio "refers to himself and other immigrant authors like him as 'expatriates.'" Ruberto and Sciorra (2017, 5) state that "the half-million or so Italians who immigrated to the United States between 1945 and 1973 can be classified as either working-class or elite." They cite Pasquale Verdicchio who writes that "to this day, professionals who have lived outside of Italy for decades have difficulty defining themselves as emigrants/immigrants."

[3] See Carravetta's (1994) insightful review essay.

[4] See Papini's (2007) review of the 2005 translation by Roberta L. Payne of Cecchetti's (1967) *Diario nomade*.

[5] The short stories of *Danza nel deserto* are: "Danza nel deserto," "Il telefono," "Il molo," "Il viale dei pirati," "La baia secca," "Le lettere," "Gl'ingessati," "Il castello," "Gl'ingabbiati," "Il cassone," "La macchina dell'aria," and "L'ascensore."

[6] In the novel *Il deserto dei tartari* (Buzzati [1997]), Giovanni Drogo, a lieutenant, is sent to a distant fortress on the edge of the desert from which an invasion of the Tatars is expected. The invasion does not take place, and the constant training becomes monotonous and without meaning. Many years pass and one day Drogo, now old, becomes ill just as the much-anticipated event happens: The Tatars advance from the desert without him being able to take part in the defense preparations, and Drogo dies, forgotten by all.

[7] The first lines of *La parola difficile* (Difficult Word) are " – Nuova York! Nuova York! Avevo compiuto ventitre anni e ancor non conoscevo mio padre, emigrato in America sei mesi prima che io nascessi." (New York! New New York! I was twenty-three years old and I still did not know my father, who migrated to America six months before I was born.)

[8] The trilogy and *Il ritorno* (Tusiani 1992b) signal a return to Italian.

[9] It is important to note that the trilogy is also the biography of Tusiani's family in America and a grand tour of Italian American history as he understands it.

[10] Also see "Song of the Bicentennial" (Tusiani 1978).

[11] For a more complete analysis, see Siani (1999).

[12] Tusiani studied Italian in school and at the university and spoke it when he was not at home, but his native language is the dialect spoken in San Marco in Lamis (Gargano, Apulia). This is his first language, the language that is full of cultural significance; this can be said about most Italians who grew up speaking dialect at home.

[13] The bibliography on Tusiani is vast. For more information on his treatment of the emigration question, see the bibliography of the Fondo Tusiani (Università

del Salento, founded and curated by Emilo Bandiera until his retirement, and in particular the studies listed in the Works Cited below. See the Fondo Tusiani for his writings in Latin and dialect.

WORKS CITED

Buzzati, Dino. 1997. *Il deserto dei tartari*. Milan: Mondadori.

Carravetta, Peter. 1994. "Review Essay: Border Writing: The Multidimensional Text. D. Emily Hicks Minneapolis: University of Minnesota Press, 1991." In *Differentia: Review of Italian Thought*, edited by Peter Carravetta, 6. Stony Brook, NY: Stony Brook University Press.

Cecchetti, Giovanni. 1967. *Diario nomade*. Padua: Rebellato.

Cecchetti, Giovanni. 1981. *Il villaggio degli inutili*. Venice: Rebellato.

Cecchetti, Giovanni. 1980 *Nel cammino dei monti*. Florence: Vallecchi.

Cecchetti, Giovanni. 1985. *Danza nel deserto*. Venice: Rebellato.

Cecchetti, Giovanni. 1992. *Forum Italicun* 26 (May): 251–252.

Chiappelli, Fredi. 1975. "Sulla poesia di Cecchetti." *Forum Italicum* (June/September): 123–130.

Fontanella, Luigi. 2003. *La parola trasfuga. Scrittori Italiani in America*. Fiesole: Cadmo.

Fontanella, Luigi, and Paolo Valesio, eds. 1993. "Italian Poets in America," a special issue, *Gradiva: International Journal of Italian Literature* 5.1, Stony Brook, NY.

Garofalo, Piero, Elizabeth Leake, and Dana Renga. 2019. *Internal Exile in Fascist Italy: History and Representations of confino*. Manchester, UK: Manchester University Press.

Giordano, Paolo A. 1991. "From Southern Italian Emigrant to Reluctant American: Joseph Tusiani's *Gente Mia and Other Poems*, in *From the Margin: Writings in Italian Americana*, edited by Anthony J. Tamburri, Paolo A. Giordano, and Fred L. Gardaphé, 314–326. West Lafayette, IN: Purdue University Press.

Giordano, Paul, ed. 1994. *Joseph Tusiani Poet Translator Humanist: An International Homage*. New York: Bordighera.

Hicks, D. Emily. 1989. *Border Writing: The Multidimensional Text*. Minneapolis: University of Minnesota Press.

Lettieri, Michael. 1989. "Danza nel deserto: intervista a Giovanni Cecchetti." *Ipotesi* 80(June): 123–130.

Marazzi, Martino. 2011. *A occhi aperti. Letteratura dell'emigrazione e mito americano*. Milan: Franco Angeli.

Papini, Maria Carla. 2007. "Review of Giovanni Cecchetti. *Nomad diary* (Diario nomade)," *Italica* 84, no. 2/3: 651–53.

Perez-Firmat, Gustavo. 1994. *Life on the Hyphen: The Cuban-American Way*.

Petrillo, Raymond, ed. 1997. *Contrappunti / Counterpoints: Selected Prose of Giovanni Cecchetti*. New York: Peter Lang, International Academic.

Ruberto, Laura, and Joseph Sciorra, eds. 2017. *New Italian Migrations in the United States: Art and Culture Since 1945*, Vol. 2. Champaign-Urbana: University of Minnesota Press

Siani, Cosma. 1999. *L'io diviso. Joseph Tusiani fra emigrazione e letteratura*. Rome: Cofine.

Siani, Cosma. 2000. *Two Languages, Two Lands. L'opera letteraria di Joseph Tusiani*. San Marco in Lamis: Quaderni del Sud.

Tamburri, Anthony Julian. 1991. *To Hyphenate or Not to Hyphenate? The Italian/American Writer: An Other American*. Toronto: Guernica.

Tamburri, Anthony Julian. 1998. "Rethinking Italian/American Studies: From the Hyphen to the Slash and Beyond." In *Beyond the Margin: Readings in Italian Americana*, edited by Paolo Giordano and Anthony Julian Tamburri, 243–283. Madison-Teaneck, NJ: Farleigh Dickinson University Press.

Tamburri, Anthony Julian. 2016. "Un rimpatrio linguistico, ovvero un recupero culturale? Il ritorno di Joseph Tusiani." *Italica* 92(2): 338–356.

Tusiani, Joseph. 1978. *Gente mia and Other Poems*. Stone Park, IL: Italian Cultural Center.

Tusiani, Joseph. 1982. "The Themes of Deracination and Americanization in *Gente Mia and Other Poems*." *Ethnic Groups* 4: 149–176.

Tusiani, Joseph. 1988. *La parola difficile: autobiografia di un Italo-Americano*. Bari: Schena.

Tusiani, Joseph. 1991. *La parola nuova autobiografia di un Italo-Americano*. Bari: Schena.

Tusiani, Joseph. 1992a. *La parola antica: autobiografia di un Italo-Americano*. Bari: Schena.

Tusiani, Joseph. 1992b. *Il ritorno*. Bari: Schena.

Valesio, Paolo. 1989. "Writer between Two Worlds: Italian Writing in the United States Today." *Differentia* 3-4 (Spring/Autumn): 259-276.

Valesio, Paolo. 1993. Introduction to "Italian Poets in America," edited by Luigi Fontanella and Paolo Valesio. *Gradiva* 5.1: 5-8.

Valesio, Paolo, and Peter Carravetta, eds. 1993. *Poesaggio*. Quinto di Treviso: Pagus.

Viscusi, Robert. 1981. "*De vulgari eloquentia*: An Approach to the Language of Italian American Fiction." *Yale Italian Studies* I(3): 21-38.

West, Rebecca. 1981. Review of Cecchetti's *Cammino dei monti* (Firenze: Vallecchi, 1980). *Forum Italicum*.

Dancing with Italians in American Culture

Fred Gardaphé

> Since we all inevitably embody our own very particular cultural perspectives, we must do more than look at movement when we write about dance.
>
> Deidre Sklar
> "Five Premises for a Culturally Sensitive Approach to Dance"

This essay is intended to be the first step in the development of an observation that concerns the way Italian American gendered ethnicity has been displayed through the dancing of Italian American male characters in U.S. film and literature, beginning with Rudolph Valentino and ending with John Travolta. Through observations of the cinematic scenes in which Italian American men dance, I believe we can observe the ways Italian notions of masculinity have confronted wider traditional American notions of masculinity to form what I will call Italian American masculinities.

Notions of Italian American masculinity are the result of the interaction of centuries of Italianate masculinities coming into contact with a variety of others that have developed into one type of "American man," a man who was expected to protect the honor of his family by controlling his women. A woman's purity—the chastity of a daughter and the faithfulness of a wife—reflected a man's public esteem. Over the years, men devised ways of restraining women's desires, monitoring female behavior, and rectifying violations.

It wasn't until the great wave of Italian immigration of the early twentieth century that American masculinity began to feel threatened by aspects of Italian masculinity. Most of the earliest Italian immigrants were men who came to make money and planned to return to Italy. A great number of these men lived with fellow Italian workers or boarded with Italian families. Other Americans were fearful of the early Italian immigrants, who were characterized in newspapers and literature as dark, dirty, and dangerous strangers. Newspapers were filled with accounts of urban crime attributed to the Italian immigrants. It was felt that without the refining influences of women, and lacking the traditional social controls that modified male behavior, the men would not only become corrupted but also turn their corrupting behavior toward American women. Such thinking led to the characterization of the Italian immigrant man as the brute. Even Henry James, an Italophile, disassociated himself from Italian immigrants, characterizing them once as "gross aliens to a man" (James 1907, 231).

While viewed as transgressive in many ways, the Italian male was deemed threatening only in the context of ethnic neighborhoods or workplaces until he began to appear in yellow journalistic accounts of crime and in movie theaters, via the early depictions of dark criminals in films such as *The Black Hand* (1906) and *The Musketeers of Pig Alley* (1912) and the swarthy seducer through Rudolph Valentino (*The Sheik* 1921) and *The Four Horsemen of the Apocalypse* (1921). Valentino's impact on American masculinity has been well documented by Gaylyn Studlar, Giorgio Bertellini, and others. Early on, as Studlar (1996) writes, "Valentino was easily dismissed as one of the 'menial and sensual' immigrants who made their living by exploiting women's desire for the morally and sexually dubious pleasures that surrounded night club and tango tea dancing" (152). During the 1960s, traditional notions of American manhood were being challenged by feminism and gay liberation. Italian American men evidence a traditional patriarchal sense of manhood derived from an Italian model that confronted the American model of the strong, silent, level-headed, and prone-to-violence male earlier presented in television and film portrayals of cowboys, soldiers, and detectives. Therefore, they made good foils for these new ideologies. The American idea of using shows of strength and violence to establish and maintain honor was still clung to even as the efficacy of patriarchy was disappearing.

The all-consuming nature of U.S. popular culture during this period presented opportunities for men like Joe DiMaggio and Frank Sinatra to project Italian American manliness onto a national screen and become role models for American men. One way of proving unquestionable masculinity as well as loyalty to the United States was performing military service during World War II; nearly 500,000 Italian Americans served in the armed forces, a higher proportion than any other ethnic group. Another means of expressing masculinity would be the display of the proper place for a man during such ritual actions as public dancing. This Italian American manliness has usually gone hand-in-hand with a certain troublesomeness to the greater American way of thinking, however. From the sweaty workers in the Boston Common who alarmed Henry James (1907), to the exotic Rudolph Valentino's sensuous strides across the silver screen and into the hearts of American women, from the cocky strut of dapper gangsters across TV screens, to the gold-chained disco dude played by John Travolta, the Italian American man has been called on whenever a breach of status quo civility needed to be displayed, especially through the body.

Using examples from the films *The Four Horsemen of the Apocalypse, Little Caesar* (1921), *The Godfather* (1972), *The Godfather Part II* (1974), and *Saturday Night Fever* (1977), I will demonstrate that the development and reception of images of Italian American masculinities have derived and depended on those images first presented by the characters Valentino portrayed in his films. What I want to consider is the impact Valentino had on subsequent generations of Italian American performers who have carried the torch as "Latin Lovers" for three generations, and the role he played in shaping the future of American masculinity through to the era of the metrosexual man. I will focus on the dancing performances of Italian American characters in these films to show how Italian American masculinity avoided and then incorporated the Valentinian flair, turning it into an acceptable expression of American manhood. In the end, I argue that in a little over fifty years, the marginalized version of Valentino's masculinity becomes an accepted mainstream performance by the time we get to John Travolta's portrayal of Tony Manero in *Saturday Night Fever*.

RUDOLPH VALENTINO

Valentino early on was looked at as the exotic, foreign Other—"considered to be especially cunning in his exploitation of woman's 'dance madness.' Tango pirates of suspect lower-class, often immigrant backgrounds were believed to be using their access to middle-class women at afternoon tango teas to begin relationships that elevated them up the class ladder," and it is these immigrants who "inevitably defied normative standards of robust, ebulliently childish American masculinity," in the process becoming "an insidious threat to the nation" for their ability to mix itself into the nation's blood (Studlar 1996, 152).

Valentino is responsible for one of the earliest displays of Italian American masculinity on display through dances, and while he is not playing an Italian American character in *The Four Horsemen of the Apocalypse*, his dancing in it carried over beyond the film to represent Italianate masculinity in U.S. culture, one that is more inclined to do what is necessary to please and pleasure his woman. What surfaces in the scene in which Valentino dances the tango is the way a man could assert himself among other men and take control of a woman through dance. This scene is also one of the earliest in which an Italian American actor dances on the screen. The key component in this scene is the closeness of Valentino (as Julio Desnoyers) to Virginia Warwick (as Chichi). Throughout the dance he tantalizes Chichi and, in the process, forces American masculinity to confront new possibilities, as Studlar (1996) notes:

> In *Four Horsemen of the Apocalypse* dance also provides a nuanced physical revelation suggesting that the beautiful but misogynist man possesses a latent capacity to be another kind of lover, one who combines strength and tenderness. In dance, the hero's authoritative masculinity promises sexual excitement, but women spectators, like romance readers, may see something else in his refined face. They may see, in Radway's words, that he is

Dancing with Italians in American Culture

also "a man who is capable of the same attentive observation and intuitive 'understanding' that they believe women regularly accord to men." (174)

This understanding includes total concentration on the dancer's partner, which is something that is eventually lost as the Valentino image makes its way through Italian American performance history. Through Valentino, writes Studlar, Hollywood "generated a fantastic vision of the reconciliation of masculinity and femininity through a privileging of the dancer's body as a site of expressive knowledge and sexual understanding" (198). Valentino's subsequent performances moved away from this "threatening" vision of the "woman-made man." In later films such as *The Eagle* (1925) he took on a more "American" one that is a more reserved and calculated display of masculinity, which Studlar suggests makes for "a more athletic Fairbanks-style Slavic hero" (198).

With the contrast between the Fairbanks and Valentino styles suggested, it is curious/intriguing that we see Fairbanks's son Douglas Jr. cast as the Italian American gangster turned dancer in the 1931 film *Little Caesar*. This might have been a role that could have been offered to Rudolph Valentino had the actor lived long enough and successfully made the transition to the talkies. Fairbanks's Americanized Italian dancer Joe Massara presents a version of masculinity that contrasts that of the old-fashioned gangster, Rico Bandello, played by Edward G. Robinson. Bandello presents what Peter Lehman (2007) calls "a failed masculinity" that leads to his ruin (Studlar 1996, 193).

In the major dance scene of this film we get a different version of the Italian American dancing. Here we see Fairbanks playing an Italian American gangster turned professional dancer. He and his partner Glenda Farrell (as Olga) are both wearing formal clothes, and the distance between the two as they dance is safe and socially acceptable. Dance represents a way that a former gangster can become a legitimate success, and this message becomes the final scene in the film in which the dying Rico gazes up at the billboard featuring the success of his former gangster accomplice turned dancer.

This movement toward assimilation can be seen in the effect it has on subsequent representations of Italian American men dancing in films. As Giorgio Bertellini points out, in order to achieve public recognition Italian immigrants needed to achieve a sense of national belonging, which they were encouraged to seek through such institutions as "the Italian Catholic Church, the ethnic press, and urban popular entertainments" (691). Bertellini shows us how Mussolini fit the white American sense of manliness which was "centered on personality, attractiveness, perfectibility and self-creation through consumption ... while still indebted to Victorian precepts of character, athleticism, self-reliance and integrity" (699). It is this middle-class sense of masculinity we see portrayed in later films with Italian American men dancing in the American way. In such films Italian American men begin moving away from the exotic manly Otherness represented by the "deviant masculinity" of Valentino (Bertellini 2005, 691). Bertellini explains, "Caught between urgencies of national identity and pressing experiences of popular culture and new gender relations, the Italian American press offered a familiar polemical devaluation of mass culture as feminine and an equally familiar and polemical endorsement of high modernist notions of masculinity and national identity as the realm of discipline, vigorous character, and self-control" (699).

POSTWAR FILMS: *THE GODFATHER* AND *SATURDAY NIGHT FEVER*

This is the very assimilation we find reflected in the dancing scenes of *The Godfather*. Early on in the film we see Don Corleone (Marlon Brando) dancing a waltz with his wife, showing that the dancing man has his place in proper social/familial settings. Later in the film, Michael Corleone (played by Al Pacino) dances at his wedding in Sicily. In both of these scenes, the dancing Italian American men gaze not at their partners, but at the audience that surrounds them. Public dancing becomes more of a performance of a social expectation and responsibility than a show of attraction, seduction, or intimacy. Attention is drawn to the dancer only when something goes wrong. For example, in a scene from *The Godfather Part II* Fredo's wife dances with another man at the evening reception and falls on the dance floor—an exhibition of the loss of self-control. The shot cuts from the falling wife to Fredo, standing at a table. Fredo's masculinity is further dismantled as he observes his wife. The woman is escorted away, shouting about how Fredo is a mama's boy, and ultimately the message is that Fredo cannot control his woman. The Italianate notion of *bella figura*, or the importance of maintaining one's composure in the face of trouble, making a good impression through dress and behavior, does not allow for public dancing to turn into a spectacle, and so Fredo and his wife demonstrate *brutta figura*, making herself and her husband look bad in public. This theme of dancing as proper between a man and his wife becomes the final sequence in the final *Godfather* film as an elderly Michael Corleone imagines, just before he dies, the dancing he's done throughout his life with his daughter and his wives.

The images of the gangster in *The Godfather* films, as I have argued in an earlier study, strongly reflect a traditional and dying notion of American masculinity, one that morphs into the new Italian American man presented in the 1977 film *Saturday Night Fever* in the character of Tony Manero (played by John Travolta). Writer and critic Bethan Roberts makes the point that "*Saturday Night Fever* brought the nostalgic Corleone masculinities into the future of the 2001 Odyssey where Italian-American-ness finally had a chance to strut without leaving a trail of bodies in its wake." But I would argue that it is not the lack of violence evoked through Travolta's character that reflects his difference from earlier portrayals of Italian American masculinity; it is rather his narcissism, reflecting the Me Generation of the 1970s and 1980s, that enables the ghost of Valentino to return to tantalize American women and men.

Travolta's character struggles with his masculinity everywhere but on the dance floor. He does this first through interactions with his father, who teases his son throughout the film. As David Buchbinder writes, the conflict between father and son in *Saturday Night Fever* is one that "can be understood as a rite of passage that gives the central male character—the dancer—entry into the community of men as autonomous and fully masculine" (Buchbinder 2004). "The male body is thus often represented in motion, self-absorbed (even, as in the case of Travolta and Swayze, when there is a female partner present) sexualized and eroticized through the very action of putting itself on display" (Bertellini 2005, 717).

We see this in one of the early dance scenes of the film. Tony Manero takes to the dance floor and performs a memorable solo without a partner and in the process creates a spectacle of himself that attracts the attention and admiration of women and men. Jeff Ynac (1996) suggests that it is Travolta who connects the divide between traditional American masculinity and the exotic challenged version posited by Valentino. Ynac writes:

> The ... representation(s) of the male body (specifically the body of Travolta) as erotic spectacle and their attempts to repair the rift between Hollywood's traditionally polarized definitions of active masculinity/power and passive femininity/objectification form a fascinating look into Hollywood's strategies for fetishizing the eroticized male body ... the film's objectification of Travolta's body is countered by a blatantly overdetermined construction of masculinity, most notably achieved through Travolta's narcissistic gaze upon himself. However, one representation does not overrule the other, but rather the two work together to create a multiplicity of potential sexual identities and pleasures for the viewing audience, indicating the potential fluidity of cultural gender identities contained within this single male figure. (Ynac, 39)

As evidenced in the dance contest scene toward the end of the film, Travolta's Italian American masculinity turns an about-face from Valentino's as Tony Manero rarely looks into the eyes of his dancing partner and shows his face to the audience as though he were performing solo. With this character Travolta reflects what has been characterized by sociologist Donald Tricarico (1991) as guido culture, an Italian American youth subculture that looks to popular culture and entertainment for fashioning self-expression.

And while Tricarico suggests that guido culture was created in response to the film, I would argue that the opposite is the case.

Saturday Night Fever showed the Italian American male at work and play, but mostly playing at work, living for the escape that a nightclub might offer: a chance, for some, to strut their stuff in public and be someone who gets attention from the people around them. The key of this film is that the Italian American male is once again in the spotlight, performing, but this time without the overt threat to his "masculinity" that Valentino faced. If the distance between men and women when dancing can show the degree of seduction, then a comparison of the space between Julio Desnoyers and his partner and Tony Manero and his has much to say about the change from an Italianate masculinity to an Italian American masculinity.

Real testaments from Italian American participants in the real Disco World upon which the *Fever* film was based report that it distorted the image of the Italian American man. Carl Capotorto's (2008) memoir *Twisted Head* captures the film's shortcomings: "When *Saturday Night Fever* came out, a couple of years later, my friends and I scoffed: Travolta's game was corny. He wasn't doing it right. His partner couldn't dance at all. We were the real thing, and we knew it" (Capotorto 210). Capotorto comments on the real-life dancing:

> I loved the stillness and swivel in the hips as the feet worked fancifully; the elegant, high-speed port de bras; the drama of the dance itself, swelling with the swell of the music; loved the look on my partner's face, my hand on her hip, our wordless communication, my authority in leading. I earned a reputation for making any girl, no matter how inexperienced, look good on the dance floor. (Capotorto, 211)

Looking good on the dance floor is what matters now, as dance is no longer about seducing the woman but about showing off the self and seducing the audience. While the notion of *sprezzatura*, or the art of making an action look effortless, still is maintained, the purpose of the show has changed. An interesting aside here is that throughout his career Travolta's sexuality has been questioned by tabloids just as was Rudolph Valentino's, and Travolta was chosen to star in the biopic that was to be made on Valentino. But who either of them has slept with matters not, especially when you consider that Valentino's masculinity, and to some extent Travolta's, are both shaped by women. That is to say that there is a different sensitivity and expression to Italian masculinity that challenges very strict notions of old-fashioned American masculinity.

It is a short distance from the guido to the contemporary idea of the metrosexual: "a young man with money to spend, living in or within easy reach of a metropolis—because that's where all the best shops, clubs, gyms, and hairdressers are. He might be officially gay, straight, or bisexual, but this is utterly immaterial because he has clearly taken himself as his own love object and pleasure as his sexual preference" (Capotorto 2008, 210). And there can be no doubt that both actors have had a role in developing this version of American masculinity. Women have always played a role in the creation of masculinity. Michael Morris (1991) noted that Valentino's performances of masculinity were certainly shaped by his second wife Natacha Rambova, and Mario Puzo revealed that he based Don Vito Corleone on his mother (Gardaphé 2006).

It has taken over two generations for the woman-made marginalized masculinity of Rudolph Valentino to make it into the center of U.S. masculinity. We have come a long way from the criticized Italian dancer to the emulated Italian American dancer, and throughout the process the evolution has retained a strong thread fashioned by Valentino back in the 1920s that passed through the fabric of the Tonys and Guidos straight into the heart of U.S. masculinity. Study of Italian American actors and characters dancing in films such as Michael Cimino's *The Deer Hunter* (1978), Andrew Bergman's *The Freshman* (1990), and Martin Brest's *The Scent of a Woman* (1992) would enhance continued exploration of dance performance and its impact on the representation of Italian American masculinity.

WORKS CITED

"Badham: Sex and Spaghetti." http://www.spikemagazine.com/0996godf.php,SpikeMagazine.com, September 1 (accessed May 31, 2009).

Bertellini, Giorgio. 2005. "Duce/Divo: Masculinity, Racial Identity, and Politics among Italian Americans in 1920s New York City." *Journal of Urban History* 31.5: 685–726.

Buchbinder, David. 2004. "The Sign of the Dancing Men: Negotiations of Masculinity in Film Musicals." https://performing.artshub.com.au/news-article/bits-and-blogs/performing-arts/professor-david-buchbinder/the-sign-of-the-dancing-men-negotiations-of-masculinity-in-film-musicals-66700 (accessed October 15, 2020).

Capotorto, Carl. 2008. *Twisted Head: An Italian American Memoir*. New York: Broadway Books.

Gardaphé, Fred. 2006. *From Wiseguys to Wise Men*. New York, NY: Routledge.

James, Henry. 1907. *The American Scene*. London: Chapman & Hall.

Lehman, Peter. 2007. *Running Scared: Running Scared: Masculinity and the Representation of the Male Body*. Detroit: Wayne State University Press 109.

Morris, Michael. 1991. *Madame Valentino: The Many Lives of Natacha Rambova*. New York: Abbeville Press.

Roberts, Bethan. 1996. "Francis Ford Coppola: *The Godfather*: *Saturday Night Fever*: John Badham: *Sex and Spaghetti*." *Spike* magazine. https://spikemagazine.com/0996godf/ (accessed October 15, 2020).

Sklar, Diedre. 2001. "Five Premises for a Culturally Sensitive Approach to Dance." In *Moving History/Dancing Cultures*, edited by Ann Dils and Ann Cooper Albright, 30–32. Middletown, CT: Wesleyan University Press.

Studlar, Gaylyn. 1996. *This Mad Masquerade*: *Stardom and Masculinity in the Jazz Age*. New York: Columbia University Press.

Tricarico, Donald. 1991. "Guido: Fashioning an Italian American Youth Style." *Journal of Ethnic Studies* 19.1(Spring): 41–66.

Ynac, Jeff. 1996. "More Than a Woman: Music, Masculinity and Male Spectacle in *Saturday Night Fever* and *Staying Alive*." *Velvet Light Trap, New Masculinities* 38: 39–50.

"He made us all look like gavones": Marking *Cafoneria* and Policing the Boundaries of Propriety, Taste, and Ethnic Identity among Italian Americans

Joseph Sciorra

On March 12, 2012, Queens College's John D. Calandra Italian American Institute screened Abel Ferrrara's 2010 film *Mulberry St.* as part of its Documented Italians film and video series. The documentary details preparations for the annual San Gennaro *festa* in New York City's Little Italy. Ferrara explains in the film that the street feast "brings all the characters out," as he introduces viewers to individuals like Butchie the Hat, Cha Cha, Joey Cigar, Baby John, and other local nicknamed personalities who reminisce about the feast in the time before Mayor Rudolph Giuliani intervened to rid the popular event of organized crime. *Mulberry St.*, with its indecorous characters, recurrent profanity, and non-linear narrative, is neither a conventional documentary nor an attempt at ethnic boosterism.

The film elicited a wide range of reactions from the audience, which was an eclectic mix of scholars and the general public, during the post-screening Q&A with the director. One audience member, an older woman[1], visibly irate, told the director, "The people in that film are a bunch of gavones, and you're the king of gavones!" She concluded by telling Ferrara bluntly that he should burn his film. This exchange, while passionate at times, eventually led to a more tempered conversation about the role of documentary films, a director's point of view, the history of Italian Americans in New York City, and cinematic depictions of that group.

The judgmental sentiment and power of the contemporary pejorative *gavone* (also spelled *gavon*), and its Italian source word, *cafone*, are pervasive among Italian Americans, especially on the East Coast. In his Italian American "cultural lexicon," literary scholar Pellegrino D'Acierno (1999a) declares that *cafone* "is one of the key terms in Italian American social language" (xxxvii).[2] In its most rudimentary definition *cafone*/gavone signifies a person who exhibits bad taste and engages in low-class behaviors. (While the two words share common meanings, differences exist in the U.S. context, as I explore below.) But the fungibility of the words' meanings point to not only their evolution in the United States but also to the situational and historically grounded context of their use: "a simple, country bumpkin" (Tedesco 1999, 360); "a vulgar fool" (Gambino 1975, 309); a "cultureless" individual (Firmani 2017, 66); a "man of no soul" (Covello 1972, 80); a gluttonous "pig" ("gavone" 2004); or a "rough punk, gorilla" (Rieder 1985, 28).[3] The words' shifting definitions highlight the need to be aware of who is speaking and in what context in order to understand the social implications of *cafoneria*—the state of gavoneness—for such opinions often reveal less about the people being discussed and more about the individuals ascribing value judgment.

This emic reproach of aesthetics and morality is of critical concern for formulating group identity. My interest is principally with the consequences of taste regimes on group identity and less on the individual engagement by Italian Americans in their everyday lives with in-group judgments about taste. My contention is that *cafoneria*/gavoneness is at the heart of Italian American cultural praxis, a practice that functions both historically and in the contemporary moment to shape and construct both an aesthetic and a moral topography. While this near-obsessive judging of perceived slights in decorum of personal presentation has existed historically, this criticism has also become a significant way for policing perceived infractions of group representations, especially in mass media. Specifically, self-appointed Italian ethnic leaders, often heads of regional and national voluntary associations, have taken up the charge of monitoring the public image of Italian

Americans in recent times by issuing rebukes of fellow ethnics based on alleged lack of class-based refinement that is informed by the lingering specter of the gavone.

The Italian American marking of *cafoneria* in the public sphere is fundamentally about delineating the porous borders of distinction around class-based interpretations and definitions of group identity. This policing of the gavone is also informed by highly gendered and racialized understandings of the term whereby it primarily refers to particular notions of masculinity and whiteness that have developed in twentieth-century United States. This gendered and racialized preoccupation with taste is the product of a stigmatized identity that is the legacy of an economically exploited Southern Italy and its peoples who have been historically stereotyped as provincial, underdeveloped, and violent in the popular imagination as well as the racialized bigotry and, at times, violent discrimination in the United States against Southern Italian immigrants and their American-born children. Ultimately this internalized inferiority is fueled by Italian Americans' deep-seated preoccupation with their historical denigration by non–Italian Americans, most importantly middle-class white Americans.

I approach this cultural apprehension through a three-pronged reading of Pierre Bourdieu's examination of taste regimes, Erving Goffman's understanding of stigma, and Robert Viscusi's discussion of the internalized colonialism afflicting self-esteem. I begin by tracing the sociolinguistic formulations of the term *cafone* in Italy, in particular Southern Italy, and then among Italian immigrants in the United States. My cultural history continues with a look at the emergence of the Italian American word *gavone* in popular discourse, literature, and consumer culture, with a focus on an episode of the TV show *The Sopranos* (HBO, 1999–2007). Finally, I examine contemporary ethnic spokespeople's public critiques of media images concerning perceived breaches in behavior through the lens of the 2017 Anthony Scaramucci scandal. My intention is to shed light on the supremacy of the endemic concept of gavone for Italian Americans so as to illuminate the ways by which group identity is shaped, managed, and policed in the public sphere.

CAFONE IN ITALY

One cannot properly understand the Italian American term *gavone* without an overview of its origin word *cafone* in Italy, in particular its development as an expression of class disparagement in the Mezzogiorno (Southern Italy). The word has come to be associated with a stigmatized and racialized South that has durable permutations. Despite changing meanings over time and space, the stigma the two related words convey has historical reverberations that impact contemporary scenarios.

According to the Garzanti Italian dictionary, *cafone* has two meanings: *contadino* (peasant), used primarily in the South, and by extension, *persona villana, zotica, maleducata* (a rude, boorish, ill-mannered person) ("cafone" 1990, s.v.). Garzanti's Italian-English dictionary translates the word as "oaf, lout, clod" ("cafone" 1972, s.v.). Philologist Antonio Vinciguerra, responding to queries about the word's origins and debunking popular derivations on the website of the Accademia della Crusca—the authoritative society dedicated to the Italian language—states that *cafone* comes from Southern Italian languages (dialects) and that its etymology harkens back to the Latin word *cavare*, "to dig up the dirt." The word's association with peasants, the land, and the agricultural world is evident from various Southern Italian terms that Vinciguerra offers, such as *pane cafone* (peasant bread, Campania), *cafoneria* (a large room for workers in a farm house, Apulia), and *cafunishe* (a shepherd's terracotta bowl, Abruzzo) (Vinciguerra 2017).

Perhaps no better example of the usage of the word *cafoni* to signify *peasants* can be found than in Ignazio Silone's 1933 Fascist-era novel *Fontamara*, in which their abysmal conditions as landless agricultural workers in Abruzzo are starkly and cogently presented. Importantly, given the specifics of the Italian language and the context here, *cafoni* refers to both men and women:

At the head of everything is God, the Lord of Heaven. Everyone knows that.
Then comes Prince Torlonia, lord of the earth.
Then come Prince Torlonia's guards.
Then come Prince Torlonia's guard's dogs.
Then, nothing at all.
Then, nothing at all.
Then, nothing at all.
Then come the *cafoni*. And that's all. (Silone 2000, 26)[4]

This harrowing passage provides a succinct view of the subaltern position of Southern Italian peasantry with regard to the word *cafone* and its various permutations and associations as they developed in Italy and subsequently in the United States. Given this economic, social, and political subjugation, it is no surprise that the culture of subaltern Italian peasantry—that is, their knowledge and skills, or what Antonio Gramsci (1991) refers to as "folklore," which he defines as their "conception of the world and life" that historically was positioned "in opposition . . . to 'official' conceptions of the world" (189)—was in turn devalued and deemed worthless, a dominated aesthetic.

The semantic shift from *peasant* to *ill-mannered* highlights the way in which the term has traveled across fluctuating boundaries where different social classes meet and interact. This linguistic transference occurs first in Neapolitan and Sicilian languages (not Tuscan-based Italian) during the eighteenth century, if not earlier, according to Vinciguerra (2017) who notes that the new meaning develops among urban dwellers who saw rural workers/*cafoni* as boorish, leading to the word *cafone* becoming associated with anyone exhibiting such traits.[5] This shift occurs in other parts of Italy as well where the words *villano* and *bifolco*, used for different rural workers, come to take on negative connotations similar to *cafone*. The Italian understanding of urbanity, or *civiltà*, is bound up with townspeople's notion of proper behavior—decorum, refinement, education—that is enacted through the cultural capital of language, dress, and comportment (Silverman 1975, 4) to help establish and maintain a sense of identity and belonging that stands in marked contrast to the culture and practices of the countryside. This marking of distinctions, what Pierre Bourdieu (1984) suggests is "a practical mastery of distributions" (465), in which classifications of subtle and glaring differences and aesthetic dispositions among social classes are noted and all too often judged, are manifested in the habitus of everyday life (Bourdieu 1991, 82–83), from embodied practices to consumer products. The defining of *civiltà* emerges with the mixing of social classes, as lower-class individuals find themselves in situations and among others in which their class-based knowledge, practices, and aesthetics come up against the dominating class and its practices, which have been deemed normative and hegemonic. Thus, the rough behavior of an ill-bred person becomes pronounced in social situations where class borders are breached. The resulting condescension toward peasants deepened as Italy experienced historical shifts toward modernity and nation building after unification in 1861, resulting in an entrenched disdain for what would be characterized as a *cultura negata*, or a denied culture (Carbonaro and Nesti 1975), of subaltern peasantry.[6]

A noteworthy development in the term's loaded and layered cultural meanings is its entrance into the Italian national vocabulary, which occurs after the unification of Italy (Vinciguerra 2017). The *cafone* as peasant/lout became racially coded in the developing national imaginary as specifically Southern Italian and imbued with a litany of negative attributes in the ideological construction of the Other in keeping with the contiguous epithet *terrone* (of the land) applied against Southern Italians by Northern Italians. This stigmatization is rooted in the subaltern conditions of the impoverished Mezzogiorno, which Northern elites, in control of the government, the economy, and the media, not only militarily occupied and subjugated the South to an internal colonization but also othered its people in a racialized discourse of essentialized inferiority. As Gramsci notes in "Some Aspects of the Southern Question," in the Mezzogiorno political subjugation and economic exploitation by Northern politicians and businessmen were coupled with a racializing project of ascription and abjection:

"He made us all look like gavones"

> It is well known what kind of ideology has been disseminated in innumerable ways of the propagandists of the bourgeoisie among the masses of the North: The South is the ball and chain that prevents a more rapid progress in the civil development of Italy; Southerners are biologically inferior beings, either semi-barbarians or out and out barbarians by natural destiny; if the South is underdeveloped it is not the fault of the capitalist system, or any historical cause, but by the nature that has made Southerners lazy, incapable, criminal, and barbaric. (1995, 20)[7]

The Mezzogiorno was not merely backward but was linked inextricably to nonwestern and "uncivilized" spaces like Africa and Asia, with all the associated pathologies of these non-European topographies (Dickie 1999, 106); thus it and its inhabitants were racialized as inferior. The national project involved the promotion of a *civiltà italiana* (Gabaccia 2000, 8–9; see also Choate 2008) that is based on cosmopolitan Northern Italian elite culture, which privileged idealized depictions of ancient Rome and the Renaissance and did so in standard Tuscan Italian. The alterity of the Mezzogiorno as a marginalized place out of time with a modern, progressive Italy and its uneducated and racialized inhabitants was established at that moment when Italy's impoverished and desperate citizenry, its *cafoni*, were compelled to migrate in order to survive.[8]

CAFONE IN IMMIGRANT UNITED STATES

For immigrants in the United States, *cafone* still referenced their former subaltern status in Southern Italy, an internalized inferiority that spurred many toward a form of economic justice that the possibility of an industrialized United States could offer to some. And by and large the word, when used in English, became mostly associated with men and different forms of masculinity. For the protagonist of *The Grand Gennaro*, Garibaldi Lapolla's 1935 novel, a *cafone*'s hurt and resentment at an exploitative system of oppression is palpably articulated. Early on in the novel, when a discussion during dinner in a Harlem boarding house turns to repatriation, the immigrant Gennaro Accuci declares in an angry outburst that he will not return to his Calabrian village where he once bowed in servility to his social superiors: "What was I out home?[9] A nobody, dirt off the street-walks, a *cafone*! There were those that were my better.... Here I am Gennaro Accuci and proud of it. I bow to no one" (Lapolla 2009, 37). In the diaspora this fictionalized character can reject Italy's exploitative system that led to his emigration while at the same time battling a new world capitalism in his "making America" (8).

The concept of the low-class *cafone* among Italian immigrants was exacerbated by the bigotry they experienced in the United States at the hands of the dominant host society. Many of the racist ideologies developed in Italy about Southern Italians migrated along with immigrants to the United States and informed the xenophobia and violence waged against Italian immigrants deemed unfit for U.S. citizenship due to ascribed negative attributes (e.g., violent criminality, a "pagan" form of Catholicism, adherence to radical politics). An internalized inferiority was honed and made acute in response to the racialized prejudice, discrimination, and at times violence against the four and half million Italian citizens who migrated to the United States and their American-born children (Luconi 2007, 33–44; Stella and Franzina 2009, 283–311). All too often internal differences were marked by Italian immigrants through the frame of the deleterious larger U.S. society and the broad-brush strokes in which all Italian immigrants were painted. The *cafone* quickly became imbued with the emotional and intellectual responses to white America's discrimination against all Italians at the time.[10]

In the first quarter of the twentieth century the opprobrium of the *cafone* moniker could also refer to those Southern Italian immigrants who wanted to "make America" by working in order to repatriate expeditiously to their hometown, buy property, and live above their previous status. According to an unpublished account of one Sicilian community in New York City, members of a "superior class" of immigrants from Cinisi (Palermo province) for whom "a good name for the Italians is a requisite of their progress," referred to their compatriots who did not "feel injured whenever the Italian name is hurt" because their primary concern was in working and making enough money for their eventual return home as *caffoni* (a Sicilian spelling) (Park and Miller 1921, 104). This anecdotal account reveals the class differences and divergent priorities between the emergent *prominenti* (literally, the prominent ones) of immigrants—those well-to-do immigrants who positioned themselves as community leaders—and the vast majority of the working class.[11] As had happened in Italy, it was the *prominenti*'s ideology and interests, often conservative and self-serving, that in their attempt to circumvent a racialized stigma through social distinction would take precedence over those of the new-world *cafoni* and establish a pattern with lasting consequences.[12]

In the ever-changing social conditions of Italian immigrant life, especially in a cosmopolitan and global city such as New York City, which was the principal port of arrival and primary place of settlement for the large wave of Italian migrants, it became increasingly difficult to discern who was a *cafone* and who was a *prominente*. One of the ways ambitious working-class immigrants negotiated the emerging cultural landscape was through a process of mimesis in which class emulation and appropriation of objects and behaviors served to announce and mark a perceived and/or desired status change.[13] And yet they were often understood emically as arrivistes who in their social striving were unable to shed fully the habitus—that "matrix of perceptions, appreciations, and actions" (Bourdieu 1991, 83)—of their previous *cafone* selves and who lacked the cultural capital to achieve fully their new-world transformations. It was popular culture in the form of staged performances and mass-produced recordings that exposed the class affectations of the *prominenti*. Perhaps the most astute observers of these incipient immigrant parvenus were the comic lyricist Carlo "Tony" Ferrazzano and the performer Eduardo "Farfariello" Migliaccio.

FIGURE 1. Eduardo "Farfariello" Migliaccio in character. Courtesy: John D. Calandra Italian American Institute, Queens College, City University of New York.

Via numerous stage skits and musical recordings these immigrant artists expressed the trials and tribulations of the working-class poor, those who were befuddled by the topsy-turvy world of New York City, swindled out of their hard-earned pennies, belittled for their accented English, and bullied by the representatives of U.S. power such as the police and judges. With his wildly popular musical comedy routines, Migliaccio in particular was a champion of the *cafoni* and a sympathetic observer of their quotidian travails expressed in the macaronic immigrant parlance that combined Italian, Neapolitan, and English.[14] In doing so Migliaccio and Ferrazzano simultaneously held up for satirical examination the immigrant—most often identified as a man—who had succeeded financially and/or socially and who still acted and sounded like a *cafone*.[15] Musical routines like "Il Cafone Arrichito" (The *cafone* who gets rich) and "Il Cafone Presidente della Società della Festa a Sant'Antonio" (The *cafone* president of the St. Anthony Society) were caricatures of former peasants who became rich and worked their way up the immigrant social ladder but remained unaware of their delusional self-image of grandeur while exhibiting boorishness to others (Romeyn 2008, 115–116). Here is where Farfariello in particular is perhaps most trenchant because his theatrical depictions point to the emergent class of successful immigrant businessmen and leaders, who, while entering the ranks of the *prominenti*, not only remain *cafoni* but create what I consider to be a new category of Italian American, that of the *cafone prominente*, whose legacy it can be said continues to present day. The *cafone prominente* is so concerned with his self-promotion and success that everyday bounds of civility are abandoned.

In addition to and perhaps also coupled with the *cafone prominente* is the Italian immigrant who in his desire to assimilate is embarrassed by being Italian, abandons use of Italian (and/or regional languages), and enthusiastically praises the Unites States at the expense of a routinely disparaged Italy (Livingston 1918, 218). A wonderful example of such a figure is found in the 1917 song "Lu cafone patriota" (The patriotic *cafone*), which holds up for examination and criticism those that make false comparisons between Italian and U.S. society and practices:

> Quell'uomo che disprezza la nazione
> e la provincia sua è un animale,
> peggio del mio compare, un mascalzone,
> 'mbicillo e nce lo fa sapé Pasquale.
> Il mio compare, salvo in sangiovanne,
> è un grande porco, quell'animalone!
> Non parla maie, pure si lu scanne,
> la lengua italiana, quell cafone!
>
> Dice che nell'America,
> per lui e un grande scorno
> se parla 'taliano,
> per questo qualche giorno
> lo prendo a calci a paccchere,
> gli do una lezione,
> per farle rispettare
> la nostra nazione.[16]

> That man who despises the nation
> and his province is an animal
> worse than my buddy, a scoundrel,
> an idiot, like Pasquale says.
> My buddy, despite being a godparent,
> is a big pig, that huge animal!
> He won't speak Italian
> even if threatened, that *cafone*!
>
> He says that in America,
> for him it is a great scorn
> if one speaks Italian,
> that's why one day
> I'll kick him and slap him,
> to teach him a lesson,

so as to make him respect
our nation.

In time, according to Vinciguerra, these wannabe Americans were derided by their fellow immigrants with the epithet "anglocàfoni," or Anglo *cafoni* (Vinciguerra 2017). As we see, *cafone* in this period comes to define not only working-class individuals and behaviors but also successful, assimilated, and middle-class Italian Americans and their actions, who are deemed to some degree to be inauthentic and false.

Immigrants' delicate negotiation of the moral problematics involving the project of "making America" informs the interpretation of *cafone*, past and present, on the changing cultural landscape of Italian America. The perception of ethics is best articulated by an unidentified Harlem resident quoted by educator Leonard Covello for his 1944 PhD dissertation. Discussing the *giornaliero*, the propertyless agricultural day labor of the Mezzogiorno, the individual states:

> The *giornaliero* was first of all a *cafone*; i.e., rough, ill-mannered. He showed no respect for the customs and traditions of the family and society. When he could get away with it he did not consider the rights or feelings of other people. He had no ideal to rise to. He was an unfeeling clod, too dull to think of finer things in life. He was engrossed merely in material pursuits. Nothing was sacred to him. A man of no soul. (Covello 1972, 80)

This decontextualized statement stripped of identifying attributes such as gender, age, birthplace, date of immigration, occupation, etc., is a questionable one given the lack of pertinent information. Keep in mind that Covello's discussion of the past is always contingent on the present, in this case, that of 1930s New York City.[17] This proclamation about the *cafone*'s lack of a soul in his particularly masculine quest for material gain can be understood as less about the historical past in Italy and more about the speaker's Italian American contemporaries who are perceived to have sold their soul in the quest for monetary gain and societal advancement.[18] For this speaker, it could be said, they are the emerging Italian American *cafoni*.

CULTURE CAPITAL FOR THE SECOND AND THIRD GENERATIONS

Tensions around social mobility and embodied aesthetics became particularly acute for second- and third-generation Italian Americans as they shifted from working-class to middle-class status in significant numbers after World War II. This contentiousness often involved the abandonment of some and adoption of other cultural behaviors and consumer choices that were frequently fraught with significant emotional ambiguities (Gans 1965, 253) and were perceived by non–Italian Americans as acts of a gaudy parvenu operating outside their station. The stigma of vernacular Italian American culture at this time was significantly imbued with the "hidden injuries of class," to quote Richard Sennett and Jonathan Cobb's 1972 sociological study. Their book, with numerous Italian American examples, documents the feelings of inadequacy and ambiguity that individuals, predominately men in work environments, experienced in the post–World War II era as they move from the habitus of working-class white ethnic urban families and neighborhoods with their associated occupations and lifestyles into white-collar jobs and middle-class suburbs. Often this transition was expressed as shame, self-loathing, anger, inadequacy, and hypersensitivity, a bundle of feelings that has lingered for some Italian Americans well into the twenty-first century (see Lubrano 2004; Merullo 2000, B10–12).

This class shift was occurring at the same time Italian Americans had become accepted as whites and as they themselves became more fully invested in whiteness. The marking of the gavone's racialized component is best illustrated by the statement made in the mid-1970s by a Brooklyn leader of the Italian-American Civil Rights League that succinctly links class, gender, and race in a historical discourse: "The Italian used to be stereotyped as a *gavon*, as a man of no culture, like years ago when they showed Negroes spitting out watermelon seeds" (Rieder 1985, 28). Here the gavone is a cultureless man on par with the ugly trope of African Americans as lazy simpletons and insatiable gluttons. In this interpretation the gavone is located outside of the grand ideal of a *civiltà italiana*, what historian Simone Cinotto (2014) calls "white Italy," and instead is the product of a provincial, underdeveloped, and violent "black Italy" that is the Mezzogiorno (27). Thus, the monitoring of the gavone from both within and beyond Italian American environs is inextricably framed as a racialized enterprise.[19] It is interesting to note that for the Brooklyn community leader the gavone was a distant unassimilated ancestor, an entity relegated to history by the 1970s. And yet, as we will see, the gavone continues to haunt the Italian American imaginary to present day.

ENTER THE GAVONE

The Italian American pronunciation and spelling of *cafone* as gavone emerged in the latter half of the twentieth century. Retaining *cafone*'s earlier connotations of ill-mannered behavior, gavone was recalibrated with developing meanings for a certain type of man that also encompassed violence and criminality, gluttony, and/or trashiness. Use of gavone was documented for what appears to be the first time in print in none other than Mario Puzo's 1969 international best-seller mobster novel *The Godfather*.[20] In a passage describing the various crime families traveling from different parts of the United States to a peace summit in New York City the word appears: The reader learns that the male members of the Boston gangsters were "*gavones*, or uncouth louts; ruffians" (1978, 300; italics in the original). In addition, the fictional Massachusetts crime family was also unstable, chaotic, lacking control, and was headed by a man who not only cheated his underlings but did "not have the respect of his 'people'" (300). Sixteen years after *The Godfather*'s publication sociologist Jonathan Rieder in his now classic study *Canarsie: The Jews and Italians of Brooklyn Against Liberalism* describes the *gavone* — spelled without a final "e" and italicized — as "a rough punk, a gorilla, or a brutish peasant" (1985, 28). In time the meaning of gavone (often italicized) to signify a roughneck and violent man most often associated with criminal activities began to surface in popular print media.[21] By the turn of the twentieth-first century, the term *gavone* comes to be glossed with the word *lowlife* and linked directly to real and fictional *mafiosi* in the popular imagination and in particular to the acclaimed TV show *The Sopranos* (Goldberg 1999; Haberman 2006).

In addition to the violent and mobbed-up meaning of gavone, the term became widely associated with gluttony. The gavone's rapaciousness renders him simply a "pig," gastronomically speaking, as per the definition in the popular online *Urban Dictionary* ("gavone" 2004). This particular definition appears to have its origins in regional and specifically Sicilian and Calabrian etymology (Vinciguerra 2017), and given its ostensible post–World War II usage it is more than likely that this specific definition is tied to the arrival of a new wave of working class, in particular Sicilian immigrants to New York City and the East Coast in general (see Ruberto and Sciorra 2017a; 2017b).

A third, similarly more recent, element in the Americanized iteration of the *cafone* is the gavone as a "trashy" person ("gavone" n.d.) especially concerning such embodied aspects as sartorial manners and the public presentation of self. Online examples of this disparaged display often reference as examples *The Sopranos* and the reality show *Jersey Shore* (MTV 2009–2012), both of which feature Italian American characters and themes in specifically New Jersey settings. It is with these two TV shows that the gavone has become associated and conflated with the new social categories of *guido* and *goomba*, who are defined to a large degree by their ostentatiousness and often antisocial behavior.[22] Guido is a youth subculture emerging first in post–World War II immigrant Brooklyn and subsequently migrating to the suburbs around New York City that is built around consumer goods, body grooming, and club music as contemporary ways that Italian American taste and style are enacted.[23] Goomba on the other hand is an ill-defined taste style that encompass a somewhat older cohort than guido (though not completely) that dovetails with many of the ethnically marked traits exhibited by mediated Italian American *mafiosi* concerning food, clothing, consumption, and general extravagance.[24] This third definition of the gavone as trashy underlines the idea that the gavone can be said to be in a state of *brutta figura* (literally, an ugly figure), that is the public presentation of self that is deemed aesthetically and morally offensive. Italian Americans have historically scrutinized social interaction for a performer's ability to enact its antithesis, *una bella figura*, or adherence to proper comportment and the aesthetic and moral dimensions of such performance.[25]

Fear of the trashy gavone is acutely pronounced in journalist Maria Laurino's 2000 memoir *Were You Always an Italian?* about her ethnic reconciliation and emerging sense of Italian American identity. In her account, the reader learns that third-generation Laurino grew up in the New Jersey suburban town of Short Hills, with a mother who "tried hard to be modern" (46). Laurino notes that her mother's view on clothing and personal adornment was concerned with adhering to "minimalism" and preoccupied with a fear of "excess," a superfluity that would mark the wearer as a "gavone," which Laurino defines as "low class" (58) and "cheesy" (72).[26] What is particularly striking about Laurino's use of the term is not so much that she uses it in reference to a woman but that gavone is synonymous with "looking Italian American" (58). Thus, to exhibit an identifiable ethnic style is in effect to exhibit low-class elements. She states: "Italian-American clothes were colorful and baroque often worn by women with jet black hair piled high on the head: tops in turquoise, chartreuse, shocking pink, purple, and coral ... and clashing pants; dresses dripping with brocade; gold shoes" (59). As a fashion-consciousness teenager growing up in the 1970s when models were wearing "raging reds, shocking pinks, and deep purples," the striking colors associated with "that over-the-top Italian-American look" caused a crisis of style and ethnic identity for the young Laurino who found it is difficult to mark the "fine line between *gavone* and chic" (59), the boundary between uncool and cool.

Laurino's use of the word *gavon* for trashy highlights the embodied presence of difference among East Coast Italian Americans of a certain generation and the ways in which signs of perceived infractions in social decorum are linked to an unassimilated identity. This dissonance, I argue, is the inheritance of a culture denied and a legacy of insecurities manifested at a psychological level that is enacted in the social and public spheres. The convergence of class mobility, shifting ideals surrounding gender and race, and discriminatory legacies (often concerning the lingering taint of organized crime) imposed from the dominant culture resulted in a deep-seated and festering "ethnic self-disesteem" (Harney 1993, 11). Self-imposed emic distinctions and judgments for historically stigmatized groups like Italian Americans reveal what sociologist Erving Goffman (1986) has identified as "identity ambivalence" (107), that is, those conflicting attitudes when encountering the ostentatiously exhibitions of ethnic cohorts. He states: "It is in his affiliation with, or separation from, his more evidently stigmatized fellows, that the individual's oscillation of identification is most sharply marked" (107). As Laurino reminds her readers repeatedly, the distance between Italian American and gavone is measured against the matrix of white middle-class norms of behavior and beauty. Thus negotiations along the cultural borders of Italian American life exhibit themselves as triumphal proclamations of success and nagging doubts of inclusion that have filtered deep into the construction and imagining of individual and group identities. The gavone straddles this contentious and discordant realm of Italian America.

LA CIVILTÀ ITALIANA AS AN ANTIDOTE TO THE INTRACTABLE GAVONE

Laurino (2000) posits her Italian American upbringing and value judgment of aesthetics and comportment vis-à-vis a critical element in the marking of Italian American gavoneness: the encounter with Italy and Italians. During her trips as an adult to Italy beginning in 1981 Laurino encounters an Italian culture that is distinct from the familiar Italian American culture of her New Jersey childhood. She informs the reader that she unlearns several Americanized Southern Italian terms to use those same words as pronounced in standard Italian, stating she went from saying "gavone" to "cafone" (120). This linguistic shift and self-conscious behavior are part of her claim to a newly reconstituted ethnic identity more closely linked to and identified with "real Italians" (Ruberto and Sciorra 2017a, 9) as opposed or in addition to Italian Americans.[27] Laurino's account of self-discovery is not an anomaly but in fact an example of a middle-class project of ethnic uplift and "stigma management" (Goffman 1986, 51) found in a number of accounts.[28] This recalibration of Italian American identity emerging from the encounter with a contemporary Italy, its people, *una civiltà italiana*, and to a large degree its prized consumer products becomes a critical vehicle for disassociating from a Southern Italian, immigrant, and working-class background.[29]

The Italian American discovery of a contemporary Italy and Italian Americans' recasting of their ethnic identities has occurred to a large degree through consumption. Food, fashion, design, and film have been major elements of the "Italian Style" or "Made in Italy" brand that has "reinforced the shaping of an ethnically keyed, middle-class consumer-driven style" (Ruberto and Sciorra 2017b, 8; see also Cinotto 2014, 1–31) for Italian Americans. Italian consumer goods have come to represent a new way of being Italian American that is coupled with the increased travel of Italian Americans as tourists to Italy and also the emigration of "elite" Italian immigrants—often university trained and white-collar professionals—beginning in the mid-1970s to the present day who exhibit the cultural caché of the highly exported Italian style (see Ruberto and Sciorra 2017a, 17–19).[30]

The marketing of Italy for Italian American consumption is part of a long history of an expanding Italian colonial relationship with the diaspora that began at the onset of the crisis of immigration after unification (Choate 2008).[31] The cultivation of the connection between metropole and periphery was an economic imperative for Italy that involved marketing exported goods, especially foodstuffs, to immigrants with an imprimatur of the *civiltà italiana* (see Cinotto 2014, 1–31; Zanoni 2018). The consumption of Italian products was a powerful way Italian Americans negotiated their diasporic nationalism. By the late twentieth century the emotionally charged middle-class consumption of a *civiltà italiana* became a critical palliative in soothing the lingering stigma of a tainted subalternity that the intractable gavone represented.

Literary scholar Robert Viscusi (2006) argues that Italian Americans' "unconscious colonialism" (xiv) vis-à-vis an ideological Italy maintains an unequal relationship in which immigrant histories and cultures are subjugated by overarching narratives of a glorious and imagined Italian past as well as present. The acquiescence to the metropole's hegemonic claims to history and narratives of identity works to negate Italian Americans' working-class histories and expressivity by confining the former to within the borders of the nation state at the suppression of the diaspora. The allure of the Italian national project "provide(s) circus dreams of awesome display" (9) for immigrants and perhaps most especially their descendants, who through their promotion and consumption of an idyllic and mythic Italy replicate their unequal cultural position. Embracing a *civiltà italiana* as an ethnic marker at the expense of vernacular, lower-class cultural practices perpetuates an unexamined striving for prestige in U.S. society in which the "result is often an empty and unloving self-aggrandizement" (214). The search for full acceptance in U.S. society is predicated on the marking and policing of class-based and racialized borders of ethnic distinction. It is along the rickety border of *cafoneria* that Italian Americans have shaped a defensive culture of insecurity, grievance, and self-denial.

TASTE REGIMES IN *THE SOPRANOS*

Matters of taste and style among a group of fictional Italian Americans are featured frequently in David Chase's HBO drama *The Sopranos*. The show often highlights the ostentatious displays of consumer goods popularly marked as gavone and/or goomba. The *mafiosi* characters who reside in the upscale wealthy suburbs of northern New Jersey, a generation removed from their roots in Newark's former working-class ethnic slum, are often depicted as gauche parvenus. For example, in a scene from the 1999 episode "A Hit Is a Hit," Tony and Carmela Soprano's next-door neighbor Jean Cusamano derisively calls attention to the couple's bad taste during a private dinner with friends by mentioning, aghast, their "bar with the goomba Murano glass," causing some to laugh. Characterizing the "Made in Italy" Murano glass as an example of Italian American goomba culture serves a similar function as Laurino's "trashy" definition of gavone and acts as an accusation that distances the speaker from her neighbors. The fact that one person at the dinner replies, "I like Murano glass" highlights the tensions for some middle-class Italian Americans of what Laurino calls the "fine line between *gavone* and chic" (59).[32]

This judgmental sentiment is further developed in the episode "Marco Polo," from 2004, in which Tony's actions are deemed to be those of a gavone that taint the family as a whole. A scene involves the seventy-fifth birthday party for Hugh De Angelis, organized by his wife Mary and his daughter Carmela at the latter's house. Mary has invited Hugh's Navy buddy, Dr. Russ Fegoli, and his wife Lena. Before the party, Mary informs her grandson Anthony Jr. that Fegoli is retired from the Foreign Service, having been a "career assistant to the ambassador to the Vatican" and that he received a medal from the pope. "Here's someone we can all be proud of, Anthony," she instructs him. Fegoli is a successful and assimilated Italian American — "a cultured person" — with bona fides squarely grounded in a *civiltà italiana*. Indeed, at one point we learn that Fegoli has a PhD in international affairs from Princeton University.

Not unlike Laurino's ethnic self-discovery in Italy and the appeal of "real Italians," Mary is particularly attuned to the allure of Italy that Fegoli represents and the promise that it holds in conferring an alternate Italian (American) identity — different from what she understands her son-in-law Tony to embody (with or without his Mafia connections). Sitting with the Fegolis at the party, she proclaims: "You really have to go to Italy to know, and so many of them don't." This ambiguous statement obfuscates what is learned from an Italian sojourn but reveals her contempt for those Italian Americans who illustrate their ignorance by not making the effort to discover what she deems an authentic *Italian* culture. And even Tony has an affinity for high-end Italian consumer goods as both a status of economic achievement and a marker of middle-class Italian ethnicity. His gift to his father-in-law Hugh is an imported Beretta shotgun, an object that announces its fine artisanship associated with a *civiltà italiana*. Yet, despite his knowledge and consumption of such a luxurious Italian product, Tony is unable to distance himself from a working-class derived Italian American identity that causes overwhelming *agita* for his mother-in-law.

FIGURE 2. Tony Soprano meets Russ and Lena Fegoli in *The Sopranos* episode "Marco Polo." Still capture from digital file.

For Mary the encounter between Tony and Russ Fegoli is an unmitigated disaster that mortifies her and further highlights her endeavoring to cultivate ethnically marked distinctions in taste. Some of her embarrassment centers around food, when she gushes over the Northern Italian recipes (e.g., osso bucco) that the Fegolis shared with her in the past, as distinguished from the Southern Italian fare that became the staple of Italian American homes.[33] It is Tony's arrival to the backyard party twirling a string of locally made linked sausages draped around his neck (and singing with a stereotypical Italian immigrant accent) that initially creates Mary's consternation. Conflicting notions of Italian American identity

"He made us all look like gavones"

come to head when, at the end of the party, she apologies "for everything" to the Fegolis, and Carmela confronts her mother:

Carmela: You're sorry for what?
Mary: Ah.
Carmella: No, no, no. I wanna hear.
Mary: Oh, please, Carmela. The off-color jokes, the sausage twirling.
Carmela: Tony.
Mary: These are cultured Italians. Russ is a success, a diplomat. This was a shock for them.
Carmela: And he's such a diplomat he insults his host. You heard what he said to Tony. He's a pompous man. He always was.
Mary: Let's talk about this another time.
Carmela: That's why you didn't want Tony here. It had nothing to do with the marital situation. All along it was so that your cultured Italian friends, who were born and raised on Arthur Avenue, I might add, wouldn't meet your gavone son-in-law.
Mary: He made us all look like gavones.
Carmela: Whatever we are I am proud of it, unlike you obviously.
Mary: I have always been proud of my heritage.
Carmela: Bullshit! You told Aunt Rose you were glad DeAngelis didn't end in a vowel.
Mary: I never said that!
Carmela: And when Meadow came out, "Oh my God, she's so dark."
Mary: You're drunk. I'm going home.
Carmela: There are Italians all around with their closet self-loathing. I just never wanted to believe my mother was one of them. What the fuck are you crying about? [pause] Your secret is out.

This dramatic family confrontation begins with the camera slowly moving onto the mother and daughter until both are framed in close-ups, their facial expressions front and center, the shots cutting back and forth between the two. The scene encapsulates Mary's antipathy and trepidation concerning breaches in class, ethnic, and even race propriety and creatively renders the desire to control the appearance of gavoneness and its toxic embrace. Carmela exposes her mother's various ethnic fault lines by calling out Russ's origins in the once-working-class Bronx neighborhood Arthur Avenue and his lack of decorum for having slighted her husband Tony in their home. Carmela's pride in her ethnic sensibility (albeit tainted by organized crime) echoes the common use of the word *gavone* by representatives of Italian American organizations (see below). Perhaps most damning is Carmela's pointed accusation of her mother's concealed ethnic enmity, citing Mary's past statements indicating on one hand the pleasure of not having an obviously Italian-sounding married name and on the other a disquiet about her granddaughter Meadow's dark complexion that harkens back to the racial ambiguity of Italian immigrants. Carmela's cursing at her mother speaks to the emotional intensity that the anxiety and monitoring of the gavone engenders at the border between ethnic striving and self-loathing.

A Crisis in Representation: Anthony Scaramucci

Chase's parodic meta-commentary of Italian American middle-class striving is a trenchant and ludic engagement with the criticisms the show garnered from Italian American organizations. Entities like the National Italian American Foundation (NIAF), UNICO National, and the Order Sons of Italy in America as well as local organizations targeted *The Sopranos* because of its Mafia themes, often arguing in a binary fashion both against "negative" images and for "positive" depictions of Italian Americans (Guarini 2001; Petrozzello 1999). Over time, many of these ethnic organizations would raise complaints about subsequent reality shows such as *Jersey Shore* and *The Real Housewives of New Jersey* that did not deal with organized crime but that these ethnic spokespeople nonetheless found offensive for featuring individuals self-identified or ascribed as guidos, goombas, and gavones (Cohen 2010; Wyatt 2009).

These mediated "trashy Italians" — defined to a large degree by their ostentatiousness and often antisocial behavior, whose presence of difference among Italian Americans — have become a flash point for ethnic spokespeople. The public and mediated marking of distinctions — posted on websites and social media and covered by the print and TV press — serves to set up an elite group of vocal arbiters who attempt to shape an ideology of normative ethnicity.[34]

As is often the case when Italian American spokespeople become "outraged" (an operative word for many complaints) with mediated imagery deemed offensive, a roster of successful Italian Americans are enumerated as alternatives: *bella figura* as ethnic boosterism. Such was the case with NIAF's communiqué about *Jersey Shore* in which luminaries from the Garden State were listed as alternatives to the individuals depicted on screen: "Supreme Court Justice Samuel A. Alito, Jr.; General Raymond T. Odierno; Bruce Springsteen; and Governor Chris Christie" (Del Raso n.d.). The perpetual parading of "positive role models" in keeping with the "contributionism" paradigm of white ethnics' gifts to the nation (Fleegler 2013, 14–16) is an anodyne to a lingering inferiority complex.

A fly in the ointment of such Italian American championing was made evident in the form of Anthony Scaramucci. On July 31, 2017, Scaramucci was fired after ten days as White House communications director in the Trump administration after his expletive-laden interview with a journalist was made public (Baker and Haberman. 2017; Shear, Thrush, and Haberman, 2017). NIAF had honored this Harvard Law School graduate, hedge-fund manager, and self-proclaimed "proud Italian" (Stasi 2017) at its earlier March 2017 gala in New York City and subsequently issued a press release congratulating him on the federal appointment. Then-President of NIAF John M. Viola said: "I know he will continue to make our community proud" ("NIAF Congratulates Anthony" 2017). What happens when such a heralded member of the tribe exhibits all the earmarks of the gavone, as he was quickly labeled on social media?[35] NIAF was silent, issuing no follow-up press releases (or at least none that remain online). Andre DiMino of the Italian American One Voice Coalition Executive Board distanced Scaramucci from "hard working, law abiding, and respectful" Italian Americans while expressing concern that "lazy comedy writers" would create mob-themed skits about the incident (Fredericks 2017).[36] One Italian American journalist wrote an open letter to Scaramucci (an accompanying photograph of the *Jersey Shore* cast featured Scaramucci's face photoshopped onto the body of one of the cast members) outlining the enumerable ways he had exhibited questionable behavior and as a result shamed Italian Americans as a group. She continued by contrasting him with a litany of *civiltà italiana* heroes and role models: "Let's not forget that you/I/we come from the land of da Vinci, Marconi, Michelangelo, Galileo, Columbus, Catherine of Siena, Elena Cornaro Piscopia (the first woman awarded a university degree), and Sophia Loren, the first actress to win an Oscar for a non-English-speaking part" (Stasi 2017). Scaramucci's almost treasonous act against the group and its touted achievements in the upper echelons of government set off a moral panic of disgust, fear, and rejection that revealed the Achilles's heel of some ethnic spokespeople's obsession with keeping the gavone at bay.

Conclusion: The *Cafone*'s Dream

Despite such aversion to gavones, goombas, and guidos by social and cultural arbiters of a sanitized Italian America, and perhaps in resistance to such public attacks, some Italian Americans have embraced these vilified monikers and outlier identities as expressions of an *italianità* (Italianness) suited to their twentieth-first century lives. One can only wonder what the driver of the car whose New York State vanity license plates reads "GAVONE" was hoping to signal as he drove on the Henry Hudson Parkway in the Bronx in 2018.[37] Sicilian immigrant Giuseppe Lassoni had a "dream to open a restaurant and name it *il cafone*," according to Roberto Oliveri, his former business partner and current chef at Trattoria Il Cafone in Lyndhurst, New Jersey, which he did in 1997 (telephone conversation with Roberto Oliveri, May 25, 2019).[38] It comes as no surprise that such individuals are often working-class immigrants who arrived in the 1960s, 1970s, and 1980s and their children whose affinities with the agricultural *cafoni* of the Mezzogiorno are strong and for whom the habitus of varied cultural practices is a source of pride. In this and in other innumerable ways we see that the semiotic battlefield that is Italian American cultural production remains a contested site of various discursive skirmishes.

FIGURE 3. The façade of Trattoria Il Cafone in Lyndhurst, New Jersey, 2019. Photograph by Joseph Sciorra.

The peasant, the boor, the greenhorn, the socially inept, the vulgar, the ruffian have historically stood synecdochically in relation to the larger community of Italian Americans. Immigrant leaders and ethnic spokespeople have actively sought to dissociate the group image from the stigma of their lower-class *paesani*, be they illiterate ditch diggers or clubbing suburbanite youths. This fear of the gavone is predicated on the idea that such individuals and behaviors will come to embarrassingly represent the group at large in the eyes of the larger U.S. society. The tainted subaltern identity has its roots in Southern Italy that was further developed in the United States in response to the racialized bigotry, discrimination, and acts of violence. A deep-seated sense of inferiority has persisted despite the embrace of an assimilated white American identity and an association with elite Italian consumption. The tensions surrounding the often conflicting notions of what constitutes Italian American culture and its authentic cultural practices and symbolic attributes are manifested in the public realm. Ultimately, such public chastisement and policing of what perceived attributes constitute appropriate group identity have resulted in limiting discourse around cultural politics and the diversity of experiences and social aesthetics in the everyday lives of Italian Americans.

ACKNOWLEDGMENTS

I am grateful to my colleagues Yiorgos Anagnostou, Simone Cinotto, and Laura E. Ruberto for their astute comments on a previous draft of this essay, and to Simona Frasca, Hermann Haller, and Rosaria Musco for assistance with the transcription and translation of "Lu cafone patriota." Many thanks to Jacqui May and Tom O'Conner for the generous use of their house as a week-long writer's retreat.

NOTES

[1] I have chosen not to identify this person by name.
[2] D'Acierno hyperbolically refers to the term as "the C-word" (1999a, 703–766) suggesting, I believe mistakenly, that it is on par with the N-word. As in-group terms, *cafone/gavone* simply do not have the same valence, historical weight, and intergroup dynamics as does the racial epithet.
[3] The word *gavone* does not appear in any standard American dictionaries.
[4] I thank Robert Viscusi for bringing this passage to my attention.
[5] This attribution is in keeping with a major shift in modern Europe as urban dwellers and cultural and religious reformers and the emergent bourgeoisie distinguished between "learned culture" and "popular culture." See Burke (1978).
[6] See Sabatino (2010) for how tensions along the urban/rural divide played out in how Italian architects, scholars, government officials, and other elites viewed vernacular architecture after unification.

7 Several works of more recent vintage have explored the history of the Mezzogiorno and its particular representation in the national imaginary: Dickie (1999); Schneider (1998); Lumley and Morris (1997); Verdicchio (1997).

8 My essay focuses on the United States and not Italy, Italian Americans and not Italians, and so I leave it to others to parse the term's evolving meaning in twentieth- and twenty-first-century Italy. Perhaps the most popular use of the term in Italy in recent times is the 1999 song "Supercafone," by Roman rapper Piotta, a satirical look at the male disco goer that references Italian American film character Tony Manero (of *Saturday Night Fever*) and thus adds a transnational and diasporic component to the pop culture circuitry of the word.

9 This original wording is meant to replicate immigrant spoken English.

10 Livorni (2019, 37–44) explores stereotypical portrayals of Italian immigrants, which she categorizes as *cafoni*, in popular music geared to the general U.S. consumer, and how those songs were reinterrupted by Italian American performers.

11 Pozzetta (1971) observed writing about New York City's *prominenti*: "Generally ultra-conservative in social outlook, poorly educated, and narrow minded, this group possessed almost total control over the immigrant community's direction. … In the face of extreme poverty and suffering on the part of many new arrivals, the *prominenti* concerned themselves almost totally with their own welfare, prestige, and public image" (232–233).

12 Writing in 1978, historian Ziffiro Ciuffoletti suggests that Italian consuls and their staff at the time viewed the Italian working-class immigrant in a not dissimilar fashion than that expressed in Silone's book, that is, not as a desperate compatriot and fellow citizen in need of assistance but instead as a mere *cafone* who "because of his boorish behavior offends his country, brings scorn down on all Italians, and embarrasses his more urban compatriots" (quoted in La Sorte 1985, 132).

13 Folklorist Elizabeth Mathias has written about how former peasants living as urban proletariats in Philadelphia borrowed prestigious funerary practices from landowners remembered from Italy that resulted in elaborate floral arrangements and enormous grave stones (Mathias 1974, 35–50).

14 See Carnevale (2009, 114–135) and Haller (2006) for more on Magliaccio.

15 A sampling of song titles includes: "Lu cafone nervosa," "Lu cafone sciampagnone," "Lu cafone cantante," "Lu figlio de lu cafone che ragiona," "La cafone ngannato," "Lu cafone Cittadino Americano," "La cafone sucialista," "Lu cafone patriota," "O cafone che ragiona," and "Lu cafone intelligente" (Livingston 1918, 223 n13).

16 I have used Hermann Haller's (2006, 92) published two verses as a base for my rendition here but modified them after consulting with Haller as well as other scholars and listening to the recording online. The phrase *salvo in sangiovanne* proved to be particularly vexing, referencing either Giovanni (John) a character mentioned later in the song or the *comparggio* or godparenting system, which in Southern Italy was often initiated on June 24, the feast day of St. John (San Giovanni). I have opted to use the latter interpretation and translate *salvo* (except) as *despite*.

17 Cinotto notes that Covello's "unquestionable acceptance of immigrants' memories as neutral, factual reproductions of the past is perhaps the greatest weakness of the work" (2004, 506).
18 One finds a similar perspective with Lapolla's (2009) character, the grand Gennaro, the *cafone* (37) who in the process of "making America" (8) at all costs transforms himself from a junk collector to a Harlem *prominente* while destroying himself and his family in the process; this is the exemplar of the *cafone prominente*.
19 It is interesting to note the links between race and perceived bad behavior embedded in the Spanish word *cafre* in Puerto Rico. See Rebollo-Gil (2005).
20 In a number of Southern Italian languages words with the letters "c" and "f" in Tuscan Italian are pronounced as "g" and "v," respectively. In addition, the final vowel is often eliminated when spoken.
21 See Heywood Gould's (1989) crime novel *Double Bang*: "So now they made threats, said they wanted a sit-down. Next thing you know they'd be bringin' alotta gavones from Atlantic City into the act. Alotta aggravation" (105); and Pete Hamill's (1989) *Esquire* magazine article on *mafioso* boss John Gotti: "The hoodlums who remained in the rackets were generally dim-brained *gavones*, reduced to hijacking, loan-sharking, stealing cars, or peddling heroin."
22 These three terms and social categories have also been used to describe the Italian Americans featured on the reality shows *Growing Up Gotti* (A&E 2004–2005), *Real Housewives of New Jersey* (Bravo 2009–), and *Made in Staten Island* (MTV 2019).
23 See Tricarico (2019) for the definitive work on guido youth culture.
24 The term *goomba* is derived from the Italian American pronunciation of *compare* (godfather), a term of endearment for fictive kinship. Actor Steven Schirripa from *The Sopranos* co-authored a nonacademic book on goomba as a lifestyle (Schirripa and Fleming 2002). The word was popularized when it was used for the evil mushroom character in the popular arcade (and subsequent platform) game Super Mario Bros. (Nintendo).
25 Writing about an event at an Italian American women's voluntary association in Chicago, Gloria Nardini (1999) suggests that *bella figura, brutta figura*'s opposite "is a central metaphor of Italian life" that is "deeply embedded as one of the primary arbiters of Italian social mores" (7). Related terms include *figuraccia* and *scostumato*. See also Scannell Guida (2020).
26 One cannot help but think of Karen, the Jewish character in Martin Scorsese's film *Goodfellas*, describing the wives of made-men she met: "What they wore was thrown together and cheap, a lot of pants suits and double knits."
27 I use the common expression *real Italian*, which designates an Italian citizen living in Italy as well as more recent Italian emigrants in the United States. Laura Ruberto and I further develop this term in our two-volume edited anthology *New Italian Migrations to the United States* (Ruberto and Sciorra 2017a; 2017b).
28 See Cinotto (2014, 1–31); Ritter (2014, 195–206); Ruberto and Sciorra (2017a, 1–32 and 2017b, 1–31); Tricarico (1989, 24–46).
29 The "explicit disgust with Italian-American folk and vernacular aesthetics" and ethnic self-loathing with the encounter with Italy is best exemplified in the writings of Grizzuti Harrison (Sciorra 2011, 4). Grizzuti Harrison's superciliousness with

regard to the messy and hybridic ways in which Italian immigrants and their children in the United States created a new culture for themselves in their homes and communities is illustrative of the historically manifested tensions surrounding aesthetics and taste and the subsequent policing in the forms of condemnation, reform, and co-optation of Italian American cultural expressivity.

[30] This ethnic uplift vis-à-vis Italian consumer products is poignantly illustrated in *The Sopranos* (2002) episode "Christopher" (co-authored by Laurino) in which a university professor addressing a group of "new Italian American women" offers a retort to negative media depictions: "Our grandmothers may have been dressed in black but we're in Moschino and Armani. For those who say Italian Americans eat smelly cheese and sip cold wine tell them we're from the land of aromatic Asiago and supple Barolo."

[31] The Italian government understood *la colonia* as both its overseas possessions—what were called "colonies of direct domination"—and emigrants abroad, that is, "spontaneous colonies" (Choate 2008, 23).

[32] In the same episode Tony dismisses the assimilated Bruce Cusamano in racialized terms: "I mean a white man like our friend Cusamano. Now he's Italian, but he's 'merigan [American]. It's what my old man would have called a Wonder Bread wop. He eats his Sunday gravy out of a jar."

[33] She comments that Tony's mother Livia and other Sopranos "skeeved" (is disgusted by) Northern Italian cuisine because of its use of butter.

[34] See Anagnostou (2017) for how Greek Americans interpreted and reacted to a reality show that featured youth from that ethnic group.

[35] For example, see comments posted on Facebook, especially by "Tommy J," on the John D. Calandra Italian American Institute's Facebook group (John D. Calandra Italian American Institute Facebook group 2017).

[36] Comedian Stephen Colbert on *The Late Show with Stephen Colbert* (2018) did just that when, alluding to a news item that mentioned a "more subtle version of Scaramucci," he stated that "everything is a more subtle version of Scaramucci including the cast of *Jersey Shore*, Joe Pesci in *Goodfellas*; and the phrase "'Ay, not for nuthin' can I get some gabagool wrapped [in] some mazzarella over here?" followed by stabbing gestures à la Pesci.

[37] My thanks to Mark Gartenberg for sharing the photograph he took of the car on October 13, 2018.

[38] I was unable to obtain an interview with Lassoni. See also DeCarlo's embrace and defense of being a self-described goomba (2003).

WORKS CITED

Anagnostou, Yiorgos. 2017. "Norms, Vulnerabilities, Paradoxes: Greeks and MTV." 155–179. *Journal of Modern Greek Studies*, 35.

Baker, Peter, and Maggie Haberman. 2017. "Anthony Scaramucci's Uncensored Rant: Foul Words and Threats to Have Priebus Fired." *New*

York Times, July 27. https://www.nytimes.com/2017/07/ 27/us/ politics/scaramucci-priebus-leaks.html (accessed February 10, 2020).

Bourdieu, Pierre. 1984. *Distinction: A Social Critique of the Judgement of Taste*. Cambridge, MA: Harvard University Press.

Bourdieu, Pierre. 1991. *Outline of a Theory of Practice*. Cambridge, MA: Cambridge University Press.

Burke, Peter. 1978. *Popular Culture in Early Modern Europe*. New York: Harper Torchbooks.

"cafone." 1972. *Dizionario Hazon Garzanti inglese-italiano*. Milan: Garzanti.

"cafone." 1990. *Il grande dizionario Garzanti della lingua italiana*. Milan: Garzanti.

Carbonaro, Antonio, and Arnaldo Nesti. 1975. *La cultura negata: caratteri e potenzialità della cultura popolare*. Rimini: Guaraldi.

Carnevale, Nancy. 2009. *A New Language. A New World: Italian Immigrants in the United States, 1890–1945*. Urbana, IL: University of Illinois Press.

Choate, Mark I. 2008. *Emigrant Nation: The Making of Italy Abroad*. Cambridge: Harvard University Press.

Cinotto, Simone. 2004. "Leonard Covello, the Covello Papers, and the History of Eating Habits among Italian Immigrants in New York." *Journal of American History* 91, no. 2: 497–521.

Cinotto, Simone. 2014. "Introduction. All Things Italian: Italian American Consumers, the Transnational Formation of Taste, and the Commodification of Difference." In *Making Italian America: Consumer Culture and the Production of Ethnic Identities*, edited by Simone Cinotto, 1–31. New York: Fordham University Press.

Cohen, Patricia. 2010. "Discussing That Word That Prompts Either a Fist Pump or a Scowl." *New York Times*, January 22. https://www.nytimes.com/2010/01/23/ arts/television/23shore. Html (accessed February 10, 2020).

Covello, Leonard. 1972. *The Social Background of the Italo-American School Child: A Study of the Southern Italian Family Mores and Their Effect on the School Situation in Italy and America*. Totowa, NJ: Rowman and Littlefield.

D'Acierno, Pellegrino. 1999a. "Cultural Lexicon: Italian American Key Terms." In *The Italian American Heritage: A Companion to Literature and*

Arts, edited by George Leonard and Pellegrino A. D'Acierno, 703–766. New York: Garland Publishing.

D'Acierno, Pellegrino. 1999b. "Introduction: The Making of the Italian American Cultural Identity: From La Cultura Negata to Strong Ethnicity." In *The Italian American Heritage: A Companion to Literature and Arts*, edited by George Leonard and Pellegrino A. D'Acierno, xxiii–liv. New York: Garland Publishing.

DeCarlo, Johnny. "The Difference Between Italian, Goomba, & Gangster." H-Net.org, h-itam discussion group. https://lists.h-net.org/cgi-bin/logbrowse.pl?trx=vx&list=h-itam&month=0301&week=e&msg=fhDVmKqz8TOXzuW6kHm19A&user=&pw= (accessed July 23, 2020).

Del Raso, Joseph V. n.d. "National Italian American Foundation Official Statement: MTV's 'Jersey Shore.'" National Italian American Foundation. https://www.niaf.org/niaf_event/national-italian-american-foundation-official-statement-mtvs/ (accessed February 10, 2020).

Dickie, John. 1999. *Darkest Italy: The Nation and Stereotypes of the Mezzogiorno, 1860–1900*. New York: St. Martin Press.

di Leonardo, Micaela. 1984. *The Varieties of Ethnic Experience: Kinship, Class, and Gender among California Italian Americans*. Ithaca, NY: Cornell University Press.

Durante, Francesco. 2014. *Italoamericano: The Literature of the Great Migration, 1880–1943*. New York: Fordham University Press.

Firmani, B.G. 2017. *Time's a Thief*. New York: Doubleday.

Fleegler, Robert. 2013. *Ellis Island Nation: Immigration Policy an d American Identity in the Twentieth Century*. Philadelphia: University of Pennsylvania Press.

Fredericks, Bob. 2017. "Italian-Americans Say Scaramucci Gives Them a Bad Rep." *New York Post*, July 28, https://nypost.com/2017/07/28/italian-americans-say-scaramucci-gives-them-a-bad-rep/ (accessed December 23, 2019).

Gabaccia, Donna R. 2000. *Italy's Diasporas*. Seattle: University of Washington Press.

Gambino, Richard. 1975. *Blood of My Blood: The Dilemma of the Italian-Americans*. Garden City, NY: Anchor Books.

Gans, Herbert J. 1965. *The Urban Villagers: Group and Class in the Life of Italian-Americans.* New York: The Free Press.

"gavone." n.d. Definition. https://definithing.com/gavone/ (accessed December 23, 2019).

"gavone." 2004. Definition. https://www.urbandictionary.com/define.php?term=gavone (accessed September 25, 2019).

Goffman, Erving. 1986. *Stigma: Notes on the Management of Spoiled Identity.* New York: Simon & Schuster.

Goldberg, Jeffery. 1999. "The Don is Done." *New York Times Magazine,* January 31. https://www.nytimes.com/1999/01/31/magazine/the-don-is-done.html (accessed September 25, 2019).

Gould, Heywood. 1989. *Double Bang.* New York: Pocket Books.

Gramsci, Antonio. 1991. *Selections from Cultural Writings*, edited by David Forgacs and Geoffrey Nowell-Smith, translation by William Boelhower. Cambridge: Harvard University Press.

Gramsci, Antonio. 1995 (1926). *The Southern Question.* Translated by Pasquale Verdicchio. West LaFayette, IN: Bordighera Incorporated.

Guarini, Frank J. 2001. "'Sopranos' Stereotypes." Letter to the editor. *New York Times*, March 6. https://www.nytimes.com/2001/03/06/opinion/l-sopranos-stereotypes-255378.html (accessed February 10, 2020).

Haberman, Clyde. 2006. "As 'Sopranos' Returns, Art Irritates Life." *New York Times,* March 10. https://www.nytimes.com/2006/03/10/nyregion/as-sopranos-returns-art-irritates-life.html (accessed September 25, 2019).

Haller, Hermann W. 2006. *Tra Napoli e New York: La macchiette italoamericane di Eduardo Migliaccio.* Rome: Bulzoni.

Hamill, Pete. 1989. "In Gotti They Trust." *Esquire,* October 1. https://classic.esquire.com/article/1989/10/1/in-gotti-they-trust (accessed February 10, 2020).

Harney, Robert F. 1993. "Caboto and Other Parentela: The Uses of the Italian Canadian Past." In *From the Shores of Hardship: Italians in Canada. Essays by Robert F. Harney*, edited by Nicholas De Maria Harney, 1–27. Lewiston, NY: Éditions Soleil Publishing.

Lapolla, Garibaldi M. 2009. *The Grand Gennaro.* New Brunswick, NJ: Rutgers University Press.

La Sorte, Michael. 1985. *La Merica: Images of Italian Greenhorn Experience*. Philadelphia: Temple University Press.

Laurino, Maria. 2000. *Were You Always an Italian? Ancestors and Other Icons of Italian America*. New York: Norton.

Livingston, Arthur. 1918. "La Merica Sanemagogna." *The Romantic Review* 9, no. 2 (April–June): 206–226.

Livorni, Isabella. 2019. "Parla comme t'ha fatta mammeta"?: Identity Formation through Sonic Code-Switching in 1920s Italian American Song." *Italian American Review* 9.1 (Winter): 26–48.

Lubrano, Alfred. 2004. *Limbo: Blue-Collar Roots, White-Collar Dreams*. Hoboken, NJ: Wiley.

Luconi, Stefano. 2007. "Anti-Italian Prejudice in the United States: Between Ethnic and the Racial Question." In *Mediated Ethnicity: New Italian-American Cinema*. edited by Giuliana Muscio, Joseph Sciorra, Giovanni Spagnoletti, and Anthony Julian Tamburri, 33–44. New York: The John D. Calandra Italian American Institute.

Lumley, Robert, and Jonathan Morris. 1997. *The New History of the Italian South: The Mezzogiorno Revisited*. Devon, UK: University of Exeter Press.

Mathias, Elizabeth. 1974. "The Italian-American Funeral: Persistence through Change," *Western Folklore* 33, no.1: 35–50.

Merullo, Roland. 2000. "Hatred and Its Sly Legacy." *The Chronical of Higher Education,* December 1, B10–12.

"NIAF Congratulates Anthony Scaramucci on His Appointment as White House Communications Director." 2017 (July 21). Press release. https://www.niaf.org/niaf_event/niaf-congratulates-anthony-scaramucci-appointment-white-house-communications-director/ (accessed February 10, 2020).

Park, Robert E., and Herbert A. Miller. 1921. *Old World Traits Transplanted*. New York: Harper & Brothers.

Petrozzello, Donna. 1999. "'Sopranos' Draws Bias Flak Italian-Americans Eye HBO Protest to Denounce Stereotyped Badfellas," *New York Daily News*, August 13. https://www.nydailynews.com/archives/entertainment/sopranos-draws-bias-flak-italian-americans-eye-hbo-protest-denounce-stereotyped-badfellas-article-1.854490 (accessed February 10, 2020).

Pozzetta, George. 1971. "The Italians of New York City, 1890–1914." PhD Dissertation. University of North Carolina at Chapel Hill.

Puzo, Mario. 1978. *The Godfather*. New York: Signet Books.

Rebollo-Gil, Guillermo. 2005. "Entre cafres y blanquitos: Perceptions of Race and Racism in Puerto Rico." PhD Dissertation. University of Florida. http://etd.fcla.edu/UF/UFE001/rebollogil_g.pdf (accessed February 7, 2020).

Rieder, Jonathan. 1985. *Canarsie: The Jews and Italians of Brooklyn Against Liberalism*. Cambridge, MA: Harvard University Press.

Ritter, Courtney. 2014. "The Double Life of the Italian Suit: Italian Americans and the 'Made in Italy' Label." In *Making Italian America: Consumer Culture and the Production of Ethnic Identities*, edited by Simone Cinotto, 195–206. New York: Fordham University Press.

Romeyn, Esther. 2008. *Street Scenes: Staging the Self in Immigrant New York, 1880–1924*. Minneapolis: University of Minnesota Press.

Ruberto, Laura E., and Joseph Sciorra. 2017a. "Introduction: Real Italians, New Immigrants." In *New Italian Migrations to the United States, Vol. 1: Politics and History Since 1945*, edited by Laura E. Ruberto and Joseph Sciorra, 1–58. Urbana: University of Illinois Press.

Ruberto, Laura E., and Joseph Sciorra. 2017b. "Introduction: Rebooting Italian America." In *New Italian Migrations to the United States, Vol. 2: Art and Culture Since 1945*, edited by Laura E. Ruberto and Joseph Sciorra, 1–31. Urbana: University of Illinois Press.

Sabatino, Michelangelo. 2010. *Pride in Modesty: Modernist Architecture and the Vernacular Tradition in Italy*. Toronto: University of Toronto Press.

Scannell Guida, Denise. 2020. "Bella figura: Understanding Italian Communication in Local and Transatlantic Contexts." *Oxford Research Encyclopedia of Communication*. https://oxfordre.com/communication/view/10.1093/acrefore/9780190228613.001.0001/acrefore-9780190228613-e-929 (accessed April 16, 2020).

Schirripa, Steven R., and Charles Fleming. 2002. *A Goomba's Guide to Life*. New York: Clarkson Potter.

Schneider, Jane. 1998. *Italy's "Southern Question": Orientalism in One Country*. Oxford: Berg.

Sciorra, Joseph. 2011. "Introduction: Listening with Accent." In *Italian Folk: Vernacular Culture in Italian-American Lives*, edited by Joseph Sciorra, 1–10. New York: Fordham University Press.

Sennett, Richard, and Jonathan Cobb. 1972. *The Hidden Injuries of Class*. New York: Norton.

Shear, Michael D., Glenn Thrush, and Maggie Haberman. 2017. "John Kelly, Asserting Authority, Fires Anthony Scaramucci." *New York Times*. July 31. https://www.nytimes.com/2017/07/31/us/politics/trump-white-house-obamacare-health.html (accessed February 10, 2020).

Silone, Ignazio. 2000. *The Abruzzo Trilogy*. South Royalton, VT: Steerforth.

Silverman, Sydel. 1975. *Three Bells of Civilization: The Life of an Italian Hill Town*. New York: Columbia University Press.

Stasi, Linda. 2017. "Anthony Scaramucci Lost His Wife, Dignity and Right to Call Himself a 'Proud Italian' All in One Week." *New York Daily News*, July 29. https://www.nydailynews.com/news/politics/stasi-scaramucci-lost-wife-dignity-shaming-italians-article-1.3365080 (accessed December 23, 2019).

Stella, Gian Antonio, and Emilio Franzina. 2009. "Brutta gente: Il razzismo anti-italiano." In *Storia dell'emigrazione italiana, Vol. II. Arrivi*, edited by Piero Bevilacqua, Andrea De Clementi, and Emilio Franzina, 283–311. Rome: Donzella Editore.

Tedesco, Jo Ann. 1999. "Sacraments: Italian American Theatrical Culture and the Dramatization of Everyday Life." In *The Italian American Heritage: A Companion to Literature and Arts*, edited by George Leonard and Pellegrino A. D'Acierno, 353–386. New York: Garland Publishing.

Tricarico, Donald. 1989. "In a New Light: Italian and Italian-American Ethnicity in the Mainstream." In The *Ethnic Enigma: The Salience of Ethnicity for European-Origin Groups*, edited by Peter Kivisto, 24–46. Philadelphia: The Balch Institute Press.

Tricarico, Donald, 2019. *Guido Culture and Italian American Youth. From Bensonhurst to Jersey Shore*. London: Palgrave Macmillan.

Verdicchio, Pasquale. 1997. *Bound by Distance: Rethinking Nationalism through the Italian Diaspora*. Madison, NJ: Fairleigh Dickinson University Press.

Vinciguerra, Antonio. 2017. "Sull'origine di cafone (con qualche osservazione e consiglio a proposito delle etimologie in rete)." http://www.accademiadellacrusca.it/it/lingua-italiana/consulenza-linguistica/domande-risposte/origine-cafone-qualche-osservazione-consigli, December 15 (accessed August 26, 2019).

Viscusi, Robert, 2006. *Buried Caesars and Other Secrets of Italian American Writing*. Albany: State University of New York Press.

Wyatt, Edward. 2009. "Two Reality Shows Stir Publicity and Anger." *New York Times*, December 6. https://www.nytimes.com/2009/12/07/business/media/07reality.html (accessed February 10, 2020).

Zanoni, Elizabeth. 2018. *Migrant Marketplaces: Food and Italians in North and South America*. Urbana: University of Illinois Press.

Media

Ferrara, Abel, dir. 2010. *Mulberry St*. MST Productions.

Migliaccio, Eduardo "Farfariello." n.d. *Lu cafone patriota*. YouTube. https://youtu.be/fIpWsckjjjg (accessed April 14, 2020).

Patterson, John, dir. 2004. "Marco Polo." *The Sopranos*. Season 5, episode 8. April 24. HBO.

Penn, Mathew, dir. 1999. "A Hit Is a Hit." *The Sopranos*. Season 1, episode 10. March 14. HBO.

Scorsese, Martin, dir. 1990. *Goodfellas*. Warner Bros.

The John D. Calandra Italian American Institute's Facebook group, comments to the posted article "'I Can Tell You 2 Fish That Don't Stink': How Anthony Scaramucci Is Bringing Mob Talk to the White House." https://www.facebook.com/search/top/?q=%E2%80%98I%20Can%20Tell%20You%202%20Fish%20That%20Don%E2%80%99t%20Stink%E2%80%99%3A%20How%20Anthony%20Scaramucci%20Is%20Bringing%20Mob%20Talk%20to%20the%20White%20House&epa=SEARCH_BOX (accessed July 23, 2020).

The Late Show with Stephen Colbert. 2018. "White House Welcomes a Disgraced Fox News Boss and His Racist Wife." July 11. CBS. https://

www.cbs.com/shows/the-late-show-with-stephen-colbert/video/_5XdgkZljJRgCz9_abfa47MzpAaKWo6E/white-house-welcomes-a-disgraced-fox-news-boss-and-his-racist-wife/ (accessed December 23, 2019).

Van Patten, Tim, dir. 2002. "Christopher." *The Sopranos*. Season 4, episode 3. September 29. HBO.

How Cultural Memory Builds a Narrative Past in Forming Individual Identity

Donna M. Chirico

> i wanted to know who i was because i felt so entirely alone
> discussing terms with others we stand upon our memory of resource
> just that no one mentions it does not mean no one knows who you are
>
> but of course we do not really know how anybody knows
> when we love people we rest on trust and good memories
> what we understand of one another may not always be clear
>
> — Robert Viscusi, *Ellis Island*

Early on in *Let's Wake Up, Italics!*, Piero Bassetti (2015, 22) proposes a "progressive redefinition of identity." He asserts, "We should free ourselves from the idea of belonging to a territory that is spatially defined, and forcefully bring new identitary reference points to the fore" (51). It becomes, then, not the elimination of identity but instead creating an identity that encompasses both the local—country of origin—and the global—an international community of citizens. Bassetti makes this sound easy. This idea of glocalization[1] reflects a significant change in how a person comes to a personal identity that transcends borders.

Regardless of how clearly this adaptation is described or the willingness of the participants to make the change, the task of eliminating a territorial or cultural attachment is problematic, if not impossible. This is because redefining cultural identity necessarily involves restructuring cultural memory. Personal identity is derived, in part, from that which came before us, involving transformative historical experiences, and it is then tailored for each individual based on personal experiences and unique interpretations. Despite what most people believe, memory is not a static function linked solely to the past; rather, it is a complex and dynamic cognitive process that not only references the past but brings the past into the present as it creates movement toward the future, including the future self. This cognitive flow means that there is a constant reinterpretation of existing memory as the individual modifies the past to suit the present self, while also using the past to direct future development of identity. If the past self does not correspond to the present self, then something must be revised or possibly eliminated. The result is a revisionist personal narrative that allows the past to better serve the present interpretation of the self. Two important questions then emerge: Who decides what cultural memory to preserve? And how can cultural memory be modified?

The ongoing controversy surrounding the naming of Columbus Day is an example of the persistence and influence of cultural memory and illustrates the role of Christopher Columbus as an identity marker divorced from physical place. The figure of Columbus was used to create a collective ethnic identity among Americans of Italian heritage and to bolster their U.S. national pride; his significance is negligible to Italians in Italy. And as is well-known, today within the Italian American community the topic of Columbus's import is a growing source of disharmony and uncivil discourse. In the United States there was and still is a need for immigrants to band together and create communities of support. This was the historical function that Columbus Day served and the reason there was such an effort among earlier Italian immigrants to make it a national holiday. This action brought symbolic recognition of Italian heritage and, more critical, an awareness of the struggle of Italian immigrants in their new world. The word *pride* has come to be used as an expression of support for these immigrants, usually accompanied by slogans, symbols, statues, and marches or parades. Semiotics tells us that the meanings attached to these expressions are complex, deeply held, and, as Charles Sanders Peirce (1960) asserted, continuously changing. This premise is consonant with the continually evolving sense of self.

Cultural Memory and Individual Identity

The disagreements lately provoked by the Columbus debate have produced a division that stems from both differences in the meanings assigned and disinformation or a lack of knowledge regarding historical fact; those individuals pressing to retain Columbus are relying on cultural memory without allowing for adaptation of meaning to adjust to a present-day context. If one is to transcend local boundaries, then the Columbus debate can be examined in a larger, global context by determining what value there might be in maintaining or eliminating the central role of Columbus from a shared history: Is this aspect of cultural memory of value to Italian Americans beyond the first generation? Is Columbus needed as a source of pride?

The battle is between those in the Italian American community and beyond who want to maintain the cultural memory that exalts Columbus versus those who want to eliminate the significance of that memory and establish a modern narrative that suits present needs as a community. It has become a matter of Columbus as hero versus Columbus as villain. Underlying this from the perspective of personal identity is that by saying Columbus is bad, what is understood by the person who has incorporated a positive idea about Columbus is that my heritage is bad, consequently I am bad. This diminishes the personal sense of self and makes it easier to understand why there is a need to hold on to the Columbus-as-hero narrative. If you discard Columbus, you must necessarily discard part of yourself.

Such a process is inextricably linked to memory. While most people are aware that there is short-term memory and long-term memory, many are unaware of the complexities of memory and the interplay among the types of memory. There is, for example, also sensory memory, which is extremely brief, but still important because this is how a sense of images fleetingly experienced is maintained. It is why we remember that vandalized statue of Columbus we saw for a moment while riding in the car. What is generally less understood is that within long-term memory there are multiple ways information is stored depending on the characteristics of those memories. Some memory is related to performing everyday tasks and is largely unconscious. These are the procedural memories related to motor functions such as driving a car or getting dressed. Imagine someone with dementia as such quotidian actions are "forgotten." There is a struggle to recall what once required no thought to access. Episodic memory is autobiographical, largely conscious, and relates to personal experiences. These memories include names, times, places, and emotions. It is not only the memory of your sixth birthday party, it is also the happiness you experienced as you were handed the puppy or the sadness you felt when your sibling blew out the candles before you could. There are aspects of memory that connect us to our cultural past. Cultural memories are those institutionalized memories that come through established sources as a symbolic heritage communicated through formal texts, rituals, monuments, celebrations, objects, sacred texts, and other forms of media. Personal memory, communicative memory, is limited to the recent past, typically defined as three to four generations, whereas cultural memory stretches back through time and can last for thousands of years.

It is essential to understand that *all* memory is faulty. As professor of religious and cultural studies Jan Assmann has stated, cultural memory is "the faculty that allows us to build a narrative picture of the past and through this process develop an image and an identity for ourselves" (Meckien 2013). This is why libraries, for example, the repositories of cultural memory, are targets in civil war and imperialist conquest. From the burning of the library in Alexandria to, in more recent history, the Serbian destruction of the National Library of Sarajevo (now rebuilt), all are attempts to destabilize cultural memory. To quote Assmann again, "This was the strategy of the totalitarian regime to destroy the past, because if one controls the present, the past also comes under control, and if one controls the past, the future also comes under control" (Meckien 2013). The burning of books has been replaced by blocking access to the Internet by a nation's dominant regime. Both are attempts to subvert cultural memory. The latter act is particularly insidious because in an instant history can be rewritten and the previous version can disappear.

Cultural Memory and Individual Identity

Language is an integral part of cultural memory, especially in those instances where words are not easily translated. Bassetti's term *italics* is a good example. In *The Monolingualism of the Other*, Jacques Derrida (1998) testifies to aspects of his acculturation as an Algerian Jew with respect to learning language, education, becoming a citizen, and the "dynamics of cultural-political exclusion and inclusion" (15-17). The statement that stands out from Derrida is, "I have but one language—yet that language is not mine" (25). Derrida points out that language is a type of possession and subject to actions by the dominant culture. Going back to asking who preserves cultural memory, think of what language is spoken in a school. Dialects and indigenous languages are often prohibited in school to maintain the authority of the ruling party. It still persists in the United States, despite how much is known about the value of multilingualism, that immigrants are discouraged from maintaining the language of their birth. Of course, for the children of immigrants, that their parents speak poor English can be an embarrassment. It is evidence that the person does not belong.

Separate from Columbus, while most immigrants must learn the language of the receiving culture, it should be no surprise that there is a psychological component where in later generations the development of identity includes a desire to recover the lost language of origin. There is a fierce effort to trace the self to the past, assuming that what is found will enhance the person in the present. This is seen in the remarkable rise in the numbers of people having their DNA tested. It also highlights the distinction between personal memory and cultural memory. Individuals who assume a certain heritage are flummoxed when the test reveals an alternate ethnic heritage to the one in which the person was raised. This disconnect must then be resolved cognitively, which means that a revised personal narrative must be formulated to accommodate what is revealed. The cognitive process is the same when those who revere Columbus are confronted with a historical reality that challenges their positive image of him.

This brings us to identity development as informed by cultural memory. A group of psychologists at the University of Bologna investigated the age and density of early memory by looking at young adults in extended family households versus nuclear family households. They found that those who grew up in extended families with multiple generations present had earlier and denser memories; denser means richer memories with more detail that tend to last longer (Artioli et al. 2012). There is also research to indicate that what is remembered and what is forgotten are tempered by the cultural-historical perspective in which the individual is developing:

> Remembering is forced to use all kinds of tricks to resist the villain's assaults and to guard the treasure—the accumulated wealth of past experience and knowledge. While Remembering strives to defend this precious treasure, maintaining it as untouched as possible, Forgetting never tires of trying to steal and destroy it (or at least to damage or, insidiously, to distort and falsify it). In this way, the conflict about the treasure of the past takes on still another dramatic dimension: it becomes a struggle for truth. (Brockmeier 2002, 15)

One way immigrants remember is to return to the land of origin. This has given rise to an inventive industry, namely "diasporic tourism." The return arouses tension when the person goes "home" and finds that that place is not how it is remembered. What has been discovered in research is what was often assumed, which is that you cannot go home again because home as you knew it no longer exists.

According to Sabine Marschall (2017), "African transnational migrants undertake touristic journeys to their former homes, expecting to reconnect with their former lives, manifested in ordinary and familiar material traces and social relations, yet the visit reveals what kind of person the migrant has become; for some, it induces awareness of a self-transformation that can never be reversed" (221). Loretta Baldassar (2011) has done similar work with Italian migrants to Australia. She found that the primary reason for a return journey to the place of origin for Italians is the moral obligation to care for aging parents. This is an example of cultural memory connected to national identity because it is understood, even in the second generation, that Italian children are responsible for their parents. This is a common pattern for multiple ethnic groups.

It is the case too that refugees return to the site of the camps where they first came to a country, as these are places of expression of their group belonging. Alessandro Triulzi (2016) at the University of Naples writes about the Archive of Migrant Memories in Lampedusa. This archive contains the migrants' own recollections of leaving their homes and traveling to a safer place. Triulzi tells the story of how personal effects, letters, documents, photos, and other items, "lie to decompose as a vivid expression of what is not to be remembered in the nation's past" (149). The archive was created to make the invisible visible. It is an effort to create a collective memory, a narrative that has the potential to become a cultural memory. Will Lampedusa be remembered as a safe haven for refugees or as a dumping ground for the detritus of humanity? This will depend on how the story is written and who is doing the writing.

The Archive of Migrant Memories is an example of how major cultural events need to be summarized in ways that can be fitted into a personal narrative that drives identity formation. The archive may seem peculiar at first, but history museums are commonplace. In New York City alone, there are the Tenement Museum, the Museum of Jewish Heritage—A Living Memorial to the Holocaust, and, more recently, the 9/11 Memorial & Museum. These become sacred places where the abstractions of memory can become concretized. Entering these spaces arouses awe in the individual by arousing both cultural and personal memories. This is a similar mental and physiological response that is stimulated when an émigré returns to the homeland, even when the person is generations removed from the immigration experience. A closer to home example are the shrines created at the site of a traffic accident. The shrines are often maintained for lengthy periods of time, usually by those closest to the victim. There is a sense that if the site is not marked, then the memory of the person will disappear.

Whether it is visiting museums or traveling to a home that no longer exists, these places become where we believe we can confront our cultural legacy and integrate this into the present self we have become. The narrative created at the intersection of cultural memory and the reality of the present will inform the future development of individual identity. The need is to find the missing pieces so that an impression of feeling whole is accomplished.

Identity is inextricably linked to the idea of place. Returning to the quest toward glocalism, this is why abandoning a territory that is spatially defined is especially difficult: The person initially defines themselves within a set of physical and psychological borders because memories of experiences within the borders contribute to the building of identity. Returning to Robert Viscusi's (2013) quote in the epigraph, "when we love people we rest on trust and good memories/what we understand of one another may not always be clear" (96). The feeling of trust that is aroused is not clear because it comes from that shared, yet distant, cultural memory. Discarding such memories is impossible, and revising them, as in the case of Christopher Columbus, is challenging. Discussing such contentious terms with others presupposes standing on our shared memory of resource. It means that you have to be willing to jump off the parapet and assume that you will fly.

NOTES

[1] Although the term *glocalization* had been used in the business sphere since the 1980s and is cited in the 1991 edition of *The Oxford Dictionary of New Words*, it was the sociologist Roland Robertson who introduced the term to the social sciences in 1995, prior to Bassetti's use of the word.

WORKS CITED

Artioli, Frederica, Pera Carla Cicogna, Miranda Occhionero, and Elaine Reese. 2012. "'The People I Grew Up With': The Role of Sociodemographic Factors in Early Memories in an Italian Sample." *Memory* 20.2: 189–197.

Baldassar, Loretta. 2011. "Italian Migrants in Australia and Their Relationship to Italy: Return Visits, Transnational Caregiving and the Second Generation." *Journal of Mediterranean Studies* 20.2: 1–28.

Bassetti, Piero. 2015. *Let's Wake Up, Italics!, Manifesto for a Global Future*. New York: Calandra Italian American Institute.

Brockmeier, Jens. 2002. "Remembering and Forgetting: Narrative as Cultural Memory." *Culture & Psychology* March. 8.1: 15–43.

Derrida, Jacques. 1998. *Monolingualism of the Other; or, The Prosthesis of Origin*. Palo Alto, CA: Stanford University Press.

Marschall, Sabine. 2017. "Migrants on Home Visits: Memory, Identity and a Shifting Sense of Self." *International Journal of Tourism Research* 19: 214–222.

Meckien, Richard. 2013. "Cultural Memory: The Link between Past, Present, and Future." Institute of Advanced Studies at the University of Saõ Paulo. June 7. http://www.iea.usp.br/en/news/cultural-memory-the-link-between-past-present-and-future (accessed January 11, 2020).

Peirce, Charles Sanders. 1960. *Collected Papers of Charles Sanders Peirce*, Vols. I and II. Cambridge: Harvard University Press.

Triulzi, Alessandro. 2016. "Working with Migrants' Memories in Italy: The Lampedusa Dump." *Crossings: Journal of Migration & Culture* 7.2: 149–163.

Viscusi, Robert. 2013. "16.12" *Ellis Island*. New York: Bordighera Press.

Italian Diaspora Studies and the University: Professional Development and Curricular Matters

Anthony Julian Tamburri

A DESCRIPTION

We have seen over the decades a plethora of complaints about the representation of Italians and Italian Americans in the media.[1] Letters of protest have come from just about all corners of the Italian/American[2] population. Organizations big and small, national and regional, have engaged in such criticism and disapprobation. I, too, have engaged in such acts, especially with regard to a blog post by political commentator Michael Kinsley (2009), a MillerCoors LLC ad (Mullman 2009), and a 2017 truffles ad by Eataly Chicago. Such acts of protest are surely warranted. How else might non-Italian Americans come to understand what offends? But the mere act of protest, or the seemingly successful receipt of a letter of apology, if not the cancellation of a commercial, are all unacceptable endgames.[3] On the contrary, they should be the first step in a more concerted effort to counter such stereotyping. We cannot speak of the representation of Italian Americans in any of the media, especially in terms of "negative" stereotypes, without also discussing possible remedies to such depictions and what responsibility lies within and among Italian Americans themselves. In avoiding this second step of proactively seeking out remedies, we run the risk of falling into the old trap of victimization, for which "Woe unto us" becomes the mantra that, when said loud enough, abrogates any and all responsibility that otherwise might very well rest with ourselves.

In what follows, I would like to underscore, at times via anecdotes and examples, further ways in which all of us who lament and deplore such representations can more productively spend our time and energy. When the John D. Calandra Italian American Institute held an event on guido culture in January 2010, none of the loudest voices who had spoken out earlier against the MTV show *Jersey Shore* (2009–2012) showed up — this, in spite of the fact that I had actually given more than fifteen minutes of air time the previous month, on the Institute's *Italics* TV program, for someone to speak against *Jersey Shore*. Instead, a few actually made veiled email threats against the Institute.

Now, with the onset of MTV's *Made in Staten Island* (2019), some Italian/American spokespeople are going out of their way to complain about (1) the representation of Italians and/or Italian Americans on television, and (2) that the children and grandchildren of *mafiosi* are profiting off their relatives' notoriety. I will concede that there are better ways to use such notoriety. That said, allow me, in the form of questions, to suggest some actions that can surely lead us to that path of success in furthering a more complete picture of Italian America with the concerted desire that our history, in the end, be better understood in all of its facets and complexities:

> How about organizing something more constructive than simply carping?
> How about organizing workshops for young Italian Americans?
> How about organizing workshops for the recognized or self-proclaimed leaders of Italian/American associations?
> How about funding serious scholarship about these social phenomena?
> How about organizing workshops for professionals, high-school teachers, and college educators alike?
> How about convincing elected officials to put their time, effort, and funding behind some remedies to these pressing issues?

At the above-mentioned guido culture symposium, our audience of approximately 125 people included one elected official, New York State Senator Diane Savino. Of all the local and regional Italian/American elected officials, she was the only one to express interest in what we had announced, a lecture on guido culture by one of our City University of New York (CUNY) colleagues, Donald Tricarico. Her sense of pro-action is something we had hoped to witness as a more widely exhibited response. This did not happen. Savino, to the contrary, did attend; she spoke, and stayed for close to the entire event. In the wake of our event, others continued to condemn *Jersey Shore* and those of the Italian/American population who did not condemn it, thus denigrating any and all who did not side with them in an outright denunciation of the program and a total refusal to engage in any sort of discussion about the origins of guido culture. They resorted to the tactics of derision and dismissal as opposed to dialogue and debate.

As Fred Gardaphé has often stated, Italian Americans have spent an inordinate amount of time and energy fighting fictional characters as opposed to the real thing. More recently, in an essay in which he underscores "the disease of literalism," he states:

> A recent site for observing this disease is in many of the responses of individuals and organizations to such programs as *The Sopranos*. More unified acts by Italian Americans have been launched against fictional portrayals of the Mafia than were ever mounted against the real *mafiosi* in the United States.
>
> The complete opposite is true in Italy where people have risked and lost their lives in pursuit of reality. So what is it about irony deficiency that leads to such behavior? (Gardaphé 2016, 6)

In engaging with Gardaphé's much-repeated declaration, let us address the real problems along with the fictional characters through (1) education, (2) scholarship, and (3) workshops for the public at large, for Italian Americans, for Italians, and for educators. So, as we say in Italian, "Diamoci da fare!" (Let's get to work!) Because anything short of the above is simply tilting at windmills.

Italian Americans need to be sure that Italian and Italian/American history and culture are part of U.S. curricula at the public-school level, K-12. We also need to be sure that courses in Italian/American history and culture are taught at the college level.

Indeed, to go further, we need to work toward creating first and foremost graduate programs, as well as professorships, in Italian/American studies at the college level and not, I would underscore, only at the so-called elite colleges and universities.[4]

The success of such actions lies with us, members of the Italian/American population.[5] We need to support our own activities, such as attending Italian/American-focused events; and this means sitting through lectures that, in the end, truly do inform us toward a greater completeness of knowledge of our culture in spite of the fact that we might believe we know it all already. We need to respond with courteous yet firm indignation when—whether it be at a social event or business meeting—someone makes an offensive comment about Italians or Italian Americans in his/her feeble attempt to make a joke. We need to engage in these and other forms of what I call cultural philanthropy, something that is second to none.

More significant, it is paramount that our public officials engage in a greater degree of ethnic discourse that clearly surpasses those ethnic boundaries of social events. Namely, it is simply not enough for our elected representatives (congressional, senatorial, and at state and municipal levels) to proclaim their Italian pride at Italian/American events such as Italy's Festa della Repubblica or Columbus Day parades. They need to do so at events and in venues that are not always and only Italian and Italian/American. They should uphold the value of an Italian/American legacy in these venues precisely because, for instance, (1) what we know today as modernity has its origins in the Italian Renaissance; (2) what we know as philanthropy today has its modern roots in the Italian Renaissance; (3) what we know today as the U.S. legal system has its roots in an eighteenth-century Italian legal philosopher, Cesare Beccaria; (4) what we know of the art world is that more than 60 percent of the world's production is Italian in origin; (5) what we know of U.S. contemporary literature is that some of our best sellers are David Baldacci, Don DeLillo, Wally Lamb, Lisa Scottoline, and Adriana Trigiani, to name a few. And this does not include the vernacular, cultural articulations that abound, such as gardens, women's embroidery, domestic altars, religious street *feste* (feasts), and other manifestations of our quotidian culture—these, too, are part and parcel of our Italian legacy and Italian/American cultural history.[6] Simply stated, we need to go beyond "pizza" and "nonna"![7]

In so doing, we also need to collaborate with other ethnic and racial groups around the United States. In an effort to find communal ground, we can and should become more sensitive to their trials and tribulations. In so doing, we also come to see the analogies between our experiences and those of other groups. We come to realize, as well, that certain expressions—if still used in some situations and hence seemingly still acceptable—may actually be taboo in other situations. The examples abound and there is no need to repeat them here: We need not be a graduate or postgraduate of Ivy League institutions to understand the offensiveness of such language today. Indeed, one might suggest that we do away with such expressions in all situations.

A Prescription

Among the myriad questions that might spring forth from what I have described above, one might readily be, "How do and/or should we talk about who we are and how do and/or should we move forward?" Tackling such a therapeutic and recuperative challenge involves addressing at least seven components:

1. History
2. Acculturation vs. assimilation
3. Representation (yesterday and today)
4. Articulation of ethnicity
5. Identity
6. Interethnic collaboration
7. Education

Another aspect of the challenge is that it possesses a double-layered consciousness: Such awareness is distinguished by an internal and an external cognizance that are de facto dissimilar in origin but not in impact. And all of this is ultimately negotiated through a constitutive act that is founded on pedagogy, tutelage, and reflection.

These seven components are the building blocks for us to arrive at a consciously analytical awareness of who we are and what our Italian and/or Italian/American heritage is. In studying our history as best we can in its entirety, we come to see how Italian immigrants and their progeny developed into contemporary Italian Americans. We understand their trials and tribulations as well as their successes, a combination of facts and phenomena that add to our own sense of self. How much of this heritage we decide to appropriate and recognize as ours will determine whether we engage in either acculturation or assimilation. If we move more toward the former, then our heritage culture—sometimes referred to as a "minority" culture—succeeds in retaining those unique cultural signs such as language, food, customs, and other behavioral patterns. If instead we tend toward the latter, then our heritage culture eventually loses all its signs and markers that distinguish it as separate from the host—sometimes referred to as a "majority" culture; this includes the above-mentioned language, food, customs, and other behavioral patterns. At this juncture, then, one is an un*hyphenated* American, and that is fine; and his/her ethnic journey of discovery ends here. However, in opting for acculturation, we eventually gain an awareness, a sensitivity as well, we might say (among numerous other things), about representations of us, both yesterday and today. As we become more familiar with the historical phenomena of our past and reconcile them with current cultural experiences, we gain a greater Italian/American consciousness and hence become more efficient in our articulation of our ethnicity. We begin to develop, that is, an identity as *hyphenated* Americans, or, better, as Italian/American people.[8]

This abbreviated description of an individual's passage to hyphenation leads to the last two components I have identified above: interethnic collaboration and education. The advantages of the former bring us to understand more fully the histories of other immigrant groups, be their immigration chosen or imposed. Such an understanding then affords us the possibility to gain a more complete—and I would add complex—awareness of our own overall experience and how it then relates to their respective experiences

Italian Diaspora Studies and the University

within the greater mosaic of what we know as the United States. It is, hence, at this juncture where we reach that level of education that grounds us more firmly in our Italian Americanness.

But this seventh component of education, as I intend it here, does not figure only as the end point in one's development of his/her Italian Americanness. It has yet another facet to it, one that exhibits a dual perspective that is analogous to the double-layered consciousness I mentioned above, one that is distinguished by an internal and an external cognizance. In fact, we saw above that education is an end point, the result of an acquisition of knowledge and insight vis-à-vis one's Italian Americanness, one's ethnic identity, that is. At this level, instead, education is a concerted, transitive operation of instructing or informing those who do not know, namely inducing knowledge of Italian/American history and culture to the uninformed. In turn, the same internal and external cognizance I mentioned earlier is now representative of the necessity to approach both populations, the Italian/American, which is internal, and the non-Italian/American, which is external. Our challenge as educators is, to be sure, that as many people as possible be acquainted and conversant with the history of Italians in the United States.

THE ANTIDOTE

Now, if what I have articulated above seems to have complicated the issue, that is because the issue is complicated and necessitates complex remedies that all fall under the greater umbrella of education, as I have outlined at the end of the previous section. It is only through our labors of promulgation and propagation that we will be able to move forward. We need to yell it from the mountain top and enlist the services of those in positions of influence. Once we have the united efforts of those who can exert leverage and impact in education, be it from an internal or external point of control, we can then move forward to create a series of programs that will allow for the greater education of Italian/American history and culture at both the K-12 and college levels.[9]

In this section, I will offer a few examples that are close to failsafe in the promotion and instruction of Italian/American history and culture; and within this umbrella term of *culture*, I include the learning and teaching of the Italian language. Further still, these means are not always as expansive as one might fear and, I underscore, should not be geared only toward the highly educated, sophisticated intellectual who speaks a specialized jargon accessible to the few. Here are two: The bag lunch is an activity by its very name inexpensive and informal. Faculty can meet with students during lunch or, if the college has one, the free hour (a ninety-minute period reserved for lectures and other activities when no classes are scheduled).[10] The Italian club, to name a second type, is supported by most colleges with space and funding, though most often minimal. The student club can readily partner with a section of a department and sponsor events about Italian/American history and culture.

There are more formal activities one can organize: a lecture series, book presentations, symposia, and conferences. These are all programs that require funding, for sure, which can range from a few hundred dollars to a few thousand dollars, if not more. And this is where the negotiations with people in positions of influence come into play. Nonprofit organizations and local and regional elected officials are possible, if not probable, sources for financial assistance. Let us be frank here: Any Italian/American organization with an adequate annual budget that does not fund cultural events and activities is derelict in its duties, especially if said organization engages in protests against anti-Italianism with the abovementioned proverbial letter of apology as its end goal. Further still, if said organizations give scholarships to college students and do not require at least one year of Italian-language study, this too enters into the realm of dereliction if their mission includes Italian language in the promotion of culture.

One of the two most important pedagogical activities is to offer a course on Italian/American history and culture. Be it a small-enrollment course that also serves as a writing course, or a large-enrollment course as part of general education electives, it has the basic function of imparting knowledge of Italians in the United States, as we sometimes call ourselves.[11] It is not a quick fix by any means. It is, instead, one small part of a more concerted effort to infuse Italian/American studies into the college curriculum. It is a one-step-at-a-time building block to create that requisite network of courses from college to college; this is part of the greater, long-term challenge of educating the public at large about the history of Italians and their progeny in the United States. If there is one thing we have learned to date, it is that what we have been doing seems not to be working. For instance, if a so-called left-thinking TV personality feels comfortable in referring to political commentator Jerome Corsi as the "Godfather of the birther movement," as MSNBC correspondent Joy Reid so casually did in 2019 within a context of absolutely no reference to ethnicity, then we have not yet succeeded in educating the public—and here, especially, public figures—about anti-Italian epithets.

The second significant pedagogical enterprise is the professional development seminar, open primarily, but not exclusively, to graduate students—especially at the doctoral level—and college professors. I am referring to the type of meeting in which people gather for a significant amount of time in order to study and discuss the topic at hand. With regard to Italian/American or Italian diaspora studies,[12] we had not seen anything like this until 2014, when the Rockefeller Foundation sponsored a one-week workshop of the Italian American Studies Network (IASN) at the Rockefeller Center in Bellagio, Italy. The foundation paid all expenses for nineteen scholars and intellectuals from Italy and the United States to attend. While the majority of the attendees were professors, not all were. We had a few people who worked for cultural institutes and associations such as the John D. Calandra Italian American Institute and the Centro Altreitalie, two of the only two institutes, I would submit to you, that we can readily call an Italian diaspora studies think tank. Two of the results from the IASN Rockefeller Foundation meeting were (1) a book publication on the state of affairs of Italian diaspora studies and (2) the creation of a network of scholars and cultural managers that has solidified in the subsequent years. In fact, a group of thirty people gathered for a week in January 2018 at the Calandra Institute; it included many from the 2014 IASN Bellagio meeting and others as well from other parts of Europe and the United States.

The schedule of the 2014 IASN Bellagio meeting was actually created six months before, when Fred Gardaphé and I were in Rome for an international conference organized by ILICA, the Italian Language Inter-Cultural Alliance. In that wonderful *aperitivo* hour that Italians so smartly observe, he and I enjoyed our drinks over a conversation on how we might organize a weeklong seminar. It was an exploration for something longer than the 2014 IASN Bellagio meeting even though we had not yet identified a time or place in which to organize such a seminar. Indeed, the 2014 IASN Bellagio meeting was still only a thought; we had yet to bring the project to fruition.

After the 2014 IASN Bellagio meeting, it was patently clear that the desire for a seminar did indeed exist. Thus, having returned to the United States, we began to look into the structural and financial possibilities. Once Gardaphé and I realized that (1) the desire on the part of possible participants/fellows existed, (2) the desire to be part of the faculty was strong, and (3) there was interest on the part of Italian/ American institutions and organizations to sponsor fellowships, we launched the first edition of the Italian Diaspora Studies Summer Seminar (IDSSS) at the University of Calabria in collaboration with its Department of Humanities. After three years, we moved the IDSSS to Roma Tre University, hosted by the Department of Foreign Languages, Literatures, and Cultures, which has a strong American studies component that covers Italians in both North and South America. Further still, Roma Tre University has an interdepartmental center of American studies, Centro di Ricerca Interdipartimentale di Studi Americani.

The Italian Diaspora Studies Summer Seminar is a three-week professional development curriculum for college faculty and doctoral students. The classes have included literature, cinema, history, and vernacular culture, as well as other related subject matter. Over the first five years, we have had sixty-two participants, all of whom received a fellowship to cover 50 percent of the program costs. The population thus far has been graduate students and professors, the latter being more numerous. The graduate students also have the opportunity to earn as many as six graduate credits transferred to their home institutions.[13] In some cases, the professors attending as fellows, in turn, have been given release time and funding to cover the other 50 percent of the program costs. The table below shows the schedule of the first week of the 2019 seminar:

WEEK ONE

Seminar meetings last 1 hour 30 minutes

	June 17	June 18	June 19	June 20	June 21
8:00 — 10:00	BREAKFAST	BREAKFAST	BREAKFAST	BREAKFAST	BREAKFAST
10:00 – 11:30	*Italian American Cinema* Lecture & discussion Prof. Anthony Julian Tamburri	*Identity in the Italian Diaspora: Psychological Perspectives* Lecture & discussion Prof. Donna Chirico	*Italian American Cinema* Lecture & discussion Prof. Anthony Julian Tamburri	*Identity in the Italian Diaspora: Psychological Perspectives* Lecture & discussion Prof. Donna Chirico	SYMPOSIUM IASA
11:45 — 13:15	*Italian American Literature* Lecture & discussion Prof. Mary Jo Bona	*History of the Italians in the Diaspora* Lecture & discussion Prof. David Aliano	*Italian American Literature* Lecture & discussion Prof. Mary Jo Bona	*History of the Italians in the Diaspora* Lecture & discussion Prof. David Aliano	SYMPOSIUM IASA
13:15 – 14:30	LUNCH	LUNCH	LUNCH	LUNCH	
14:30 – 16,00	*Mapping Theories and Approaches to Italian Diaspora Studies* Lecture & discussion Prof. Laura Ruberto	*Contemporary Italian American Literature & Cinema 1* Lecture & discussion Prof. Sabrina Vellucci	*Mapping Theories and Approaches to Italian Diaspora Studies* Lecture & discussion Prof. Laura Ruberto	SYMPOSIUM *Italian American Studies Association* 2nd Annual Meeting in Italy	SYMPOSIUM IASA
16:15 — 17,45	*Workshop* Projects workshop Prof. Fred Gardaphé	DE LUISE GUEST LECTURE SERIES PROF. CLAUDIO GIOVANARDI "Come se la passa l'italiano fuori d'Italia?" Aula D	*Workshop* Projects workshop Prof. Fred Gardaphé	SYMPOSIUM *Italian American Studies Association*	SYMPOSIUM IASA
	GROUP DINNER 20:00 @ Kolping		DE LUISE GUEST LECTURE SERIES PROF. DANIELE FIORENTINO "Italy-US Relations in the 19th and Early 20th Century" 18:30 @ Kolping		

After five years of the IDSSS, we have come to learn that a number of our past fellows with teaching appointments have integrated knowledge they have acquired of the Italian diaspora through the IDSSS into their already existing courses. Even more exciting is the fact that others have returned to their home institutions and set up new courses; this is the case at Baruch College for Spring 2019. The course description of professor of history Vincent DiGirolamo's HIS 3460, Topics in American History reads as follows:

> This course explores the history and culture of Italian Americans, the seventh largest Census-reported ethnic group in the United States. Its focus spans from the contested legacy of Christopher Columbus to the Emmy Award-winning criminality of Tony Soprano. Students will examine the Italian diaspora from a variety of angles, drawing upon fiction, film, television, memoir, and folklore. We will look at their reasons for emigrating, their experience in steerage and in their communities, workplaces, and churches. Major themes include language, assimilation, Catholicism, radicalism, race relations, whiteness, gender norms, stereotypes, and the Mafia.

DiGirolamo's participation in the 2018 IDSSS and the course he has subsequently developed comprise the ideal diptych of what we see as one of the end goals of the seminar. Such courses in various departments within colleges and universities—or the addition of a unit on the Italian diaspora in an already existing course—are fundamental to the insertion of our voices into the greater discourse on U.S. history and culture. In turn, it also contributes to the greater education of the general American populace. Only by insisting that we belong will we then create the possibility, if not probability, that we shall.

CONCLUSION

Let us indeed ask for the public apology for egregious statements and depictions and let us even call for the pulling of offensive commercials, as I have referenced earlier. But once we achieve these goals, let us also recognize that the fertile terrain exists for those scholars, writers, filmmakers, and artists who will need the support to tell the stories that need to be told. Where, for example, is the community support for filmmakers such as Nancy Savoca, John Turturro, and Marylou Tibaldo-Bongiorno? As a group, do we even go to see their films, let alone help fund them? Where are the fellowships for writers to spend four to six weeks perfecting their craft? Do we even buy, as well as read, their books? Where are the think tanks that look to Italy's legacy in the United States or elsewhere, exploring also, indeed first and foremost, the history of Italian immigration to the host country? Such specific entities exist for other U.S. ethnic groups, indeed funded also from within. Yet the Italian/American population cannot seem to recognize, or to help set up, such entities unless they are funded from without.

The Calandra Institute is the closest thing in the United States to what I am underscoring here as that place of historical, cultural, and intellectual activism. We need more centers and institutes in different parts of the country that can make it possible for the public discourse in the United States to include Italian/American history and culture as part and parcel of the national conversation. As I write, we have yet definitively to prioritize this vision. If we want to command the respect that is in fact due us, we must work together to broaden consciousness of Italian/American experiences—among ourselves and with the rest of our fellow Americans.

NOTES

[1] For an overview of the history of discrimination against Italians in the United States, see LaGumina (1973) and Connell and Gardaphé (2010).

[2] In this essay I use the adjectival formulation *Italian/American* instead of *Italian American* or *Italian-American*. For more on this usage, see Tamburri (1991).

[3] In some cases, the letter of apology expressed "sorrow" at Italian Americans being offended, not regret that what the writer stated was offensive. An insignificant difference? Not by any means!

[4] I have spoken to this issue in various venues on a number of occasions; my latest is Tamburri (2014).

[5] I use the word *population* instead of *community* precisely because the latter gives the impression of an integrated monolithic group. Instead, if there is one thing we have learned from the most recent debate on Christopher Columbus it is that Italian Americans have distinctly different views on the Genovese navigator.

[6] One book that immediately comes to mind is the collection *Italian Folk: Vernacular Culture in Italian American Lives* (Sciorra 2011), eleven essays by as many scholars

who examine various phenomena such as foodways, the basement kitchen, music, pageantry, faith healing, witchcraft, etc. Other books of similar interest include: Magliocco (2009), Cinotto (2014), Giunta and Sciorra (2014), Sciorra (2015), and Bona (2015).

[7] For more on this notion of going beyond "pizza" and "nonna," see Tamburri (2014, chapter 8).

[8] Many have negotiated the notion of an Italian/American identity. Here I point out the following from which the reader can move either further back or closer to today. I have dealt with this in Tamburri (1991 and 2017a). For others who dealt originally with notions of identity and Italian Americans, or analogous groups, I mention here: Aaron (1964), Campisi (1948), Child (1943), Basile Green (1974), Richards (1999), Gardaphé (2003), and Ruberto and Sciorra (2017).

[9] I use the words *college* and *university* interchangeably in this essay.

[10] At CUNY, for example, all colleges have one to two free hours a week. At Queens College, we have hosted lectures by colleagues as well as by people invited from outside the college community.

[11] In addition to the scholars I mention in note 6, I would add the following with regard to novel concepts of labeling per se: Carravetta (2017), Fontanella (2003), Giordano (1998), Tamburri (2017b, 2018), Valesio (1989), and Vellucci (2017).

[12] In speaking about the United States specifically, we might opt for the adjective *Italian/American*, though the second half of the binomial can refer to the entire American hemisphere. That said, we might want to adopt in a broader sense the term *Italian diaspora* for the very reason that its referral to Italian emigration beyond Italy does not willy-nilly give greater value to any geographical privilege and/or hierarchy.

[13] This is dependent entirely on the individual institution where the graduate student is matriculated. Neither the IDSSS nor Roma Tre University can guarantee which colleges and universities will decide vis-à-vis accepting credit.

WORKS CITED

Aaron, Daniel. 1964. "The Hyphenate Writer and American Letters." *Smith Alumni Quarterly* (July): 213–217; now revised in *Rivista di studi anglo-americani* 3.4–5 (1984–1985): 11–28.

Basile Green, Rose. 1974. *The Italian-American Novel: A Document of the Interaction of Two Cultures.* Madison, NJ: Fairleigh Dickinson University Press.

Bona, Mary Jo. 2015. *Women Writing Cloth: Migratory Fictions in the American Imaginary.* Lanhan, MD: Lexington Books.

Campisi, Paul. 1948. "Ethnic Family Patterns: The Italian Family in the United States," *American Journal of Sociology* 53.6 (May): 443-449.

Carravetta, Peter. 2017. *After Identity. Migration, Critique, Italian American Culture.* New York: Bordighera.

Child, Irvin L. 1943. *Italian or American? The Second Generation in Conflict.* New Haven, CT: Yale University Press.

Cinotto, Simone, ed. 2014. *Making Italian America: Consumer Culture and the Production of Ethnic Identities.* New York: Fordham University Press.

Connell, William J., and Fred Gardaphé, eds. 2010. *Anti-Italianism: Essays on a Prejudice.* New York: Palgrave Macmillan.

Fontanella, Luigi. 2003. *La parola transfuga.* Florence: Cadmo; in English as *Migrating Words: Italian Writers in the United States.* New York: Bordighera, 2012.

Gardaphé, Fred. 2003. "Identical Difference: Notes on Italian and Italian American Identities." In *The Essence of Italian Culture and the Challenge of a Global Age. Cultural Heritage and Contemporary Change,* Series IV, Vol. 5, edited by George McClean and Piero Bassetti, 93–112. Washington DC: The Council for Research in Values and Philosophy.

Gardaphé, Fred. 2016. "Running Joke: Criticism of Italian American Culture through Comedy in *The Sopranos.*" In *Forme, strategie e mutazioni del racconto seriale,* A. Bernardelli, edited by E. Federici and G. Rossini eds., *Between,* Vol. VI.11. http://www.betweenjournal.it. (accessed January 31, 2019).

Giordano, Paolo. 1998. "Emigranti, espatriati e/o esiliati: Italiani e letteratura negli Stati Uniti." In *Lo straniero,* edited by Mario Domenichelli and Pino Fasano, 169–84. Rome: Bulzoni.

Giunta, Edvige, and Joseph Sciorra, eds. 2014. *Embroidered Stories: Interpreting Women's Domestic Needlework from the Italian Diaspora.* Jackson, MS: University Press of Mississippi.

Kinsley, Michael. 2009. "Bailing Out Organized Crime." *Washington Post,* March 6. http://www.washingtonpost.com/wp-dyn/content/article/2009/03/05/AR2009030502824.html (accessed February 17, 2019).

LaGumina, Salvatore A. 1973. *WOP! A Documentary History of Anti-Italian Discrimination in the United States.* New York: Straight Arrow Books.

Magliocco, Sabina. 2009. *The Two Madonnas: The Politics of Festival in a Sardinian Community,* 2nd ed. Long Grove, IL: Waveland.

Mullman, Jeremy. 2009. "Miller Pulls Ad for Lite Protest." *AdAge,* June 3. https://adage.com/article/news/miller-pulls-sopranos-esque-ad-lite-protests/137064 (accessed February 17, 2019).

Richards, David A. J. 1999. *Italian American: The Racializing of Ethnic Identity*. New York: New York University Press.

Ruberto, Laura E. and Joseph Sciorra, eds. 2017. "Introduction: Real Italians, New Immigrants." In *New Italian Migrations to the United States*, Vol. 1: *Politics and History since 1945*. Champaign, IL: University of Illinois Press.

Sciorra, Joseph, ed. 2011. *Italian Folk: Vernacular Culture in Italian American Lives*. New York: Fordham University Press.

Sciorra, Joseph. 2015. *Built with Faith: Italian American Imagination and Catholic Material Culture in New York City*. Nashville, TN: University of Tennessee Press.

Tamburri, Anthony Julian. 1991. *To Hyphenate or Not to Hyphenate: The Italian/American Writer: Or, an* Other *American?* Montreal: Guernica Editions.

Tamburri, Anthony Julian. 2014. *Re-Reading Italian Americana: Generalities and Specificities on Literature and Criticism*. Madison, NJ: Fairleigh Dickinson University Press;

Tamburri, Anthony Julian. 2017a. "The Coincidence of Italian Cultural Hegemonic Privilege and the Historical Amnesia of Italian Diaspora Articulations." In *Re-Mapping Italian America. Places, Cultures, Identity*, edited by Sabrina Vellucci and Carla Francellini, 53–75. New York: Bordighera.

Tamburri, Anthony Julian. 2017b. "Re-Thinking Labels: The 'Italian' Writer as Exemplar, or Distinct Categories as Quixotic," afterword. In *New Italian Migrations to the United States*, Vol. 2: *Art and Culture Since 1945*, edited by Laura Ruberto and Joseph Sciorra, 193–202. Chicago: University of Illinois Press.

Tamburri, Anthony Julian. 2018. *Un biculturalismo negato: La letteratura "italiana" negli Stati Uniti*. Florence: Franco Cesati.

Valesio, Paolo. 1989. "The Writer between Two Worlds: The Italian Writer in the United States." *Differentia* 3/4: 259–276.

Vellucci, Sabrina. 2017. "Re-Mapping the Field." In *Re-Mapping Italian America. Places, Cultures, Identity*, edited by Sabrina Vellucci and Carla Francellini, xiii–xxiii. New York: Bordighera.

CONTRIBUTORS

MARY JO BONA is Professor of Women's, Gender, & Sexuality Studies and English at Stony Brook University. Her authored books include *Women Writing Cloth: Migratory Fictions in the American Imaginary*; *By the Breath of Their Mouths: Narratives of Resistance in Italian America*; *Claiming a Tradition: Italian American Women Writers*, and a book of poetry, *I Stop Waiting for You*. Bona edited *The Voices We Carry: Recent Italian American Women's Fiction*; co-edited *Multiethnic Literature and Canon Debates*; and is series editor of Multiethnic Literatures for SUNY Press. Bona also serves on the SUNY and Bordighera editorial boards. Bona's essays appear in the *Routledge History of Italian Americans*, *La Mamma: Interrogating a National Stereotype* (Palgrave) and, forthcoming, on women and archives in *Tulsa Studies in Women's Literature*. Bona's current manuscript, *The Daughter's Abduction: Mothers, Mobility, Narrative*, revisits motherhood studies through the lens of diasporic time and gendered space.

PETER CARRAVETTA is Professor of Philosophy at SUNY/Stony Brook. He held the D'Amato Chair in Italian and Italian American Studies 2008-2018. He is the author of nine books of critique, including: *Del postmoderno. Critica e culture in America all'alba del duemila* (2009), *The Elusive Hermes. Method, Discourse, Interpreting* (2012), *Sulle tracce di Hermes. Migrare, narrare, riorientarsi* (2013), and *After Identity. Migration, Critique, Italian American Culture* (2017). He has also published eight books of poetry, including *The Sun and Other Things* (1997), *L'infinito. Poesie 1972-2012* (2013; premio Montano, *Anterem*), and *The Other Lives* (2014). Carravetta is the founding editor of *DIFFERENTIA review of Italian thought* (1986-1999), (accessible at https://commons.library.stonybrook.edu/ differentia/about.html), and the translator of Martino Oberto's avant-garde opus *Anaphilosophia* (1993) as well as G. Vattimo & P.A. Rovatti's *Weak Thought* (2014). He was a Fulbright lecturer in Rome (1991) and Madrid (2003) and visiting professor at universities in Paris, St. Petersburg, Nanjing, and at Columbia University.

DONNA M. CHIRICO is Professor of Psychology at York College/CUNY. Her research explores transcendent imagination in personal development, attainment of goals, and psychological wellbeing. Related to this, identity formation is considered to understand how ethnicity contributes to the psychological development of the self, specifically in Americans of Italian heritage and more broadly within the Italian diaspora. Professor Chirico is the president of the Italian Language Inter-cultural Alliance;

chair of the Italian/American Faculty and Staff Advisory Council to the John D. Calandra Italian American Institute; National Board member of the National Organization of Italian American Women; and, Executive Board member for the Italian American Studies Association. She serves on the editorial board of the journals *Italian American Review* and *Diasporic Italy*, has published numerous papers in the area of Italian American and Italian Diaspora Studies, and is a sought-after speaker on matters vital to the Italian diaspora.

FRANCESCO DURANTE was born in Anacapri (Campania province). He taught the culture and literature of Italian Americans at the Università Suor Orsola Benincasa in Naples. As one of Italy's foremost journalists and literary critics, he wrote for various Italian newspapers and journals. He was the author and editor of numerous books, including the groundbreaking *Italoamericana. Storia e letteratura degli italiani negli Stati Uniti, 1776–1943*, in two volumes (the second was published with the same title by Fordham University Press in 2014); *Figli di due mondi. Fante, DiDonato & C: narratori italoamericani degli anni Trenta e Quaranta*; *Scuorno (vergogna)*; *I napoletani*; and, together with the late Rudolph J. Vecoli, *Oh Capitano! La vita favolosa di Celso Cesare Moreno in quattro continenti*. He edited two volumes of Mondadori's prestigious Meridiani series on John Fante and Domenico Rea. In addition to various editions of mannerist and baroque poets and American writers, he translated seven volumes of John Fante's works, two books by Bret Easton Ellis, and writings by William Somerset Maugham, George Arnold, and William Dean Howells, among others. Durante served as the artistic director of the annual Salerno Literary Festival. His last book was *La letteratura italoamericana* (2017).

DONNA R. GABACCIA is Professor of History Emerita at the University of Toronto and past director of the Immigration History Research Center at the University of Minnesota. She is author of many books and articles about gender, class, and labor in Italy's many diasporas and an enthusiastic participant in multiple interdisciplinary organizations and projects linking history, social sciences and humanities. She currently serves as general editor of a new two-volume Cambridge History of Global Migrations. An amateur textile artist, she is also engaged in weaving into a coherent narrative for siblings and cousins the story of their own family's secrets.

FRED GARDAPHÉ is Distinguished Professor of English and Italian/American Studies at Queens College/CUNY and the John D. Calandra Italian American Institute. He is past-president of MELUS, IASA, and the Working Class Studies Association. This year he celebrates his forty-fourth year of teaching. His books include *Italian Signs, American Streets: The Evolution of Italian American Narrative*, *Leaving Little Italy*, and *From Wiseguys to Wise Men: Masculinities and the Italian American Gangster* and the short fiction collection, *Importato dall'Italia*.

SIÂN ELAINE GIBBY is writer/editor at the John D. Calandra Italian American Institute (Queens College, CUNY). She earned a BA from Indiana University in Italian language and literature and an MSArch from the University of Cincinnati. Beginning in 1998 she has worked as an editor and writer, including stints at *Slate* magazine, *Tablet*, and the Jewish Theological Seminary before coming to the Institute in 2010. She is the translator of Quinto Antonelli's *Intimate History of the Great War: Letters, Diaries, and Memoirs from Soldiers on the Front* (2016), Francesco "Kento" Carlo's *Resistenza Rap* (2018), and Luigi Fontanella's *God of New York* (forthcoming). She has written a play about Italian American poet Pascal D'Angelo titled *The Preliminary Creed*.

PAOLO GIORDANO, PhD, is Neil R. Euliano Professor (Emeritus) of Italian and Italian American Studies at the University of Central Florida. He has held teaching and administrative appointments at Loyola University Chicago, Loyola University Rome Center, the Scuola Italiana of Middlebury College, and Rosary College in River Forest, Illinois. Giordano's research and teaching interests are in the literature of Italian migration, the Italian Renaissance, and twentieth-century Italian literature. The Italian government honored him with the title of "Cavaliere, Stella della Solidarietà Italiana" in 2004, and he was given by Southern Connecticut State University with the "Distinguished Alumnus Award" in the same year. The Association of Teachers of Italian bestowed on him a lifetime distinguished service award. In 2012, his native city of Bordighera, Italy, acknowledged him with the "Parmurelu d'oru" (Golden Palm) for lifetime achievement. He is co-founder of Bordighera Press.

DONATELLA IZZO is Professor of American Literature at "L'Orientale" University, Naples, Italy. Her research fields include American literature, American studies, ethnic studies, literary theory, and comparative literature. She is the author of many essays and books on American literature and has edited or co-edited volumes and journal issues on literary theory, Asian American literature, Italian American studies, American TV series, the graphic novel in the United States, and the culture and politics of Hawai'i. A former president of AISNA, the Italian Association of American Studies, and of the Henry James Society, she is a co-director of the Futures of American Studies Institute at Dartmouth College. In 2012, with Giorgio Mariani, she launched OASIS—Orientale American Studies

International School—on the isle of Procida, a biennial school aimed at creating a new venue for conversations among Americanists from the United States, southern and Eastern Europe, North Africa, and the Middle East.

JAMES J. PERICONI is an independent researcher, Wertheim Research Scholar at the New York Public Library from 2018 to the present, and a private collector of Italian-language American imprints. His *Strangers in a Strange Land: A Catalogue of an Exhibition on the History of Italian-Language American Imprints (1830-1945)* (2012), reprinted by Bordighera Press (2013), accompanied his exhibition of these works at the Grolier Club of New York in 2012, at Brooklyn College in 2013, and at Seton Hall in 2014. He is the bibliographic editor of the American edition of *Italoamericana: The Literature of the Great Migration, 1880-1943* (2014), edited by Francesco Durante (Robert Viscusi was the editor of the American edition). *The Routledge History of Italian Americans* (2018) contains his latest research on Italian language bookselling and book publishing in the United States. Periconi has a BA in English Literature from Columbia University (1970); was a Danforth Graduate Fellow at the University of Virginia (M.A.1972); and graduated from NYU School of Law (J.D.). He practices environmental law in Manhattan.

JOSEPH SCIORRA is Director of Academic and Cultural Programs at the John D. Calandra Italian American Institute, Queens College, City University of New York. As a folklorist he has conducted ethnographic research on vernacular expressivity and published on religious practices, material culture, and popular music. He was the editor of the interdisciplinary journal *Italian American Review* and of *Italian Folk: Vernacular Culture in Italian-American Lives* (Fordham University Press, 2011) and co-editor of *Embroidered Stories: Interpreting Women's Domestic Needlework from the Italian Diaspora* (University Press of Mississippi, 2014), *Neapolitan Postcards: The Canzone Napoletana as Transnational Subject* (Rowman & Littlefield, 2016), and the two-volume *New Italian Migrations to the United States* (University of Illinois Press, 2017). Sciorra is the author of *Memorial Wall Art* (Henry Holt and Company, 1994; Thames and Hudson, 2002) and *Built with Faith: Italian American Imagination and Catholic Material Culture in New York City* (University of Tennessee Press, 2015), which won the Italian American Studies Association's 2016 nonfiction book award.

ANTHONY JULIAN TAMBURRI is Dean of the John D. Calandra Italian American Institute and Distinguished Professor of European Languages and Literatures. He is co-founder of Bordighera Press, past president of the Italian American Studies Association and of the American Association of

Teachers of Italian. Concentrating on cinema, literature, and semiotics, he has authored sixteen books in both English and Italian and more than 120 peer-reviewed essays and book chapters. His books of the past decade include *Una semiotica dell'etnicità. Nuove segnalature per la scrittura italiano/americana* (2010); *Re-viewing Italian Americana: Generalities and Specificities on Cinema* (2011); *Re-reading Italian Americana: Specificities and Generalities on Literature and Criticism* (2014); *Scrittori Italiano[-]Americani: trattino sì trattino no* (2018); *Un biculturalismo negato: La scrittura "italiana" negli Stati Uniti* (2018); and *Signing Italian/American Cinema: A More Focused Look* (2021). The Italian government honored him with the title of *Cavaliere dell'Ordine al Merito della Repubblica Italiana* in 2010. He is executive producer and host of the Calandra Institute's TV program, *Italics*, produced in collaboration with and aired on CUNY TV. He also writes a column for *La Voce di New York*, "The Italian diaspora." For more information, www.anthonyjuliantamburri.org.

INDEX

abjection, 12–13, 198–199
Abruzzo, 31, 116, 196
acculturation, 170, 237, 247, 248. *See also* Americanization; assimilation
African Americans, 15, 118, 206–207, 238
alienation, 63, 163, 169
Alito, Jr., Samuel A., 217
allegory, 28–32, 34–36, 40–41, 43–46, 48, 51, 53, 57, 58–59, 78, 164
American Dream, 63–65, 69, 73, 77–82
Americanization, 169–172, 185, 208, 210. *See also* acculturation; assimilation
anarchists, 116–117, 119–120
antifascism, 118–119. *See also* fascism
aphorism, 69
Apulia, 168, 196
Arbib-Costa, Alfonso, 93
Archive of Migrant Memories, 239
assimilation, 19, 63, 73, 94, 169, 171–174, 186, 203, 205, 207, 209–210, 213, 220, 247, 248, 254. *See also* acculturation; Americanization
Assman, Jan, 236
autobiography, 161, 169, 171, 173, 236. *See also* memoir
avant-garde, 57, 58, 120

Baldacci, David, 246
Baldassar, Loretta, 238–239
Barre, Vermont, 116
Barsotti, Carlo, 91

Barthes, Roland, 162
Bartoletti, Efrem, 119–120
Baruch College, 253–254
Basile Green, Rose, 1–2, 10
Bassetti, Augusto, 89–110
Bassetti, Piero, 233, 237
Beato Roberto, 31, 36
Beccaria, Cesare, 246
Beecher Stowe, Harriet: *Uncle Tom's Cabin*, 14, 17
Beerbohm, Max, 44
bella figura / brutta figura, 187, 209, 217
Benjamin, Walter, 75, 77–78
Bergman, Andrew: *The Freshman*, 190
Bertelli, Giuseppe, 119–120
Bertellini, Giorgio, 182, 186
biculturalism, 162, 173
bilingualism, 162, 171–172. *See also* language
Black Hand, The, 182
Bollettino della Sera, 117
Bonaparte, Napoleon, 28
Boston, 183, 207
Bourdieu, Pierre, 195, 198
Brest, Martin: *The Scent of a Woman*, 190
Bronx, 175, 216, 218
Brooklyn, 206, 207, 208
Brooklyn College, xi
Browning, Robert, 31, 44
Buzzati, Dino: *Il deserto dei tartari*, 163–164

Caesarism, 13
cafone, 123, 124, 125, 193–220. *See also* peasants
Calvi, Giusto, 119–120

Campania, 196
canon, literary, 9–11, 14–18, 61–66, 82–83. *See also* literature, Italian American
capitalism, 11, 55, 56, 62, 63, 65–66, 73–78, 82, 124, 126, 199, 200
Capotorto, Carl: *Twisted Head*, 189–190
Carducci, Giosuè, 119
Carnevale, Emanuele, 44–45
Carpi (Modena province, Emilia-Romagna), 115–116
Carravetta, Peter, 5
Carroccio, Il, 117, 118, 145, 150
Catherine of Siena, 218
Catholicism, 76, 80, 186, 200, 254
Cecchetti, Giovanni, 162–168, 174; *Danza nel deserto*, 163–166; *Diario nomade*, 163; *Nel cammino dei monti*, 163
Centro Altreitalie, 251
Centro di Ricerca Interdipartimentale di Studi Americani, 252
Cereghino, Giovanni, 91
Chase, David, 212, 216
Chiappelli, Fredi, 163
Christie, Chris, 217
Ciancabilla, Giuseppe, 116–117, 118–120
Cianfarra, Camillo, 116–118
Cimino, Michael: *The Deer Hunter*, 190
Cinisi (Palermo province, Sicily), 200–201
Cinotto, Simone, 207
City University of New York, 244–245
civiltà (civility), 197–198

civiltà italiana, 199, 207, 210–214, 218
class, 3, 10–11, 47, 66, 72, 73, 75, 78, 115, 184, 194–198, 200–201, 203, 206, 210, 212, 216; low, 3, 184, 194, 198, 200, 209, 212, 219–220; middle, 184, 186, 195, 205–206, 210–214, 216; upper, 13; working, 15, 61–62, 65, 201, 203, 205–206, 208, 211–212, 214, 216, 218–219
clothing, 73, 187, 197–198, 208–209, 211. *See also* style; taste
Cobb, Jonathan, 206
colonialism (of Italian immigrants), 12, 13–14, 18, 20, 117, 123, 125, 128, 195, 211–212
Columbus, Christopher, 5, 43–46, 55, 152–153, 218, 234–235, 237, 240, 246, 254
communication, 3, 105, 164–167, 170, 172
consumerism, 71, 73, 77, 105, 186, 195, 198, 206, 208–209, 211–214, 220
contrapuntal reading, 66, 74
Cordiferro, Riccardo, 118, 119
Cornaro Piscopia, Elena, 218
Corsi, Jerome, 251
Costa, Andrea, 119
Covello, Leonard, 205
credit (concept), 74, 76–78, 80, 82. *See also* debt
cultural capital, 66, 197–198, 201
culture wars, 16

D'Acierno, Pellegrino, 194
D'Angelo, Pascal, 44–45
D'Annunzio, Gabriele, 117

INDEX

da Vinci, Leonardo, 218
Dante, 18, 43, 44, 48, 50, 51, 56, 120, 151–152
De Biasi, Agostino, 117
De Gaudenzi, Angelo, 93
debt, 73, 75–78, 80–82. *See also* credit
decorum, 194, 197–198, 209–210, 216
DeLillo, Don, 11, 246
Derrida, Jacques, 237
desert, 163–164, 167–168
desire, 29, 73, 75, 77, 156, 181, 182. *See also* sexuality
di Donato, Pietro, 11, 16, 19, 44–45, 51–52; *Christ in Concrete*, 1, 2, 18–19, 61–83
diaspora studies, 9, 251–254. *See also* Italian American studies
diaspora, Italian, 200, 211–212, 238
dictionaries, 89–110, 196, 208
DiGirolamo, Vincent, 254
DiMaggio, Joe, 183
DiMino, Andre, 217–218
discrimination, 11, 195, 200, 210, 220
domus, 13, 15
dreams, 34–35, 45–46, 49, 65, 67, 68, 69, 72, 75–76, 79–81, 101, 129–131, 134–135, 166, 167, 169, 170–172, 174–175, 212, 218. *See also* American Dream

Eagle, The, 185. *See also* Valentino, Rudolph
East Coast, 194, 208, 209–210
Eataly Chicago, 243

education, 2–3, 16, 30, 61, 197, 205, 237, 244, 245, 247, 248–251, 254; lack of, 20, 36, 196, 199
Emerson, Ralph W., 54, 63
emigration. *See* migration
epistemology, 27–30, 33–34, 36, 41, 55
ethnic leaders, 194–195, 216–219. *See also prominenti*
ethnic literature, 15, 17, 45, 47, 186. *See also* literature, Italian American
ethnic studies, 9, 18, 43
ethnicity, 11, 49, 54, 58, 63, 66, 72–73, 181–183, 193, 194–195, 206, 208–217, 234, 237, 239, 246–249, 251, 254, 255. *See also* idenity; whiteness
exile, 31, 137–139, 155, 163, 168, 173–174
existential dilemma, 27, 29–30, 33, 35, 36, 39–42, 43, 75–76, 78, 163, 174

Fante, John, 11, 16, 20–21, 44–45
fascism, 19, 118–119, 196. *See also* antifascism
feminism, 9, 16–17, 182
Ferrara, Abel, 193: *Mulberry St.*, 193
Ferrazzano, Carlo, 201, 203
Fetterley, Judith, 17
fiction, 11, 14, 15, 61, 254. *See also* literature
film, 181, 182, 186, 193, 254–255
Fitzgerald, Francis Scott: *The Great Gatsby*, 61–83
folk culture, 20, 29, 47, 50, 120, 197, 207, 212, 246–247, 252
folklore studies, 55, 254

food, 68, 69, 116, 134–135, 208–209, 211, 214, 248. *See also* gluttony
Ford Coppola, Frances: *The Godfather*, 183, 186–187; *The Godfather Part II*, 183, 187; *The Godfather Part III*, 187; *The Godfather* trilogy, 9–10, 187
Forum Italicum, 162–163
Four Horsemen of the Apocalypse, The, 182, 183, 184–185. *See also* Valentino, Rudolph
Frugone, Francesco, 93, 109

Galileo, 218
gangsters. *See* organized crime
Gardaphé, Fred, 4, 73, 245, 252
gavone, 193–220
gay liberation, 182
gender, 32, 54, 181, 186, 188, 195, 205, 206, 210, 254. *See also* feminism; masculinity
genealogy, 29–30, 33–42, 51
Giordano, Paolo, 4
Giovannitti, Arturo, 20, 120
Giuliani, Rudolph, 193
gluttony, 194, 206–208. *See also* food
Goffman, Erving, 195, 210
goomba, 208–209, 212–213, 216–217, 218
grammar books, 89–110
Gramsci, Antonio, 197, 198–199
guido, 188–190, 208–209, 216–218, 243–244
guilt, 13–14, 75, 76–77, 78

Hoover, Herbert, 119
hyphenation, 2, 5, 6, 248

ideals, 3–4, 45, 46, 137–140, 199, 207, 210
identity, 16, 30, 43, 45–46, 50, 53, 54, 57–58, 94–95, 186, 194–198, 209–215, 220, 233–240, 247–249. *See also* ethnicity
immigration. *See* migration
Irish Americans, 101, 108, 119
Italian, North, 198–199, 214; South, 76, 120, 195–200, 205, 207, 210–211, 214, 218–220
Italian American One Voice Coalition Executive Board, 217–218
Italian American studies, 1, 4, 10, 16–17, 20, 27, 29, 30, 246, 251–255. *See also* diaspora studies
Italian American Studies Network (Bellagio meeting), 9, 251–252
Italian Diaspora Studies Summer Seminar, 251–254
Italian Language Inter-Cultural Alliance, 252
Italian-American Civil Rights League, 206
italianità (Italianness), 19, 31, 50, 218. *See also* ethnicity; identity
Italics, 243–244

James, Henry, 63, 182, 183
Jeopardy!, 9–10, 21
Jersey Shore, 208, 216–218, 243–245
John D. Calandra Italian American Institute, xi–xii, 193, 243–244, 251–252, 255

Kinsley, Michael, 243

INDEX

L'Araldo Italiano, 117
L'Aurora, 116
L'Eco d'Italia, 89, 90, 91–92, 109
La Guardia, Fiorello, 118
labor, 29, 37, 55, 62, 66–83, 121–131, 137–140, 143–145, 200–201, 203, 205. *See also* capialism; class, working
Lamb, Wally 246
Lampedusa, 239
language, 2, 3–4, 16, 18–19, 37, 44–45, 47, 49–50, 62–63, 161, 169, 174–175, 194–197, 237, 247; abandonment of, 203, 210–211; acquisition of, 89–110, 249–250; dialects, 3, 16, 29, 32, 37, 94, 118, 169, 171, 174, 196–197, 201, 203, 208, 237; English, 19–20, 115, 161–163, 249–250; Italian, 4, 89, 161–163, 196; loss of, 169–173, 203, 237; multilingualism, 162, 169–174, 237; problem of, 55, 94, 169–173
Lapolla, Garibaldi, 11; *The Grand Gennaro*, 13, 199–200
Lassoni, Giuseppe, 218
Latin Lovers, 183. *See also* masculinity
Laurino, Maria: *Were You Always an Italian?*, 209–211, 213
Lazzarato, Maurizio, 77, 82
Lehman, Peter, 185
literature, 45; American, 14–16, 61–63, 246; Italian, 63, 119, 168, 174; Italian American, 1–2, 9–21, 63, 65, 115, 161–162. *See also* canon; ethnic literature; fiction
Little Caesar, 13, 183, 185

Little Italy, 12
Loren, Sophia, 218
Lyndhurst, New Jersey, 218, **219**

Made in Staten Island, 244
mafia. *See* organized crime
Manhattan, 72, 73–74, 83, 91, 109, 116, 145, 148, 150–155; Greenwich Village, 118, 153–154; Harlem, 13, 199–200, 205; Little Italy, 154–155, 193
Marconi, Guglielmo, 218
Marschall, Sabine, 238
Martinuzzi, Giuseppina, 119–120
Marx, Karl, 55–56, 74, 77
masculinity, 13, 18, 181–190, 195, 199, 205. *See also* feminism; gender
Matthiessen, Francis Otto, 63
McNeill, William, 56
media, 194, 195, 198, 207–209, 216–218, 243. *See also* film; newspapers; television
memoir, 56, 189, 209, 254. *See also* autobiography
memory, 27–42, 43, 47, 49–52, 55, 58, 81, 83, 163, 170, 233–240
Mencken, Henry Louis, 115
Menotti Serrati, Giacinto, 117
Mezzogiorno. *See* Italian, South
Michelangelo, 218
Migliaccio, Eduardo "Farfariello," 201–203, **202**
migration, 10, 11, 12, 19–20, 28–29, 30, 34, 42, 43, 47, 52, 55, 89, 91–92, 101, 116, 118, 162, 168–169, 172–173, 181–182,

269

199, 200, 211, 239, 248, 254, 255. *See also* diaspora, Italian
MillerCoors, 243
modernism, 45, 61–64, 82, 186
Morris, Michael, 190
Morrison, Toni, 18
museums, 239–240
Musketeers of Pig Alley, The, 182

National Italian American Foundation, 216–217
National Library of Sarajevo, 236
nationalism, 3–4, 10–11, 46, 118, 211
nature, 47, 75, 121–122, 140–141, 164
New York City, xi, 6, 28, 32, 65, 70, 89, 90, 91–94, 101, 102–103, 106, 109, 116–118, 128, 175, 193, 200–203, 205, 207, 208, 217, 239. *See also specific boroughs*
Newark, New Jersey, 212
newspapers, 89, 90, 91, 93, 102–103, 116–118, 182, 186, 217–218
Nietzsche, Friedrich: *On the Genealogy of Morality*, 75, 76–77

Odierno, Raymond T., 217
Oliveri, Roberto, 218
ontology, 4, 47, 55, 59
Order Sons of Italy in America, 216
organized crime, 10, 12–13, 18, 64, 72, 73, 183, 185–187, 193, 207–213, 216–218, 244, 245, 254
Orsi, Robert, 13

Palumbo-Liu, David, 17, 18
Pascoli, Giovanni, 119, 147, 150
Paterson, New Jersey, 116
patriarchy, 18–19, 182. *See also* feminism; masculinity
peasants, 15, 32, 62, 126–128, 196–198, 203, 207, 219. *See also* cafone
Pecorino, Alberto, 93
Peirce, Charles Sanders, 234
Piccirilli, Attilio, 118
Piccolomini, Marietta, 91
poetry, 5, 20, 30, 41, 43–59, 82–83, 115–157, 162–163, 167–175
Postiglione, Umberto, 119–120
Progresso Italo-Americano, Il, 89, 90, 91, 109, 117
Proletario, Il, 115, 116–117, 120, 121, 123, 128, 129, 131, 132, 133, 136, 137, 140, 141, 143
prominenti, 201, 203. *See also* ethnic leaders
Puzo, Mario: *The Fortunate Pilgrim*, 17–18; *The Godfather*, 9–15, 17–18, 190, 207

Queens: Astoria, 28, 29, 30, 31, 36, 38, 39, 40, 41, 42; Hell Gate, 32, 39; Sunnyside, 28–32, 36–37, 39, 41, 42, 47
Queens College, 193

race, 54, 72, 206–207, 210, 216. *See also* whiteness
racism, 14, 46, 200
Rambova, Natacha, 190
Real Housewives of New Jersey, The, 216
Reid, Joy, 251

Renaissance, American, 19, 61, 63; Italian, 191, 246
representation, 43, 46, 68, 186, 188, 190, 194, 243–244, 247–248
Rieder, Jonathan: *Canarsie*, 207
Righi, Arrigo, 116, 117
Righi, Giuseppina, 116
Righi, Simplicio (pseud. Rosina Vieni), 115–157
Roberts, Bethan, 187
Rockefeller Foundation, 251
Roma Tre University, 252
Rome, ancient, 13, 191
Rondani, Dino, 116
Roosevelt, Franklin Delano, 119
Ruotolo, Onorio, 118

Said, Edward, 66
Saturday Night Fever, 183–184, 187–190
Savino, Diane, 244–245
Savoca, Nancy, 254–255
Scaramucci, Anthony, 195, 216–218
Scottoline, Lisa, 246
self-loathing, 206, 215–216
Sennett, Richard, 206
sexuality, 182–185, 188, 190. See also desire; feminism; gender; masculinity
shame, 206, 218
Sheik, The, 182. See also Valentino, Rudolph
Short Hills, New Jersey, 209
Silone, Ignazio: *Fontamara*, 196–197
Simmel, Georg, 56
Sinatra, Frank, 183
Sklar, Deidre, 181
Socialist Labor Party, 115, 116

socialists, 115–120, 125, 127
Soldati, Mario: *Addio diletta Amelia*, 118–119; *America primo amore*, 118, 161
solitude, 164
Sopranos, The, 13, 195, 208, 212–216, **214**, 245, 254
sprezzatura, 189–190
Springsteen, Bruce, 217
stereotypes, 195, 206, 214, 243. See also representation
stigma, 195–196, 198, 201, 206, 210–212, 219–220
Studlar, Gaylyn, 182, 184–185
style, 185, 208–209, 211–212. See also taste regimes
success, 15, 31, 32, 36, 47, 73, 101, 168, 185–186, 203, 205, 210, 213, 215, 217, 248

taste regimes, 194–195, 208–209, 212–214
television, 182–183, 217, 244
temporality, 35, 53, 75, 81
Tibaldo-Bongiorno, Marylou, 254–255
transnationalism, 18, 66, 238
trashiness, 207–210. 213, 217
Travolta, John, 181, 183–184, 187–190
Tricarico, Donald, 188–189, 244–245
Trigiani, Adriana, 246
Triulzi, Alessandro, 239
Turturro, John, 254–255
Tusiani, Joseph: *Gente Mia and Other Poems*, 169–170; *La parola antica*, 169, 171–172, 174–175; *La parola difficile*, 169; *La parola nuova*, 169

UNICO National, 216
Unification (Italy), 198, 211
University of Bologna , 216, 237-238
University of Calabria, 252
University of Naples, 239

Valentini, Ernesto, 118
Valentino, Rudolph, 181-190
Valesio, Paolo, 161-162; *Italian Poets in America,* 173-174
Vico, Giambattista, 47, 58
Vieni, Rosina: See Righi, Simplicio
Vinciguerra, Antonio, 196, 197, 205
Viola, John M., 217
violence, 11, 28, 31, 50, 117, 169, 182, 187, 195, 200, 207-208, 220
Viscusi, Robert, 1-6, 9-10, 43-45, 73, 94, 195, 212. *Astoria,* 27-42, 46-47, 48; *Buried Caesars and Other Secrets of Italian American Writing,* 2-4, 10-16, 18-20, 41, 42, 47-48, 62-64, 78-79; *Ellis Island,* 43, 48-59, 233, 240; *Max Beerbohm, or the Dandy Dante,* 44, 48; *An Oration upon the Most Recent Death of Christopher Columbus,* 5, 43-46, 48, 55
voluntary associations, 118, 194-195, 216, 243, 245, 250, 252

West, Rebecca, 163
whiteness, 186, 195, 200, 206-207, 210, 217, 220. *See also* race

Whitman, Walt, 48, 56, 63, 120
Wilde, Oscar, 44
work. *See* labor
World War I, 117
World War II, 19, 183

Ynac, Jeff, 188

Zanolini, Francesco, 91, 93

SAGGISTICA

Taking its name from the Italian—which means essays, essay writing, or non-fiction—*Saggisitca* is a referred book series dedicated to the study of all topics and cultural productions that fall under what we might consider that larger umbrella of all things Italian and Italian/American.

Vito Zagarrio
The "Un-Happy Ending": Re-viewing The Cinema of Frank Capra. 2011. ISBN 978-1-59954-005-4. Volume 1.

Paolo A. Giordano, Editor
The Hyphenate Writer and The Legacy of Exile. 2010. ISBN 978-1-59954-007-8. Volume 2.

Dennis Barone
America / Trattabili. 2011. ISBN 978-1-59954-018-4. Volume 3.

Fred L. Gardaphè
The Art of Reading Italian Americana. 2011. ISBN 978-1-59954-019-1. Volume 4.

Anthony Julian Tamburri
Re-viewing Italian Americana: Generalities and Specificities on Cinema. 2011. ISBN 978-1-59954-020-7. Volume 5.

Sheryl Lynn Postman
An Italian Writer's Journey through American Realities: Giose Rimanelli's English Novels. "The most tormented decade of America: the 60s" ISBN 978-1-59954-034-4. Volume 6.

Luigi Fontanella
Migrating Words: Italian Writers in the United States. 2012. ISBN 978-1-59954-041-2. Volume 7.

Peter Covino & Dennis Barone, Editors
Essays on Italian American Literature and Culture. 2012. ISBN 978-1-59954-035-1. Volume 8.

Gianfranco Viesti
Italy at the Crossroads. 2012. ISBN 978-1-59954-071-9. Volume 9.

Peter Carravetta, Editor
Discourse Boundary Creation (LOGOS TOPOS POIESIS): A Festschrift in Honor of Paolo Valesio. ISBN 978-1-59954-036-8. Volume 10.

Antonio Vitti and Anthony Julian Tamburri, Editors
Europe, Italy, and the Mediterranean. ISBN 978-1-59954-073-3. Volume 11.

Vincenzo Scotti
: *Pax Mafiosa or War: Twenty Years after the Palermo Massacres.* 2012. ISBN 978-1-59954-074-0. Volume 12.

Anthony Julian Tamburri, Editor
: *Meditations on Identity. Meditazioni su identità.* ISBN 978-1-59954-082-5. Volume 13.

Peter Carravetta, Editor
: *Theater of the Mind, Stage of History. A Festschrift in Honor of Mario Mignone.* ISBN 978-1-59954-083-2. Volume 14.

Lorenzo Del Boca
: *Italy's Lies. Debunking History's Lies So That Italy Might Become A "Normal Country".* ISBN 978-1-59954-084-9. Volume 15.

George Guida
: *Spectacles of Themselves. Essays in Italian American Popular Culture and Literature.* ISBN 978-1-59954-090-0. Volume 16.

Antonio Vitti and Anthony Julian Tamburri, Editors
: *Mare Nostrum: prospettive di un dialogo tra alterità e mediterraneità.* ISBN 978-1-59954-100-6. Volume 17.

Patrizia Salvetti
: *Rope and Soap. Lynchings of Italians in the United States.* ISBN 978-1-59954-101-3. Volume 18.

Sheryl Lynn Postman and Anthony Julian Tamburri, Editors
: *Re-reading Rimanelli in America: Six Decades in the United States.* ISBN 978-1-59954-102-0. Volume 19.

Pasquale Verdicchio
: *Bound by Distance. Rethinking Nationalism Through the Italian Diaspora.* ISBN 978-1-59954-103-7. Volume 20.

Peter Carravetta
: *After Identity. Migration, Critique, Italian American Culture.* ISBN 978-1-59954-072-6. Volume 21.

Antonio Vitti and Anthony Julian Tamburri, Editors
: *The Mediterranean As Seen by Insiders and Outsiders.* ISBN 978-1-59954-107-5. Volume 22.

Eugenio Ragni
: *After Identity. Migration, Critique, Italian American Culture.* ISBN 978-1-59954-109-9. Volume 23.

Quinto Antonelli
: *Intimate History of the Great War: Letters, Diaries, and Memoirs from Soldiers on the Front.* ISBN 978-1-59954-111-2. Volume 24.

Antonio Vitti and Anthony Julian Tamburri, Editors
   The Mediterranean Dreamed and Lived by Insiders and Outsiders. ISBN 978-1-59954-115-0. Volume 25.
Sabrina Vellucci and Carla Francellini, Editors
   Re-Mapping Italian America: Places, Cultures, Identities. ISBN 978-1-59954-116-7. Volume 26.
Stephen J. Belluscio
   Garibaldi M. Lapolla: A Study of His Novels. ISBN 978-1-59954-125-9. Volume 27.
Antonio Vitti and Anthony Julian Tamburri, Editors
   The Representation of the Mediterranean World by Insiders and Outsiders. ISBN 978-1-59954-113-6. Volume 28.
Philip Balma and Giovanni Spani, Editors
   Translating for (and from) the Italian Screen: Dubbing and Subtitles. ISBN 978-1-59954-141-9. Volume 29.
Antonio Vitti and Anthony Julian Tamburri, Editors
   Mediterranean Memories. Memorie Mediterranee. ISBN 978-1-59954-142-6. Volume 30.
Anthony Julian Tamburri, Editor
   Interrogations into Italian-American Studies: The Francesco and Mary Giambelli Foundation Lectures. ISBN 978-1-59954-143-3. Volume 31.
Susanna Nanni and Sabrina Vellucci, Editors
   Circolazione di idee e di persone: Integrazione ed esclusione tra Europa e Americhe. ISBN 978-1-59954-155-6. Volume 33.

www.ingramcontent.com/pod-product-compliance
Lightning Source LLC
Chambersburg PA
CBHW031431160426
43195CB00010BB/690